Aspects of Dramatic Form in the English and the Irish Renaissance

Aspects of Dramatic Form in the English and the Irish Renaissance

The Collected Papers of Muriel Bradbrook
Volume 3

M. C. BRADBROOK

*Professor of English Emerita,
University of Cambridge and Fellow of
Girton College*

THE HARVESTER PRESS · SUSSEX
BARNES & NOBLE BOOKS · NEW JERSEY

First published in Great Britain in 1983 by
THE HARVESTER PRESS LIMITED
Publisher: John Spiers
16 Ship Street, Brighton, Sussex
and in the USA by
BARNES & NOBLE BOOKS
81, Adams Drive, Totowa, New Jersey 07512

© M. C. Bradbrook, 1983

Editor: Sue Roe

British Library Cataloguing in Publication Data

Bradbrook, M. C.
    Aspects of dramatic form in the English and
    Irish Renaissance. – (The Collected papers
    of Muriel Bradbrook; v. 3)
    1. English literature – History and criticism
    I. Title   II. Series
    820'.9   PR403
    ISBN 0-7108-0406-7

Library of Congress Cataloging in Publication Data

Bradbrook, M. C. (Muriel Clara), 1909–
    Dramatic forms in the age of Shakespeare.
    (The collected papers of Muriel Bradbrook; v. 3)
    1. English drama – Early modern and Elizabethan, 1500–1600 – History and
    criticism – Addresses, essays, lectures.   2. English drama – 17th century – History
    and criticism – Addresses, essays, lectures.
    3. Shakespeare, William, 1564–1616 – Criticism and interpretation – Addresses,
    essays, lectures.   4. English drama – Irish authors – History and criticism –
    Addresses, essays, lectures.
    I. Title.   II. Series: Bradbrook, M. C. (Muriel Clara), 1909–
    Collected papers of Muriel Bradbrook; v. 3.
    PR653.B67 1983   822'.3'09   83-6014
    ISBN 0-389-20296-7

Photoset in 10 on 11 pt Linotron Sabon by
Rowland Phototypesetting Ltd
Bury St Edmunds, Suffolk

Printed in Great Britain by
The Thetford Press Ltd, Thetford, Norfolk

THE HARVESTER PRESS PUBLISHING GROUP
The Harvester Press Publishing Group comprises Harvester Press Limited (chiefly
publishing literature, fiction, philosophy, psychology, science and trade books),
Harvester Press Microform Publications Limited (publishing in microform
unpublished archives, scarce printed sources, and indexes to these collections) and
Wheatsheaf Books Limited (chiefly publishing in economics, international politics,
sociology and related social sciences), whose books are distributed by The Harvester
Press Limited and its agencies throughout the world.

Contents

Foreword

Half a century's work is reflected in this third volume of Muriel Bradbrook's Collected Papers. The essays range from her early, subtly suggestive close reading of Marlowe's *Hero and Leander* (originally published in *Scrutiny* in 1933), to the revaluation of 'Thomas Heywood, Shakespeare's Shadow', written in 1982. Although the volume begins with George Peele and the drama of the 1580's and early 1590's, includes important essays on Shakespeare, Webster, and other seventeenth century dramatists, and ends with Yeats and Beckett, its actual scope is even greater than that indicated by the Contents page. Professor Bradbrook has always been an associative and allusive critic, quick to grasp telling connections, the creative indebtedness or dissent which may link writers widely separated in time. Readers of this collection will find that she has much to tell them about Chaucer and Spenser, about ballads, Walter Scott or Edward Bond as well as about the drama of the English and Irish Renaissance. They will find, too, that in her later essays, as in those written at the beginning of her career, she remains open and responsive to new writing and ways of thought. She is one of those rare critics who is not afraid to change her mind, to modify an earlier position in the light of recent scholarship, or because she has come to see an issue or a particular work differently. Entirely characteristic here is her decision to re-draw the distinction originally made in her *English Dramatic Form* between 'Theatre of the Icon and Theatre of the Dream' (p. xiv), or her ability not only to welcome the new, two-text theory of *King Lear*, but to perceive its implications for Heywood (pp. 113–14).

Muriel Bradbrook's work has always been marked by catholicity of taste, a refusal to entrench herself in one century, genre, language, or critical position. And yet, as she herself says of Shakespeare's

plays, there is a sense in which these essays are 'alternative statements, varied embodiments of those deep-seated and permanent
impulses which underlie all [her] work and make it, in spite of its
variety, a vast and comprehensive whole' (p. 55). One of the most
valuable of these impulses is her life-long concern and respect for
plays in performance. An indefatigable and eager playgoer, she is as
likely to be found sheltering intrepidly under an umbrella during the
undergraduate, open-air production of some minor Elizabethan
comedy as watching Shakespeare, or the first performance of a new
play, at The National Theatre, The Barbican, or The Royal Court.
Unlike many academics, who go to the theatre to have their pre-
judices confirmed and, when they are not, dismiss the production,
she always hopes to be both delighted and surprised. I have often felt
ashamed of myself upon discovering, at the end of some mediocre
rendering of *Hamlet* or *The White Devil* from which I allowed my
mind to wander, that she had gained from an intonation, some
gesture or momentary stage grouping, an insight into the text not
previously available. It may have been the twenty-sixth time she was
seeing *Hamlet*, but the intelligent attention she brought to the theatre
with her was undiminished.

I have sometimes been tempted to tease 'Brad' by suggesting that
she would be capable of claiming that there was something to be
carefully observed and respected in 'Pyramus and Thisbe' as performed by the rude mechanicals of *A Midsummer Night's Dream*, or
in Don Adriano de Armado's ludicrous impersonation of Hector in
Love's Labour's Lost. But I have been checked just in time by
remembering that, after all, Shakespeare thought so too. This critic's
constant awareness that plays are texts to be performed, and that the
audience is the most indispensable of the performers, has always
been one of her greatest strengths. It puts her in touch with sixteenth
and seventeenth century attitudes, allowing her to show us once-
popular but now neglected works like *Titus Andronicus*, *The Jew of
Malta*, *Selimus* or Peele's *Edward I* in something of the way contemporaries saw them. It also gives her an insight into Elizabethan
collaborative writing, into verbal repetition as a device for putting
words across 'through the noise of crowds and stage battle' (p. 99),
or into Yeats's pressing need for 'something like the choristers'
theatres of Elizabeth's time, where savage and disjunctive visions of a
broken world were emodied in song and dance, by boy actors playing
old men' (p. 171). An interest not just in the way individual texts
come to life and are changed in performance, but in the complex
relationship between dramatist, actors and audience informs almost
all the essays in this volume.

After meticulously reconstructing the probable social and theatrical circumstances which produced the stripped-down text of Peele's *The Old Wives' Tale*, Muriel Bradbrook can change the way we have been reading this riddling and apparently incoherent play by reminding us of its place within 'a folk tradition, where the marvellous must always be familiar, though it cannot be rational' (p. 5). She restores a missing dimension to Peele's comedy, set within its 'frame' of Madge, Clunch the smith, and the three pages lost in the wood, by pointing out how it must have seemed when performed by The Queens' Men on tour: 'written for noble players, who, fallen on evil days, gave it to country audiences, an Induction which shewed country folk entertaining courtly players supplied a looking glass or mirror for actual performance' (p. 8).

Few critics are as adept as Muriel Bradbrook at unravelling the intricacies of Elizabethan word-play, more responsive to the tone and quality of dramatic speech, whether it is that of Shakespeare, Marlowe, Yeats or Beckett. In one of the most brilliant essays in the present collection, 'Yeats and the Elizabethans', she analyzes the influence of Spenser, Shakespeare and the ballad tradition on Yeats's poetry, arguing that the development of Elizabethan love poetry – 'a high Petrarchan idealism, leading to a sharp and bitter poetry, which includes many of the same negative emotions as Jacobean lyric, or drama' (p. 132) – is mirrored in Yeats' own artistic development, and helps to explain why it was that he took different things from the sixteenth century at different stages of his life. Only a critic who was both steeped in Elizabethan literature and possessed the most sensitive ear for cadence and for shadowy but pervasive verbal echoes could have written this piece. Equally impressive, in another critical mode, is her detailed comparison of Beckett's *En Attendant Godot* with its later, English version. As originally written, she argues, the play reveals 'its origin in his life in France', a myth 'based on memories that he could best communicate in French, and which have grown and changed since its first appearance' (p. 185). She brings to Beckett's French here the same alertness to the functioning of language that characterizes her work on Yeats, or on the dramatic poetry of the sixteenth and seventeenth centuries in England.

The ability to come to terms with alien languages and artistic forms, making them available without distortion to a different culture, is arguably one of the measures of a distinguished, as opposed to a merely 'good' critic. Immediately after the War, Muriel Bradbrook wrote with passion and precision about Ibsen, a dramatist whose language she had taken pains to learn. Many years later, she went for the first time to Japan. There, she not only made a number of academic and personal friends who have subsequently remained important to her, but discovered Noh drama as a still-vital and living form. She came to realize that Noh dancers move to a rhythm 'far slower than the beat of the heart'. That description seems for an instant to put them beyond Western comprehension – but then she reminds us that we have heard that rhythm too: in 'the muffled drums of some great funeral cortège' (p. 162).

This is a sensitive, 'blood' reaction, that of a critic who has some of the instincts of a poet, and who is not afraid to bring her own, lived experience to bear on what she reads. So, she can shear through the interminable debate as to Macduff's culpability in leaving his wife and children defenseless in Scotland by remembering the high-ranking French naval officer she met in London during World War II, a man who had escaped from France during the German occupation in order to attack that regime from England: 'He too left his wife and child exposed to the retaliation of the enemy. In those days no one asked him why' (p. 57). But she can also be tartly witty, as when she remarks of Massinger's tragedy *The Virgin Martyr* and its stoically Christian heroine: 'Martyrdom was the one profession open equally to both sexes' (p. 109).

Such vivid rapprochements between literature and life exist side by side in these essays with the scholar's recognition that the traditional shape of the Noh stage 'strangely resembles an Elizabethan stage with its "heavens" and its "lord's room"' (pp. 163–4), the unexpected affinity she discerns between the sinister partnerships in certain Elizabethan plays, in which 'evil at last eats up itself', and the stage worlds created by Edward Bond (p. 98), or the way Buddhist doctrine is shouldered aside in the final moments of Yeats's *At The Hawk's Well* by the spirit of Marlowe (p. 165). She has a gift for finding memorable and precise ways of formulating ideas and responses of which one has been dimly aware oneself without being able to give them shape – as when she observes that the witches in *Macbeth* are so horrible 'because we do not know what they are – it would be a relief to meet Mephistopheles' (p. 67), or says of Shakespeare's heroines disguised as boys that, often, the sharp contrast between their two roles gives 'an effect as of shot silk, as the boyish wit or the feminine sensibility predominates' (p. 38). I myself became a pupil of Muriel Bradbrook's in Cambridge during the 1950's. This position, as the essays in this volume forcefully but pleasantly remind me, remains essentially unchanged.

Anne Barton
New College, Oxford
Spring, 1983

Introduction

This collection of papers is a contribution to the book I have been trying for fifty years to write and have not yet written. It repeats the shape of my *English Dramatic Form in the Old Drama and the New*, juxtaposing the English Renaissance with the New Drama of this century – in these islands, at first centred on Dublin.

As I tried to show in *Shakespeare and Elizabethan Poetry*, Elizabethan drama (in the strict sense) was nourished by epyllions, lyrics and versified history of that reign. Drama is so complex that it requires maturity in each of the blending or merging 'languages'. By the turn of the century it was itself to become the point of growth verbally, as Heywood in his *Apology for Actors* was to testify: 'Our English tongue, which hath been the most harsh, uneven and broken language of the world, is now, by this secondary means of playing, continually refined.' By the end of the 1590s, the best London actors had evolved a set of genres, in a 'market situation' where plays were written in workshop conditions, to meet the needs of an audience at first unified, then diversified by the arrival of the choristers' new indoor theatres, Hamlet's 'little eyasses'.

In form more mature than any of his plays, Marlowe's *Hero and Leander*, a love-debate and love-conflict, prompted Shakespeare; epyllion and drama mingle in the vital interplay between these two. (Perhaps I should have put 'Dr Faustus and the Eldritch Tradition' here rather than in Volume I.) Peele is more significant than Greene, and Heywood than Dekker, because Peele and Heywood, like Shakespeare, were actively involved in performance. Yet each of these and their successors, down to Fletcher and Webster, could furnish a delicate lyric for an emotional climax; this may almost be taken as the test of poetic drama. Peele reappears in the two general studies – 'Bogeymen, Machiavels and Stoics' and 'Thomas

Heywood, Shakespeare's Shadow' which together span the whole period from 1589 to 1641. The first revises a section on Types of Tragedy that I wrote fifty years ago for *Themes and Conventions of Elizabethan Tragedy*; the second was presented to the *Société Française Shakespeare* at the Sorbonne in October 1982.

I should want now to rephrase the distinction in *English Dramatic Form* between Theatre of the Icon and Theatre of the Dream, as Theatre of Ritual and Theatre of Games. A ritual effectually works upon those who perform it (as in baptism or burial); games provide a mirror-image. The ritual of communal celebration in London often took the form of local or national legends, strengthening the sense of community. Games developed into parody or burlesque, the breaking of tradition to transform it, as in Shakespeare's *The Taming of the Shrew*; by the end of the 1590s, the workshop evolution of genres, attested chiefly by parody, helped playwrights and actors quickly to meet growing demands, and spectators to respond with alertness. The Lord Mayor's Show, Elizabethan street theatre, survives today: it was built up by popular playwrights.

Shakespeare's dramatic form could hardly be compassed in a single volume. I have written four books on Shakespeare, two within the last few years: the bulk of the papers in Volume 1 of these Collected Papers are also given to him. The four essays included here mark certain points of stress. The contest with Marlowe; development of acting potential through the basic convention of disguise; struggles to combine two genres, in *All's Well that Ends Well* – now, today, a stage success. Finally, the tragedy where, in transforming the ground of his earlier chronicle histories, he also transformed his own internal forms; *Macbeth* is his most concentrated work.

The crucial years of the so-called Theatre War, when young gentlemen took to writing plays, saw questioning and scepticism invading the stage; Ben Jonson was provoked to his counter-plays and efforts at definition – interesting dramatic failures like *Cynthia's Revels* and *Poetaster*, which he put into print with additional matter, thus presenting the *literary* drama, altering the status of the text. Perhaps he saw himself as Minister for Arts!

Shakespeare did not respond with counter-theory; he wrote *Hamlet*, after which nothing could be the same again. The stress may be measured in his problem plays; the final mastery in his last plays, triumphs of open form.

The history of these crowded years 1599–1602 was sketched in my *Shakespeare the Craftsman* and *Shakespeare the Poet in his World* (the chapter entitled 'Enter, Fighting, at Several Doors'); and in *The Living Monument* I glanced at Jonson's love-hate relationship with his audience.[1]

Wit – the kind of wit John Donne displayed – had ruled in the choristers' theatres; the tragedies of Webster and Beaumont and Fletcher's baroque drama, written for Shakespeare's company, blend his influence with Jonson's. They are closely linked to more sophisticated acting, their form disjunctive. Webster follows *Macbeth* with a tragedy where

> Light thickens and the crow
> Makes wing to the rooky wood.

In *The Faithful Shepherdess*, Fletcher reverted with a difference to the form of *The Old Wives' Tale*; Beaumont burlesqued Heywood. Shakespeare's last plays also reverted to earlier forms – with a difference.

Shakespeare's mature forms were complex, volatile, self-generative, popular, magnetic, adjustable, allusive, sympathetic and only partly susceptible of formulation. His well-organised subconscious mind, his intuition, did much of his work for him, as Dryden observed: 'All the images of Nature were still present to him, and he drew them not laboriously but luckily; when he describes anything, you more than see it, you feel it too.'

Hamlet's definition of the end of playing, though based upon the Ciceronian definition 'imitationem vitae, speculum consuetudinis, imaginem veritatis', is significantly varied to show the reciprocity of performance and to suggest the constantly modifying process of the poetic individuality: 'both at the first and now, was and is, to hold the mirror up to nature, to show virtue her feature, scorn her own image, and the very age and body of the time his form and pressure' (III ii 20–4). The word 'mirror' has had volumes written upon it,[2] representing as it does both tragic and comic art. The multiple plots of Jacobean times (especially Shakespeare's and Middleton's) coincide with the emergence of tragi-comedy, a modern Italian form; Marston's *Malcontent*, played by Shakespeare's company and by the choristers, was supplied with a mirror-like Induction by John Webster; it would have been recognised by Guarini. Tragi-comedy, the art of surprise, the mirror as illusion, became the dominant form for Fletcher and his successors.

Among early forms had been the Romance, combining strange adventures with local worthies; Heywood, publishing his *Four Prentices of London* in 1615, apologises for its form which 'some fifteen or sixteen years ago' was the fashion. This was the equivalent of modern star wars. The medley or gallimaufrey was the ancestor of the modern revue; the major, hybrid form was the Revenge Play. Adaptation of classical tales enabled dramatists to avoid the framework of Christian ethics on Revenge, Suicide and other tragic themes like Ambition: English Revenge drama bore as little resemblance to Seneca as the 'Characters' of Jonson to Theophrastus.

Throughout Jacobean times, great plays continued to be written in collaboration (*Eastward Ho! Pericles, The Changeling, The Witch of Edmonton*) and in plays of single authorship, the contrast of plot and sub-plot allowed poetry of the gaps to emerge through juxtaposition (Middleton, and Heywood in his marital dramas). The actors (or their backers, like Henslowe and Beeston) were in control. No author alone could plan a two-part play, for this waited on consumer-demand. Perhaps successful 'parts' might be given formal unity; Heywood's *Four Ages* may owe something to Shakespeare's English chronicle histories. Sequels to old favourites were supplied; to Shakespeare's *Taming of the Shrew* (*The Women's Prize*). Adapting was to be carried much further by Dryden's generation. Adaptation was already being used to bring new kinds of spectacular effects to the new indoor theatres; Heywood's definition of plays was 'bewitching, lively action'; he opposed the printed form.

What Ovid and Seneca were to Marlowe and Shakespeare, Shakespeare himself has been to modern poetic drama. In a study contrasting the English and Irish Renaissance[3] Philip Edwards concludes 'Yeats's Shakespeare is an honorary Celt', whilst 'Yeats is a consequence of Shakespeare' (pp. 207, 211).

Yeats worked on the popular sub-soil of fairy-tale and legend as his great forerunners had done; he was involved not only in writing but in all the process of creating a theatre, a form not native to Ireland, being essentially of the city, rather than of the countryside. However, he created not so much a national as an international art.[4] Two essays represent his double inheritance – the language of Shakespeare, the history of Ireland. John Synge fled to Aran to escape 'the squalor of the poor and the nullity of the rich'; Dublin's rejection of Synge turned Yeats towards the theatre of ritual; the ancient drama of Japan freed him as a poet to forge new and stronger images – partly out of his own history, and the new turbulence of Ireland. He ended with the tragic *Purgatory*, in which Eliot said he gave speech to modern drama. It appeared in his last work *On the Boiler* (1938), where he also wrote:

> Because the will and energy is greatest in tragedy, tragedy is the more noble; but I will add that 'Will or energy is eternal delight' and when its limit is reached, it may become a pure aimless joy, though the man, the shade, still mourns. (p. 35)

This he also declared is the mood of *Hamlet* and *King Lear*. Yeats and Beckett being visionaries, remain more profoundly political today than Synge or O'Casey (who flirted with Expressionism and other ideological fashions). All four, descended from Protestant families, paid a specially heavy toll for their loyalty to a country with which they could not completely identify. They were grafts of another stock – and have in some quarters been rejected as Anglo-Irish. Theirs is very precisely the tragedy for our time.

Beckett not only fled, but adopted another language. He found himself in that desolate scene with the single withered tree which started with the Noh drama of *At the Hawk's Well*, and reappeared in *Purgatory*; this scene prefigured Yeats's ancestral, Beckett's native Ulster of today. They hold up a mirror which is also the shield of Perseus, by which the Medusa may be confronted. Yeats and Beckett can compass a situation more than political – and not religious either; the situation of the human condition itself.

Beckett, more remote from popular drama than Yeats, is also closer to the life of the body. His one popular Irish drama is *All that Fall*, written not for the stage but for broadcasting. *Godot* is in 'a tradition biblical rather than classical, prophetic rather than philosophic, a tradition of which not form but energy is the ground.'[5]

In the modern theatres, which I dealt with in Volume II of these Collected Papers, Gordon Craig, Artaud and Strindberg, like Yeats, turned to ritual; yet the playwrights Pirandello, Lorca and Beckett knew drama as a game, subtle as chess, violent as wrestling; a game where energy is manifest.

Notes

1 *The Living Monument* (1976) and *Shakespeare the Poet in his World* (1978). The two earlier, *Shakespeare and Elizabethan Poetry* (1951) and *Shakespeare the Craftsman* (1969) were reprinted in the group of six entitled *A History of Elizabethan Drama* (Cambridge, 1980).
2 Marie-Madeleine Martinet, *Le Miroir de l'esprit dans le théâtre Elizabéthain* (1980).
3 Philip Edwards, *Threshold of a Kingdom* (1979).
4 See Karen Dorn, *Players and Painted Stage* (1983): Katherine Worth, *The Irish Drama of Europe, From Yeats to Beckett* (1978).
5 Kathleen Raine, *The Inner Journey of the Poet* (1982), p. 176.

Bibliographical Note

A bibliography of my publications is included in *English Drama: Forms and Development*, ed. Marie Axton and Raymond Williams, a book of essays presented to me (Cambridge, 1977). Since then, I have published two books: *Shakespeare the Poet in his World* (1978) and *John Webster, Citizen and Dramatist* (1980): and a booklet on George Chapman (1977). The bibliography also contains a selection (about fifty) of my reviews. The six volumes published as a collection by Cambridge in 1980 and entitled 'A History of Elizabethan Drama' contains two genre studies *Themes and Conventions of Elizabethan Tragedy* and *The Growth and Structure of Elizabethan Comedy*, one social study, *The Rise of the Common Player:* and three books on Shakespeare, dealing with his earlier, his middle and his later years (*Shakespeare and Elizabethan Poetry, Shakespeare the Craftsman* and *The Living Monument*).

Three inter-related studies of Jacobean theatre are: 'The Politics of Pageantry; Social implications in Jacobean London' in *Poetry and Drama 1500–1700, essays in honour of Harold Brooks*, ed. A. Coleman and A. Hammond, 1981; 'Publication and Performance in Early Stuart Drama; Jonson, Webster, Heywood' in *The Mirror up to Shakespeare, essays in honour of G. R. Hibbard*, ed. J. C. Gray (University of Toronto Press, 1983): 'Lawyers' Pageantry and London Theatre' in *Renaissance Essays in honour of C. L. Barber*, ed. P. Erickson and Coppélia Kahn (University of Delaware Press, 1983).

The English Renaissance

I.

Peele's *The Old Wives' Tale*

As its form emerged from pageant shews and rhetorical set speeches, Elizabethan courtly comedy was defined as a dream or shadow of the courtly life and distanced by a remote mythological setting.[1] Although he early mastered the transition from dream to waking, myth to court – at the end of *The Arraignement of Paris* Diana delivers the apple of gold into Elizabeth's own hands – George Peele (1556–97) achieved his masterpiece in a more traditional kind. *The Old Wives' Tale*, surviving only in an uncertain text dating from 1595, but possibly originating in the late 1580s, rests half-way between shew and drama. Weaving in folk themes and recollections of other plays, Peele achieved 'a rare condition of complete simplicity' that invited the audience to 'piece the play out with their thoughts'.

The play belonged to the Queen's Men, who in the mid-1580s led the London stage, but in the late 1580s and early 1590s were scarcely seen there; driven out by new actors, especially Alleyn's and Henslowe's company, they divided into two groups, who sank to country strollers. *The Old Wives' Tale*, with twenty-four named parts, for a company of seven men and two boys needed much doubling; so that characters succeed each other rapidly in small groups and may never reappear to tell the end of their adventures. Some of the many prophecies are not fulfilled, others are fulfilled, but not noted; it is clear that the play has been shortened, but one or two silent parts have been kept, because variety was a prime need.[2] The play was set elaborately in old-fashioned 'simultaneous' style, presenting on the stage at least two separate 'pavilions' with curtains (the old wife's cottage and Sacrapant's study); a wood with a crossroads and a 'well of life' from which an enchanted head arose; a piece of 'enchanted ground', with a hillock, where some characters dug and others were blasted with flames of fire.[3] These sets, which in medieval times at least were miniature in scale,[4] must have been carried round in property carts. A country audience, as Shakespeare's Holofernes knew, would be delighted with 'a shew, or ostentation or firework', accompanied here by an 'invisible' character, a magic banquet and much other spectacle. But it seems unlikely that they would enjoy literary satire or burlesque, or be prepared to recognise Gabriel Harvey in the figure of Huanebango. They would not know Harvey from Adam. It is unlikely too that a company which was still apparently acting plays like *Clyomon and Clamydes* – another of the Queen's Men's works which they did not release till 1595, though it was then about twenty years old – would at the same time burlesque the tradition of the romance.[5]

The Queen's Men did not share the light mockery of the boys' troupes under Lyly, or their more robust mockery under Nashe. The repertoire consisted of close-packed plays like the old *King Leir, The Famous Victories of Henry V* or *Five Plays in One;* when it was first formed, the leaders of this troupe dealt in lusty, extemporal clowning – they included Tarlton (who dressed as a countryman), Laneham and Robert Wilson. Peele, perhaps an actor and certainly a great deviser of city pageants, had come down from Oxford in 1571, and so grew up in the decade before the rise of Alleyn, Greene, Marlowe and Nashe. He is placed where he really belongs by the traditional, apocryphal *Merry Jests of George Peele*, that is, as a companion of Tarlton, Knell and Bentley – which last two he challenged young Alleyn to equal.[6]

In *The Old Wives' Tale* there is no need for information, orderly sequence of plot, or dramatic connection, since the enchanted princess 'as white as snow and as red as blood'; her two brothers, who seek her; the wicked enchanter; the wandering knight; the beggar with his two daughters, one fair and curst, the other foul and patient; the Spanish Knight with his two-handed sword have all been met with by the audience many times before the play began. They had no need to play an action: merely to display themselves for what they were. 'When I was a little one, you might have drawne me a mile after you with such a discourse.'

So, whether as the result of the actors' cutting or not, when the Two Brothers meet Erestus, the enchanted knight – who is also addressed as 'the white bear of England's wood' (a title from medieval romance) and once as 'Father Time', – he does not need to be told their story, but can ask at once 'Is she fair?' In performance, this seems perfectly natural; the perplexity felt by a reader melts away. When, through simultaneous setting, the audience is released from the confines of place, they cannot be tied to narrative progression.

The fluid life of such plays, like that of ballads, belonged within folk tradition, where the marvellous must always be familiar, though it cannot be rational. Recognition of the familiar and delight by the unexpected must be evenly balanced for the audience to be 'rapt'. Consistency of mood, the power to absorb the fancy and lull the feelings, binds simplified characters together in a fantastic action, dependent on riddles and magic shews. Each figure was so familiar that as he came forward to give his sequence, it would have been natural for the audience, if pleased, to demand a little more – to cry for the braggart to come back; in Bottom's phrase, 'Let him roar again.' In fact the first sequence of the boastful Spaniard, Juan y Bango (Huanebango) may have been inserted as an addition in this way; it is somewhat out of key with the rest of the play, the Clown is given a different name in it, and it contains specific literary allusions which place it in or about 1591.[7] The core of the play consists of adventures familiar from tales of wandering knights, many of which had been turned into plays;[8] but the groupings of these characters are drawn from medley plays, which the Queen's Men had given at other times. In these plays there is no narrative sequence: instead, variety of spectacle effects unity of mood or temper.

Medleys usually included two or more pairs of lovers, a hermit or magician, a speaker of riddles and prophecies, and a clown. *The Cobbler's Prophecy* (published 1594) was written by Wilson of the Queen's Men; in it, the Cobbler is given the gift of riddling prophecy that in Peele belongs to Erestus: The Cobbler's mad wife Zelota destroys the villain as Erestus's mad, betrothed wife, Venelia, destroys the enchantments of Sacrapant. Both plays require simultaneous settings with two pavilions; in *The Cobbler's Prophecy* smoke arises as 'the Cabin of Contempt is set on fire' for the finale. In one of the plays of Derby's Men, *The Rare Triumphs of Love and Fortune* (1582–3), a brother pursues his fleeing sister, and is struck dumb by an enchanter; whereas in Peele, two brothers in seeking a sister are reduced to servitude, and the clown and braggart knight struck blind and deaf. The hermit of the one play is all-powerful; in the other, he is a victim of enchantment. In each, the princess is threatened with death in the final scene, but by meek submission dissolves the last spells.

It seems therefore that much of the material of *The Old Wives' Tale* was common to the stages of the 1580s; and when a few lines from Greene's *Orlando Furioso* (1591) (another Queen's play) together with the name Sacrapant are found to have crept in, this may illustrate a general habit of building up scenes fairly freely upon the basis of a scenario or 'plot'. *The Old Wives' Tale* as it stands, adapted to the needs of a small troupe of country strollers, consists of brief sequences, with as much scenic variety and multiplication of characters as could be achieved. As a later apologist was to say

> Of actors we did lack a many,
> Therefore we clipt our play into a shew.

The illusion of variety pleased. Familiar parts would have been recognisable even in mime; the outline could be filled out to whatever extent the audience desired and the occasion warranted. To extend a part would be as plausible as to repeat a song; the Queen's Men had long been famous for extemporising. It has recently been suggested that 'plots' or scenarios were supplied by playwrights to the actors, and that Antony Mundy's fame as 'our best plotter' depended on his ability to do this.[9]

The poetry of Peele's play lives in the songs, transforming another folk tradition — that of rural seasonal games. A company of harvesters suddenly enter the scene, singing of love:

> All ye that lovely lovers be, pray you for me,
> Lo, here we come a sowing, a sowing,
> And sow sweet fruits of love:
> In your sweet hearts well may it prove.

Perhaps, like Ceres in *The Cobbler's Prophecy*, at this point they 'sowed' sweetmeats among the audience. Later they appear with harvest women, to sing their second verse: 'Lo, here we come a-reaping . . .'.

As long before as 1244, plays 'of the bringing in of autumn' were forbidden in the diocese of Lincoln; they were the counterpart of May Games. 'The thesher with his flail' is referred to as an expected figure, in the prologue to Robert Wilson's *Three Ladies of London* (1583), while in Nashe's *Summer's Last Will and Testament* (1592 –3), also based on seasonal sports, harvesters enter to a drinking song:

> Merry, merry, merry, cheary, cheary, cheary,
> Trole the blacke bowl to me
> Hey derry derry, with a poupe and a lerrie,
> Ile trole it again to thee.
> Hookie, hookie, we have shorn and we have bound,
> And we have brought harvest home to town.[10]

Though Nashe's work is as long-drawn out as Peele's is brief, it too substitutes thematic imaginative coherence for narrative order. In contrast with their dream-like flatness of dialogue, both shews

(Nashe's is introduced as 'no play neither, but a shew') are filled out by rich poetic sensuousness of pastoral description, ripe fullness of the songs; these embody a lyric gorgeousness which no scenic display could give to the eye.

> When as the Rie reach to the chin,
> And chopcherrie, chopcherrie, ripe within,
> Strawberries swimming in the cream,
> And schoolboys playing in the stream,
> Then O, then O, then O, my true love said,
> Till that time come again,
> She could not live a maid.

The clustered images, spreading summer pleasure, and carrying only by suggestion the beautiful wantonness of a woman's body, are sung by one of the more sophisticated characters in Peele's Induction. In contrast, later in his play, the Enchanted Head which rises from the Well of Life bearing ears of corn and showers of gold recites a country spell, where the harvest of love and fertility is celebrated more wantonly.

> Gently dip; but not too deepe;
> For fear thou make the golden beard to weep.
> Fair maiden, white and red,
> Combe me smooth and stroke my head,
> And thou shalt have some cockell bread.

The country manners that went to the making of cockell bread were coarse enough;[11] yet Peele's fancy remains 'clean . . . without spavin or windgall.' Jack, the dead man who comes back to help the friendly stranger who out of charity had interred him, prances in to a mummer's jingle:

> Are you not the man, sir,
> Deny it if you can, sir . . .

and Juan y Bango reflects the glancing mockery of the mummers; for though in his linguistic and amorous exploits he is the prototype of Shakespeare's Don Adriano de Armado, in another light he represents Bold Slasher.

Both Nashe and Peele reserve their heaviest mockery for learning; both are quite exceptional in the extent of their reliance on folk material, and the way in which they set it at a distance through complex Inductions. Perhaps to contemporaries, this would have recalled *The Canterbury Tales* – Chaucer being an unskilled old gaffer in Elizabethan eyes. To Peele's fellow-authors a movement 'Back to Chaucer' was familiar enough.

The jesting ghost of old Will Summers draws the audience into Nashe's shew, but constantly breaks the illusion of the scene by the kind of ritual abuse common in country merriment; nor unknown at court festivities, where the audience frequently tried to 'dash' the players. Played by an adult actor named Toy, Summers would dominate physically the boy players of Nashe. He is the only human figure to appear in the allegory; his irony both controls and anticipates the audience's response.

Peele's Induction is less striking to a modern audience than his fairy-tale, because the fairy world is now less familiar. Drama however lives most fully in the Induction, as poetry resides in the songs. It is the Induction that prevents the play from being merely another medley; it supplies natural intercourse, action that follows natural laws.

Three servants of a noble lord, whose names proclaim them actors, lost in a wood, find the creature comforts of food, fire and sleep in the cottage of Clunch and Madge. Antic goes to bed and to dream offstage, while Frolic and Fantastic sit up with old Madge that they may be 'ready . . . extempore' for the morning. The tale she tells, 'of the Gyant and the Kings Daughter and I know not what' comes to life, and before the end old Madge is asleep. Dream perspective justifies the medley, as Madge's half-told, half-dreamt tale. The original and complex tradition of the medieval dream vision was not fully accessible to Elizabethans, but Peele made some use of it in his own dream-vision, *The Honour of the Garter*.

Written for noble players, who, fallen on evil days, gave it to country audiences, an Induction which shewed country folk entertaining strayed courtly players supplied a looking glass or mirror for actual performance. Actors and audience would find their representatives here, yet in such a manner that the simpler part of the spectators might respond directly, while the lord of the manor would laugh at and recognise old Madge. Contrary to the general practice of using allegorical figures for the Induction, it is here more naturalistic than the main play. Sometimes of course, a play was presented by a grave figure representing the author; and more than a century earlier Lydgate had described a story teller reciting his tale in a theatre, while mute actors came out of a tent and mimed the story as he told it.[12]

The presence of Madge, Frolic and Fantastic throws a special colour or tone over the fairy-tale, deepening the bare simplicity of the writing – its spareness or 'parsimony' as one critic has termed it. Their speech relieves the pastoral lusciousness of the poetry with studied plainness. 'When this was done, I took a piece of bread and cheese and came my way, and so shall you have too, before you go, to your breakefast.'

Romance, though still potent when Peele wrote, was diminished – like the miniature wood of his stage or like 'far-off mountains turned into clouds' – as Shakespeare later described a woodland dream. Ben Jonson mocked the wandering knight in *Every Man out of His Humour* (1599); when in the Induction to *The Knight of the Burning Pestle* (1607), Ralph and his mistress disrupt the play, their dreams of romance are farcical. Ralph the grocer's boy is at one time set to woo the King of Cracovia's daughter, at another to make a May Day speech in his own person. Yet, a year or so later, Shakespeare in his last plays wonderfully transformed and revived the old Romances of his youth.

In the 1580s, George Peele and his friends of the Queen's Men were still enjoying that happy moment when 'the obvious was supremely satisfying'. They could rely on their audience: 'the common people, who rejoice much to be at plays and interludes and . . . have at such times their ears . . . attentive to the matter and their eyes upon the shews of the stage.'[13] This audience would supply for each brief scene an amplification from its own store of legend: so that the dream play achieves with the utmost economy both theatrical depth and poetic lucidity. It belongs to a theatre of presentation and statement, where the unfolding of the action does not consist in dramatic interplay between characters, but rather in different levels of the imaginative life itself. It is a theatre in which poetry is active as recitative and song, not yet active as fully developed dramatic exchange.[14] *The Old Wives' Tale* might most fittingly have begun to be told in the late eighties, half way between the desert wastes of rant in *Sir Clyomon and Sir Clamydes*, and the full splendour of Shakespeare's *Love's Labour's Lost* or *Midsummer Night's Dream*.

Notes

1 The emergence of drama from the rhetorical set speeches has been studied by Wolfgang Clemen, *Die Tragödie vor Shakespeare* (1955). For Lyly's definition of comedy, see especially the prologues to *Endimion* and *The Woman in the Moon*.

2 For a discussion of textual problems see Harold Jenkins, *Modern Language Review*, vol. 34 (1939), pp. 177–85. The prophecy made to Eumenides is fulfilled but not noted; the prophecy to the brothers is fulfilled by Eumenides; the end of Huanebango's and the Clown's

adventures are missing. Venelia's important part in the plot is unsupported by speech but her miming would be eloquent, as would the Furies' also.

3 The well was evidently an important property, which the Revels Office once borrowed from the wardrobe kept at the Bell Inn in Gracechurch Street (Feuillerat, *Documents relating to the Revels* (1908), p. 277). By 1601 it is treated as a jest in the Oxford play of *Narcissus*. The magic head which rose from the well is probably the same as that used in Greene's *Alphonsus of Aragon, Friar Bacon and Friar Bungay*, etc. The pavilions were used in *The Cobbler's Prophecy*, another Queen's Men's play. For a recent discussion of stage properties, see Morton Pearson, in *Studies in the Elizabethan Theatre*, ed. Charles T. Prouty, 1961.

4 See Allardyce Nicoll, *Masks, Mimes and Miracles* (1931), p. 196.

5 The view that *The Old Wives' Tale* was satiric or burlesque is now fairly generally discarded. For modern views, see A. K. McIlwraith, *Five Elizabethan Comedies* (Oxford, 1934) p. xiii; Harold Jenkins, op.cit.; Hubert Goldstone, *Boston University Studies in English*, IV (1960), pp. 202–13. Mockery of scholastic pretension was a regular part of country sports; compare the clowns' use of the form of disputation, 593–605; the dispraise of scholars in Nashe's *Summer's Last Will and Testament*, put into the mouth of Winter; the clowns' play in *John a Kent and John a Cumber*. See also note 13 below.

6 See David Horne, *Life and Minor Works of George Peele* (1952), pp. 85–6.

7 Harold Jenkins thinks this passage (312–410) was intended for deletion, and that 651–6 were intended to replace it. It seems to me more likely to be an accretion; the later writer has forgotten the Clown's grand name of Corebus, which he perhaps was meant originally to assume on becoming a 'knight' errant. Change of name was important for change of role; so Delia is renamed Berecynthia. (Cf. the wholesale renaming of characters in the sub-plot of Shakespeare's *Taming of the Shrew*.) Perhaps there was still some memory of the old habit of the player's name being written on a scroll pinned to his breast.

8 William of Palerne, hero of a fourteenth-century romance, is turned into a White Bear, like Erestus. Lost plays on Sir Eglamour and Degrebell and on 'a knight called Florence' were given as early as 1443. A number of lost plays from the 1580s must belong to the same kind as *Clyomon and Clamydes* – e.g. *Hepatulus the Blue Knight*. Shakespeare's Flute hopes Thisbe is a wandering knight.

9 See I. A. Shapiro, in *Shakespeare Survey*. vol. 14 (1960), pp. 30–1. What has been retained here is the skeleton of action – the riddles – and the regular pattern of leading characters. Incidents in classic pantomime can still be fitted in to skeleton plots (as anyone who has been to the Tivoli pantomime at Copenhagen will realise). For the habits of the Queen's Men, see W. W. Greg, *Two Elizabethan Stage Abridgements* (1923), on *Orlando Furioso*. Cf. below, 'Heywood, Shakespeare's Shadow' pp. 113–14 for persistence of this habit.

10 In Cambridgeshire villages today, the harvest feast is known as 'horkey'

supper. 'Horkey' is the last load home. Compare the harvesters who enter as part of Prospero's masque in *The Tempest*. For a general discussion of harvest plays, especially in relation to Nashe's play and to Shakespeare, see C. L. Barber, *Shakespeare's Festive Comedy* (1959), pp. 58–79.

11 Cockell bread was a marriage charm. See *The New English Dictionary* s.v. cocklebreads and cf. Eric Partridge, *A Dictionary of Slang*, s.v. cockles.

12 For a discussion of this passage from Lydgate's *Tale of Troy*, see Glynne Wickham, *Early English Stages*, vol. I (1959), pp. 193–4. A late use of Induction with the author as presenter is that of *Pericles*, where Gower appears, The Induction represents an attempt to transfer from a predominantly narrative to a predominantly dramatic way of writing. The 'shew' with its 'truchman' survived as a subordinate form well into Elizabeth's reign and developed into the masque.

13 George Puttenham, *The Arte of English Poesie*, (c. 1583), ed. A. Walker and G. Willcock, Cambridge (1936), p. 82. Puttenham says that the common people enjoy 'words of exceeding great length' and that while they are attentive to 'matter' and 'shew', yet 'they take little heed to the cunning of the rime'. As he has just been advocating classical metres, this passage would suggest that Huanebango's use of hexameters would not be noticed by a common country audience, and that they would enjoy his long words with no thought of literary parody. The notion that in a theatre *any* audience is capable of this kind of literary source-hunting seems to me very largely a figment of scholarly fancy.

14 I have tried to trace the significance of spectacle and shews in the seventies, and the literary development of the 1580s in *The Rise of the Common Player*. The rhetorical questions have been considered by Clemen, and to some extent by Madeleine Doran in *Endeavors of Art* (1954). Also, more recently by G. K. Hunter in his study, *John Lyly, The Humanist as Courtier* (1962).

II.

Marlowe's *Hero and Leander*

Marlowe's *Hero and Leander* has not received scrutiny in proportion to the frequent and almost unqualified adulation which has been bestowed on it. In particular, the tone, the poet's attitude to his subject, have not been considered at all. The glowing final lines of the *Second Sestiad* have overwhelmed the critics: the earlier part is neglected, or dismissed as tapestry-weaving in the familiar *Venus and Adonis* manner.

Yet it should be obvious that *Hero and Leander* is in Marlowe's maturest style (though even that has been questioned)[1] and that in 1593 he was not likely to practise the naïveté of a *Scillaes Metamorphosis* or an *Endimion and Phœbe*. His tendency at this period was towards distortion (or 'farce')[2] and though, in *The Jew of Malta*, his material was crude and simplified, this implies a corresponding subtlety and power in its selection and arrangement.

If this tendency towards distortion or caricature in the handling of already simplified (because stock) material is remembered, these lines, which follow the elaborate description of Hero's appearance, may appear in a new light:

> So lovely fair was Hero, Venus' nun,
> As Nature wept, thinking she was undone,
> Because she took more from her than she kept,
> And of such wondrous beauty her bereft;
> Therefore, in sign her treasure suffered wrack,
> Since Hero's time hath half the world been black.
>
> (*First Sestiad*, 45ff.)

The first conceit is a familiar one, but the accent is not familiar; and that last hyperbole, with its brisk rhyme, clinches the impression of an attitude not mock-heroic (the term is too definite) but quite

detached and even faintly amused. A little later, the effect of Hero's
beauty on the general population of Sestos is described:

> So ran the people forth to gaze upon her:
> And all that saw her were enamour'd on her:
> And as in fury of a dreadful fight,
> Their fellows being slain or put to flight,
> Poor soldiers stand with fear of death dead-strooken,
> So at her presence all surprised and tooken,
> Await the sentence of her scornful eyes;
> He whom she favours lives; the other dies.
> There might you see one sigh, another rage,
> And some, their violent passions to assuage,
> Compile sharp satires: but alas, too late.
>   (*First Sestiad*, 117ff.)

The movement of the last four lines, the mock desperation of those
pauses after the third foot, and the cheerful air with which the whole
passage sums up the fate of the lovers, cap the jaunty double rhymes.
The description is clearly in a vein of delicate mockery, spoken as it
were with eyebrows raised. Yet the simile of the poor soldiers is
straightforwardly passionate, and saves the feelings from any danger
of frivolity, reversing the usual decorative and expansive function of
the simile in Marlowe.

The description of the gods' sports, as painted on the wall of the
temple, has the same deliberate overexuberance as the first passage:

> Jove . . . for his love Europa bellowing loud,
> And tumbling with the Rainbow in a cloud.
>   (*First Sestiad*, 148–9)

The splendid 'periphrasis of night' which follows has a simple and
straightforward power, for this caricature is not belittling, nor is the
degree of distortion constant. It is the variations from one level of
detachment to another that give the poem its extraordinary air of
maturity and poise. And it is Marlowe's own assent to the irresisti-
bility of love which prompts the ruthlessness to Hero's lovers, to
Hero herself, bombarded by the sophistries of Leander. The key
to the attitude is the passage which Shakespeare quoted:

> It lies not in our power to love or hate,
> For will in us is over-ruled by fate. . . .
> When both deliberate, the love is slight,
> Whoever lov'd that lov'd not at first sight?
>   (*First Sestiad*, 167–8, 175–6)

and later,

> Love is not full of pity as men say,
> But deaf and cruel when he means to prey.
> (*Second Sestiad*, 287–8)

Hero's prayers are beaten down with relish by Marlowe as well as by Cupid: here he triumphantly identifies himself with the gods against the mortals. The deliberate caricature of that passage can hardly be contested:

> Her vows about the empty air he flings,
> All deep enrag'd, his sinewy bow he bent,
> And shot a shaft that burning from him went.
> (*First Sestiad*, 370ff.)

The story of the Destinies' love for Cupid is a burlesque illustration of the same theme, not a digression. It is exhilarating to see the beautiful pair of lovers so hopelessly entangled: it is farcical to see the toothless Destinies doting on Cupid and, with characteristic Marlovian violence, reversing the order of the world for his sake. They serve exactly the same purpose as the old Nurse in *Dido, Queen of Carthage*, who is bewitched and acts as a parody of the Queen. The parallels between *Dido* and *Hero and Leander* have not, I think, been sufficiently stressed: besides that of the theme, Marlowe's attitude of adult detachment coupled with direct passion is the same in both the works. It cannot be doubted that the scene between the Nurse and Cupid[3] with its ripe luxuriance of description belongs to the same period as the poem. The prologue to *Dido*, the scene between Jove and Ganymede, has a parallel in the episode of Leander and Neptune in the *Second Sestiad*.

The self-deceptions, the half-serious efforts to escape which Hero makes, are obvious comedy. Her slyness in 'coming somewhat nigh' Leander, her 'Come hither', (which invitation slips out 'unawares'), her final attempt to 'train' him by dropping her fan as she goes, which he with unpardonable clumsiness ignores, are not the coquetries of a Cressida, but the delicacies of a Criseyde. It is in fact with Chaucer's heroine that one compares her again and again: and the end of the *Second Sestiad* forms a remarkable parallel to *Troilus and Criseyde*, III, stanzas 156–79.

> Treason was in her thought,
> And cunningly to yield herself she sought.
> Seeming not won, yet was she won at length,
> In such wars women use but half their strength.
> (*Second Sestiad*, 293ff.)

> This Troilus in armes gan hir streyne,
> And seyde 'O sweet, as even mote I goon,
> Now be ye caught, now is there but we tweyne,
> Now yeldeth yow, for other boot is noon.'
> To that Criseyde answered this anoon,
> 'Ne hadde I er now, my swete herte deere,
> Ben yolde, iwis, I were not now here.'
>   (Book III, 173)

Chaucer's exultancy is very similar to Marlowe's; it comes directly in the joy with which he packs the household off to bed:

> There was no more skippen nor to daunce,
> But boden go to bedde with mischaunce,
> If any wight was stirring anywhere,
> And let hem slepe that a-bedde were.
>   (Book III, 99)

or in the 'sheer song of ironical happiness' of stanza 152.[4]

The attitude to Hero is one of exultant ruthlessness: the attitude to Leander varies. Sometimes he is the 'sharp bold sophister', and then the fun lies in the pomposity of his pleas. Sometimes he is the complete innocent (as in the incident of the fan), and then the subdued laugh of a double rhyme goes against him.

> Leander rude in love and raw
> Long dallying with Hero, nothing saw
> That might delight him more, yet he suspected
> Some amorous rites or other were neglected.
>   (*Second Sestiad*, 60ff.)

Finally a great many of the 'sentences' which complete a couplet as if with a little aside from the author, show the same mixtures of irony and exuberance, especially those which sum up and dismiss in a sophisticated manner the feminine point of view:

> Hero's looks yielded but her words made war,
> Women are won when they begin to jar.
>   (*First Sestiad*, 331–2)

> Ne'er king sought more to keep his diadem
> Than Hero this inestimable gem . . .
> Jewels being lost are found again, this never;
> 'Tis lost but once and once lost for ever.
>   (*Second Sestiad*, 78–9, 85–6)

> Seeming not won, yet was she won at length,

> In such wars women use but half their strength.
> *(Second Sestiad, 295–6)*

And those delightful lines,

> Seeing a naked man, she screech'd for fear
> Such sights as this to tender maids are rare.
> *(Second Sestiad, 237–8)*

The general attitude is nearer to Chaucer's than that of Keats in *St Agnes' Eve* or even Shakespeare in *Venus and Adonis*. Marlowe is both ironically detached and sympathetically identified with the lovers: and this is not an unlikely point of view for the satirical wit that the few records suggest him to have been. He appears of a sensuous and passionate temper, but detached in his attitude towards other people. He enjoyed the discomfiture of his friends, whether he produced it by unpleasant practical jokes ('sudden privie injuries') or by blasphemies about the role of the Angel Gabriel in the Annunciation, and Kyd thought 'he was of a cruel heart'. At all events he seems more Mercutio than Romeo (and it is rather surprising that none of the more biographically-minded of the Shakespearian critics has yet made the equation).

How far such an attitude could have produced any satisfactory end to the story is uncertain. Chaucer found a straightforward tragedy impossible in *Troilus and Criseyde*: but his methods of evasion were not open to Marlowe, particularly as the later poem is on so much smaller a scale. *Dido* ends magnificently, but the comedy at the beginning is not so important as in *Hero and Leander*. The greater success of the poem may be defined in the greater complexity of the feelings behind it, the surer poise: so that perhaps to doubt the possibility of a suitable ending is to underestimate Marlowe's powers.

Notes

1 L. C. Martin, Introduction to the *Poems*, p. 3.
2 T. S. Eliot, 'Notes on the Blank Verse of Christopher Marlowe', *The Sacred Wood*.
3 Act IV v. There is one line in common between *Dido* and *Hero and Leander* (*Dido*, ii i 231, and *Hero*, 1 382).
4 Empson, *Seven Types of Ambiguity*, p. 86. His remarks are very pertinent to this question.

III.

Shakespeare's Debt to Marlowe

> 'Who chooseth me shall gain what many men desire.'
> Why, that's the lady! All the world desires her;
> From the four corners of the earth they come
> To kiss this shrine, this mortal-breathing saint.
> The Hyrcanian deserts and the vasty wilds
> Of wide Arabia are as throughfares now
> For princes to come view fair Portia.
> The watery Kingdom, whose ambitious head
> Spits in the face of heaven, is no bar
> To stop the foreign spirits, but they come
> As o'er a brook to see fair Portia.
> *(The Merchant of Venice,* II vii 37–47)

At the moment of high ritual when the first of Portia's suitors, the Prince of Morocco, is to make his choice, a heightening of the verse attests his ardour. The dancing rhythm, with its onward flow, its panoramic view, and its refrain, is modelled on Tamburlaine's speech at the death of Zenocrate. Her apotheosis is celebrated with images of the cosmic grandeur that have marked Tamburlaine throughout, tinged here it would seem with some echoes of the Book of Revelations; Morocco uses the ritual of pilgrimage to express his reverence, although presumably his holy place is Mecca.

Morocco like Tamburlaine is a solar figure, clad in 'the shadowed livery of the burnished sun' (II i 2), and like Tamburlaine's the conclusion of his quest is a death's head. Tamburlaine's grief at the death of Zenocrate is his first acknowledgement of mortality; he enshrines his dead Queen 'not lapped in lead, but in a sheet of gold' (2 *Tamburlaine,* II iv 131), the gold casket of Morocco's choice.

> Now walk the angels on the walls of heaven,
> As sentinels to warn th'immortal souls

To entertain divine Zenocrate.
Apollo, Cynthia, and the ceaseless lamps
That gently looked upon this loathsome earth,
Shine downwards now no more, but deck the heavens
To entertain divine Zenocrate.
The crystal springs, whose taste illuminates
Refinèd eyes with an eternal sight
Like trièd silver runs through Paradise
To entertain divine Zenocrate.
The cherubins and holy seraphins,
That sing and play before the King of Kings,
Use all their voices and their instruments
To entertain divine Zenocrate.
And in this sweet and curious harmony,
The god that tunes this music to our souls
Holds out his hand in highest majesty
To entertain divine Zenocrate.

                    (2 *Tamburlaine*, II iv 15–33)

The music is kept back for Bassanio, and for the last scene of all, but the dark quality behind the choice, the hint of regality tempered with grief, has been established. This dramatic recollection is designed to evoke audience memories, and to give a heightened audience-response in the theatre; it is more than a literary evocation.

Marlowe is found both at Belmont and Venice; the main Marlovian connections, though more diffused, lie in Shylock's role.

In making use of *The Jew of Malta*, Shakespeare may have drawn on his own memories as an actor – for the play, unlike *Tamburlaine*, was not in print, but it had been put on by Lord Strange's Men in 1592, and was subsequently given by the Admiral's Men. If Alleyn played Barabas, Burbage as Shylock acquired a subtler version of the stage Jew. Shakespeare took over certain situations, particularly from the role of Abigail the Jew's daughter, but Barabas's joy at the strategem by which his daughter recovers his gold from its hiding place –

                    O my girl,
          My gold, my fortune, my felicity!
          . . .
          O girl! O gold! O beauty! O my bliss! –
                    (*The Jew of Malta*, II i 46–53)

becomes Shylock's grief at the flight of Jessica as mocked by Solanio:

          I never heard a passion so confused,
          So strange, outrageous and so variable,

> As the dog Jew did utter in the streets.
> 'My daughter! O my ducats! O my daughter!'
> (II vii 12–15)

The subtle use of one Christian to entrap another was a practice of Barabas which Shylock greatly expands when he pleads that the law of Venice, and international confidence in its stability, demand the fulfilment of his bond. That Antonio stands surety for Bassanio is not of Shylock's contrivance, as the mutual destruction of Mathias and Lodowick is of Barabas's.

Shakespeare can assume certain conventions about his stage figure, and upon them work his own tranformation. Barabas's justification for his treacheries, that 'Christians do the like', is sufficiently demonstrated; zest in planning these as a 'savage farce' he whetted the ironic plots in earlier plays, particularly *Titus Andronicus* and *Richard III*, where malignant delight in evil extrudes itself in lively action. The most direct borrowing from *The Jew of Malta*, Aaron's death speech in *Titus Andronicus*, is closely modelled on Barabas's counsel to Ithamore (*The Jew of Malta*, II iii 165–99),

> First be thou void of these affections:
> Compassion, love, vain hope, and heartless fear;
> (165–6)

but becomes active:

> Even now I curse the day – and yet, I think,
> Few come within the compass of my curse –
> Wherein I did not some notorious ill.
> (*Titus Andronicus*, V i 125–7)

The list of crimes that make up Barabas's life story include un-provoked murders (though of a secret kind) and more elaborate stratagems; beginning

> As for myself, I walk abroad a-nights,
> And kill sick people groaning under walls;
> Sometimes I go about and poison wells;
> (*The Jew of Malta*, II iii 172–4)

and ending with the macabre image of a man hanging himself for grief, with pinned upon his breast a long great scroll 'how I with interest tormented him'. Aaron's crimes are more openly violent, but the list ends with an equally macabre image of death; he digs up dead men and sets them at

> their dear friends' door
> Even when their sorrows almost was forgot,
> And on their skins, as on the bark of trees,
> Have with my knife carvèd in Roman letters,
> 'Let not your sorrow die, though I am dead.'
> (*Titus Andronicus*, v i 136–40)

The scrolls transform these two Death figures into emblems of Judgement, which lies beyond death.

As Aaron's last dying confession, an occasion when a man was expected to give an exemplary speech, and ensure his future life by dying well, his diabolic manifesto has more force than the counsel imparted to a slave by reason of the position which it occupies. Unquenched evil holds its addict fast. Barabas's own death speech is comparatively short, and entails a triumphant acknowledgement of what he has brought about, with a final curse on Christians and Turks alike. The theological implications of his end have been studied in detail by G. K. Hunter.[1] Aaron's choice of the devil's part is explicit, and more purposefully aimed:

> If there be devils, would I were a devil,
> To live and burn in everlasting fire,
> So I might have your company in hell
> But to torment you with my bitter tongue!
> (v i 147–50)

A just doom is to set him breast deep in earth, and famish him – 'There let him stand and rave and cry for food.' This is the end meted out to the negro bond-slave in the second part of *The Pleasant History of Tom a Lincoln*: it seems symbolic of the end of Base Desire. Aaron, who would 'have his soul black like his face', is one of a line of villainous Moors, Turks and Jews who supplied the material for atrocity plays like *Selimus* and *Lust's Dominion*; but his role in the retinue of the Empress allows for a mixture of ferocious comedy in Marlowe's manner, as he kills the nurse who has delivered the black infant born to him by the Empress, or as he instructs her sons in his own diabolic arts. This diabolic, jesting vitality has a Marlovian ring, though Shakespeare's sense of natural detail is as always much nearer the soil:

> Come on, you thick-lipped slave, I'll bear you hence;
> For it is you that puts us to our shifts.
> I'll make you feed on berries and on roots,
> And feed on curds and whey, and suck the goat,
> And cabin in a cave, and bring you up

> To be a warrior and command a camp.
> (*Titus Andronicus*, IV ii 176–81)

Aaron initiates most of the action in the play; when at the end Tamora and her sons disguised as Revenge, Rapine and Murder, they are, as it were, entering a figurative level which Aaron has already presented. In a play as deeply indebted to Kyd's Revenge dramas as *Titus Andronicus*, the Marlovian ingredient has brought something more characteristic of Shakespeare the poet into the remarkably well-constructed tragedy; and into its sombre and heraldic symmetries something of the countryside. Even Aaron's final catalogue of crimes includes some that sound like country witchcraft; to

> Make poor men's cattle break their necks;
> Set fire on barns and hay-stacks in the night,
> (V i 132–3)

are crimes not really worthy of the imperial court.

Shakespeare's imitations of Marlowe, even at their closest, invite consideration of the differences between the two. Marlowe's was incomparably the most powerful dramatic voice which he encountered at the beginning of his career, and Tamburlaine's were the accents which first had liberated the drama. Blended with the voice of the Jew in Aaron is the voice of Tamburlaine, especially in his opening soliloquy:

> Now climbeth Tamora Olympus' top,
> Safe out of fortune's shot, and sits aloft,
> Secure of thunder's crack or lightning flash,
> Advanced above pale Envy's threatening reach.
> . . .
> Away with slavish weeds and servile thoughts!
> I will be bright and shine in pearl and gold.
> (II i 1–4, 18–19)

The superb assurance of these lines, the triumph over Fortune, is Marlovian, in so grand a style that the fact that Aaron sacrifices his pride to secure the life of his bastard comes with a startling reversal. It is as if recalling Marlowe pushed Shakespeare into a further degree of inventiveness. This was the thesis maintained by Nicholas Brooke in the most cogent study of their relationship, *Marlowe as Provocative Agent in Shakespeare's Early Plays*.[2] As the sequence of history plays by Shakespeare and Marlowe ricochet one from another, each is seen borrowing in turn from the other. Henry VI's weakness shows the distintegrative force of a culpable innocence that lacks all will to

power, and is in strongest contrast to Tamburlaine's power drive.
Greene's parody from that play in his warning, addressed to Marlowe, against Shakespeare, 'O tiger's heart wrapped in a woman's
hide',[3] is indeed the key to the catatonic movement by which
Margaret becomes a spirit of Nemesis. Finally, as the embodiment of
evil, Richard Crookback betters the Marlovian villain-heroes, for
while they were pupils of Machiavelli he could 'set the murderous
Machiavel to school'. His opening speech also betters theirs, for he is
his own prologue, whilst they are preceded by various kinds of
chorus.

   Edward II, Marlowe's riposte, is clearly indebted to *Richard III*,
since Mortimer's role as protector derives in some details from
Richard's (see Harold Brooks, 'Marlowe and the Early
Shakespeare'),[4] but, as the study of an obsession, the play lacks that
wider sense of the country's plight, the desolation of England's
trampled garden, so prominent in Shakespeare's counter-play,
Richard II. Here the plot of the deposed and libertine king has many
parallels with Marlowe's, but whilst for instance the ritual of the
deposition scene is greatly expanded, the homosexual element is so
played down that Bushy, Bagot and Green seem almost irrelevant.
Some of the Marlovian magniloquence heard in the opening scenes
does not come from *Edward II*, but the earlier plays.

> I would allow him odds
> And meet him, were I tied to run afoot,
> Even to the frozen ridges of the Alps.
> (*Richard II*, 1 i 62–4)
>
> O, who can hold a fire in his hand
> By thinking on the frosty Caucasus?
> (1 iii 294–5)

The two dramatists, contending with and reacting from each other,
select their material to make contrasting effects. Richard's fall is
more richly developed; 'Down, down I come like glistering Phaeton'
is mirrored in the actual descent from the uppper to the lower stage;
in the deposition scene itself, 'Fiend, thou torments me ere I come to
hell' stands in apposition to the many comparisons with Christ and
evokes Dr Faustus, whose last speech is echoed in the cry

> O that I were a mockery king of snow
> Standing before the sun of Bolingbroke,
> To melt myself away in water drops!
> (IV i 260–2)

But here there is the double image of the King's present tears, and of his former heraldic badge, the sunburst, which was applied to him in the earlier scene. The effects of *Dr Faustus* are felt most powerfully where they are most indirect, in the final moments of self-knowledge at Pomfret, though here the depth of tragic knowledge is more analytic than Marlowe's.

The question remains that this rivalry in the theatre may have accompanied rivalry outside the theatre. What is the relation of *Venus and Adonis* to *Hero and Leander*? And is Marlowe the rival poet of Sonnets 85 and 86?

The order in which the two Ovidian romances were composed is not easy to decide. *Hero and Leander* was entered to John Wolf in the Stationers' Register on 28 September 1593, only a few months after Marlowe's death on 30 May; but it did not appear till Edward Blount published it in 1598. *Venus and Adonis* was entered on 18 April 1593 to Richard Field, and was certainly in print by June. A second edition appeared in 1594 and it was frequently reprinted. G. P. V. Akrigg, in his *Shakespeare and the Earl of Southampton*,[5] called attention to the Latin poem 'Narcissus' by John Clapham, secretary to Lord Burghley, which was printed by Thomas Scarlet in 1591 with a dedication to the Earl of Southampton. It was the first dedication the young Earl had received, but it may not have been particularly welcome.[6]

For this 'short and moral description of Youthful Love and especially Self-Love' was intended as a warning fable to the young ward who was refusing to accept the plans of his guardian, Burghley, that he should marry Burghley's granddaughter, Lady Elizabeth Vere, a marriage which had been in the Lord Treasurer's mind since the previous year.

The scene is England. Narcissus visits the Temple of Love – which, like the temple in *Hero and Leander*, is painted with stories of famous victims – where he is received by Venus, and instructed in Ovid and Petrarch; but Love prophesies that Narcissus will perish of self-love. Having drunk of Lethe, and thereby forfeited self-knowledge, Narcissus is borne on an untameable horse named 'Lust' to the Fountain of Self-Love, where, according to legend, he is drowned – in despair that night has removed the image of himself from the waters.

Here, then, is the warning which was extended to the recalcitrant youth, and here much of the material which Shakespeare was to catch up and present in a far less offensive guise. The prime model for *Venus and Adonis* is not Marlowe, but Clapham, who supplies the moral, as well as reason for the inset of the horse and jennet, and the version of the story, reduced to a mere illustration in the persuasion

of Venus, that Narcissus drowned himself (and was not, as in Ovid,
pulled into the water by amorous nymphs).

> Is thine own heart to thine own face affected?
> Can thy right hand seize love upon thy left?
> Then woo thyself, be of thyself rejected;
> Steal thine own freedom and complain on theft.
> Narcissus so himself himself forsook,
> And died to kiss his shadow in the brook.
> (157–62)

Clapham has

> Deficiunt vires, et vox et spiritus ipse
> Deficit, et pronus de ripa decidit et sic
> Ipse suae periit deceptus imaginis umbra.
> (sig. B3v)

Marlowe dismisses the story of Narcissus as a mere adjunct or mark
to show Leander's surpassing beauty:

> let it suffice
> That my slack muse sings of Leander's eyes,
> Those orient cheeks and lips, exceeding his
> That leapt into the water for a kiss
> Of his own shadow, and despising many,
> Died ere he could enjoy the love of any,
> (*Hero and Leander*, i 71–6)

as the story of Venus and Adonis is merely a tale embroidered on the
hem of Hero's sleeve:

> Her wide sleeves green, and bordered with a grove,
> Where Venus in her naked glory strove
> To please the careless and disdainful eyes
> Of proud Adonis that before her lies,
> (i 11–14)

and the 'hot proud horse' an image of Leander's imperviousness to
the counsel of his father (ii 141–5). The temple of Venus, where
Marlowe's poem opens, may recall more precisely the same Temple
in Clapham's poem: although commonplace, it fits in the catena of
images linking all three poems.

Venus and Adonis shows a far closer relation with the first group
of the Sonnets (1–19); the two Ovidian poems seem rather to be
running parallel to each other, both deriving from Clapham. If

Marlowe's poem were complete as it stands (and there are precedents for such selective treatment) it would provide a persuasion to love quite devoid of warnings. Blount of course refers to it as an 'unfinished tragedy' in his dedicatory letter to Sir Thomas Walsingham, with whom Marlowe had been residing at the time of his death. But the full story would defeat the special purpose.

In Shakespeare's poem, the natural beauty of the landscape and of the animals is totally unlike the jewelled exotic world of Marlowe's poem; Shakespeare had already brought more of the natural scene into his Marlovian portrait of Aaron, and much into *Richard II*. It is one of the distinguishing marks between the imagination of the one and the other poet.

The comedy is equally contrasted; Shakespeare's is muted, incidental:

> Her song was tedious, and outwore the night,
> For lovers' hours are long, though seeming short;
> . . .
> Their copious stories, often times begun,
> End without audience and are never done,
> (841–2, 845–6)

whilst Marlowe's, enclosed in the taut couplet form, is more pervasive, an exultant triumph at the expense of mortals and gods, who are alike befooled, self-deceiving, and subjected to deflating comment:

> Albeit Leander, rude in love and raw,
> Long dallying with Hero, nothing saw
> That might delight him more, yet he suspected
> Some amorous rites or other were neglected.
> (ii 61–4)

Both are addressing an audience whose appetite for the pure honey of Ovidian eroticism is tempered by a taste for witty 'arguments of love'. This is one of the games people play when they have to lead a good deal of their private life in public, as courtiers did. Though it is so near in theme to the Sonnets, *Venus and Adonis* is a more public affair; indeed, it was licensed for printing by the Archbishop of Canterbury himself – did he actually read it, or was it one of his chaplains?

Kenneth Muir and Sean O'Loughlin noted the almost satiric outlook of *Venus and Adonis* in parts, and its ironic use of hyperbole.[7] This becomes appropriate in a context that asks for a 'correction' of John Clapham's sententiousness. This unwilling

Adonis (not a traditional role for him) must be offered a more artful persuasion to love.

As I have indicated elsewhere,[8] I think *Venus and Adonis* was also Shakespeare's response to charges of ignorance made by Robert Greene, which were couched in the form of a warning to Marlowe, the 'famous gracer of tragedians'. It was designed to obliterate the impression he had tried to make by its implicit claim to Art, set out in its motto

> Vilia miretur vulgus; mihi flavus Apollo
> Pocula Castalia plena ministret aqua . . .

Ovidian lines which Marlowe had translated

> Let base-conceited wits admire vile things,
> Fair Phoebus lead me to the Muses' springs.
> (*Elegy* xv 35–6)

If *Venus and Adonis* is an answer to Clapham's Latin, its claim as 'Art' increases.

During the winter of 1592–3, when the theatres in London were closed by the plague, poets scattered to country retreats – the kind of retreat that Boccaccio depicted in *The Decameron*, if they were fortunate, or the kind that is suggested in *Love's Labour's Lost*. It was during this period of retreat that Shakespeare wrote *Venus and Adonis* – T. W. Baldwin dates it just a few months or weeks before publication.[9] In the seventeenth century it would have been a country-house poem – as, in some respects, it is.

The danger from plague, which did not spare the young or the beautiful, lies behind its note of urgency. The plea for 'breed' was intensified by such circumstances. Here the two poets re-echo each other. 'Beauty alone is lost, too warily kept' parallels 'Beauty within itself should not wasted', and the familiar argument of usury re-occurs, Shakespeare here being the more succinct. Venus has been describing all the maladies that 'in one minute's fight bring beauty under', comparing the body to 'a swallowing grave' if it buries its own posterity – an act worse than suicide or parricide.

> Foul cank'ring rust the hidden treasure frets,
> But gold that's put to use more gold begets.
> (767–8)

Leander's sophistry lacks this pressure but his eye certainly glances from earth to heaven. Ships were made to sail the sea, strings to play upon, brass pots to shine with use, robes to be worn, palaces to live in:

> What difference betwixt the richest mine
> And basest mould but use? For both, not used,
> Are of like worth. Then treasure is abused
> When misers keep it; being put to loan,
> In time it will return us two for one.
>
> (i 232—6)

The familiar innuendo spices this trade catalogue, but Hero's reply, which is very brief, seems not amiss: 'Who taught thee rhetoric to deceive a maid?' (i 338) Marlowe is not involved; and this spirited series of conflicts – between gods, between the lovers, within Hero herself – taught Shakespeare more about how to write plays, and fit conflict within conflict.

Sonnets 85 and 86, as I believe, describe a poetry contest between Shakespeare and the Rival Poet. These contests of recitation – one thinks of the *Mastersingers* of Wagner – had been held in London since Chaucer's time at the festival of the Pui (the guild of foreign merchants); at a lower level there were scolding matches or 'flytings'.[10]

> Was it the proud full sail of his great verse,
> Bound for the prize of all-too-precious you,
> That did my ripe thoughts in my brain inhearse,
> Making their tomb the womb wherein they grew?
> Was it his spirit, by spirits taught to write
> Above a mortal pitch, that struck me dead?
> No.
> . . .
> But when your countenance filled up his line
> Then lacked I matter; that enfeebled mine.
>
> (Sonnet 86)

Marlowe was so often credited with 'inspiration' by his fellow poets, with the 'brave translunary things' that made his spirits 'all air and fire' that the fifth line does not derogate from the recognisable fitness of the opening lines to Marlowe and to him alone. (Chapman, chief alternative, had at this time written nothing, was only newly out of the Low Countries, and found composition extremely difficult and agonising by his own accounts.)

If Marlowe were the rival poet (and he seems to me the most likely candidate), this would explain why his verse re-occurred to Shakespeare in *The Merchant of Venice* within the high ritual atmosphere of a prize contest. In Sonnet 85 the winning poem was to 'reserve [its] character with golden quill', which was what happened to the prize poem at the festival of the Pui, where the winner was given a 'crown' for the song he had made in praise of the newly elected 'Prince' of that fraternity. It was then hung up under the 'Prince's' arms. (A mock challenge at wooing is set up in Jonson's *Cynthia's Revels*.) In *The Merchant of Venice* the contest is for a much nobler reward; Morocco, the first contestant, departs with the mournful echo of what he had read on the scroll, 'Your suit is cold':

> Cold indeed and labour lost!
> Then farewell, heat, and welcome, frost,
> (II vii 74–5)

whilst, after the interlude of Aragon (whom Nicholas Brooke compares with Marlowe's figure of the Guise in his contempt for things common), Bassanio approaches with that note of love and springtime which is heard in the plays as well as the poems:

> A day in April never came so sweet
> To show how costly summer was at hand
> As this fore-spurrer comes before his lord.
> (II ix 93–5)

The after-effects of *Hero and Leander* can be sensed in *Romeo and Juliet*. The resemblance is general and is a matter of the high assurance of Juliet's 'Gallop apace, you fiery-footed steeds', or Mercutio's bawdy wit (perhaps also the tragic suddenness of his death in a futile brawl may be taken to reflect Marlowe's own). The sustained note of lyric joy, the physical obstacles that separate the lovers, the blindness of destiny that opposes them do not add up to a challenge to Marlowe; they are in Shakespeare's own mode.

From time to time he looked back on Marlowe. Among Pistol's playscraps the 'hollow pamper'd jades of Asia' appear along with Callipolis and Hiren the Fair Greek. Then, in 1598, *Hero and Leander* appeared in print, and Shakespeare, for the only time in his life, identified and quoted a contemporary

> Dead shepherd, now I find thy saw of might:
> 'Who ever loved that loved not at first sight?'
> (*As You Like It*, III v 80–1)

Two scenes earlier there had been a reference to Marlowe's death:

> *Touchstone:*   I am here with thee and thy goats, as the most capricious poet, honest Ovid, was among the Goths.

Jaques: O knowledge ill-inhabited, worse than Jove in a thatched
house!
Touchstone: When a man's verses cannot be understood, nor a man's
good wit seconded with the forward child understanding,
it strikes a man more dead than a great reckoning in a little
room. (III iii 4–13)

It is generally conceded that the 'great reckoning in a little room'
recalls Marlowe's death in a quarrel over the reckoning in a tavern.
The jest about 'honest Ovid' might have brought him to mind; but
the catastrophe that when a man's verses cannot be understood it
strikes him dead also recalls Sonnet 86:

> Was it his spirit, by spirits taught to write
> Above a mortal pitch, that struck me dead?

Not literally, of course; he had 'dried' – the actor's worst fear, a fear
already described in Sonnet 23. The image here is a double one, of the
reciter 'struck dead' and that later death after 'a great reckoning in a
little room'. Tenderest of all is Rosalind's denial that any in 6000
years had met Leander's fate (untold in Marlowe's poem).

Leander, he would have lived many a fair year, though Hero had turned
nun, if it had not been for a hot midsummer-night; for, good youth, he
went but forth to wash him in the Hellespont, and, being taken with the
cramp, was drowned; and the foolish chroniclers of that age found it was
– Hero of Sestos. But these are all lies: men have died from time to time,
and worms have eaten them, but not for love. (*As You Like It*, IV i 83ff.)

The playfulness covering so much hesitant and withheld feeling,
which is Rosalind's charm, chimes with the memory of a contest for
love and favour, ended so abruptly. A later memory of Marlowe is
also associated with death. Hamlet's favourite piece of verse has a
distinctly Marlovian ring, though he cannot remember it exactly
('"The rugged Pyrrhus, like th' Hyrcanean beast" – Tis not so; it
begins with Pyrrhus' (*Hamlet*, II ii 444–5)).

This enormous icon, much bigger than life, with 'sable arms /
Black as his purpose', foreshadows, with his arrested action as he
stands over Priam, his sword held aloft, an image we are to see, of
Hamlet himself standing over the kneeling Claudius. It is something
that has risen from the depth of the mind, and that is to return; in its
primitive violence and rhetorical emphasis quite unShakespearian,
though of course very well suited to stand out from the text of this
play. This, in itself, it would appear, was the reworking of a tragedy
that had belonged to Marlowe's day.

Shakespeare's relation to Kyd, and to Lyly, is often of a more detailed kind than his relation to Marlowe, for what they offered were theatrical models of rhetorical speech and dramatic patterning. What Shakespeare learnt from Marlowe, the only figure whose poetic powers approached his own, was shown rather in reaction. The greatest of Marlowe's creations, *Dr Faustus*, makes the least identifiable contribution; yet as Macbeth stands waiting for the sound of the bell, there is but one scene with which it may be compared.

Psychologists affirm that the slighter the indication of an adjustment, the deeper its roots may well lie. Shakespeare reacted to Marlowe in a selective way, and as a person; that is to say, there is an emotional train of association in his borrowings. Marlowe, it is clear from *Edward II*, also reacted to Shakespeare; and Greene's warning to Marlowe may have gained in point and malice if the two were already known in some sense to be in contest for the poetic 'crown'. Such a contest, in the plague years, would have been part of the courting of favour that had survived in Spenser's day, but was by the mid-1590s not without its alternatives. To these Shakespeare returned, throwing in his lot with the common players.

Notes

1 'The Theology of Marlowe's *The Jew of Malta*', *Journal of the Warburg and Courtauld Institutes*, XXVII (1964), pp. 211–40. Reprinted in G. K. Hunter, *Dramatic Identities and Cultural Tradition* (1978).

2 *Shakespeare Survey* 14 (Cambridge, 1961), pp. 34–44.

3 Greene's well-known passage in his *Groatsworth of Witte* (1592): 'There is an upstart crow, beautified with our feathers, that with his *Tiger's heart wrapped in a player's hide*, supposes he is as well able to bombast out a blank verse as the best of you, and being an absolute *Johannes fac totum*, is in his own conceit the only Shake-scene in a country.' This is the first reference to Shakespeare in the literature of his time. The line is *3 Henry VI*, I iv 137.

4 In *Christopher Marlowe*, ed. Brian Morris (London, 1968).

5 London, 1968.

6 The dedication ran: 'Clarissimo et Nobilissimo Domino Henrico Comiti Southamptoniae; Johannes Clapham virtutis, atque honoris incrementum multosque annos exoptat.' For John Clapham, see Joel Hurstfield, *The Queen's Wards* (London, 1958), especially p. 263 where Clapham is quoted as saying Burghley 'oft-times gratified his friends and servants that depended and waited on him.' It was presumably for Burghley's gratification, not the dedicatee's, that the poem was written.

It is unfortunately not given in Bullough's *Narrative and Dramatic Sources of Shakespeare*. STC lists only the London copy (*STC*, 5349).

7 See *The Voyage to Illyria* (London, 1937), pp. 44–5, where it is also said Shakespeare owed most to Marlowe in this poem.

8 See my article 'Beasts and Gods; Greene's *Groatsworth of Witte* and the social purpose of *Venus and Adonis*', *Shakespeare Survey* 15 (Cambridge, 1962), pp. 62–80. *Collected Papers* vol. 1.

9 T. W. Baldwin, *On the Literary Genetics of Shakespeare's Poems and Sonnets* (Urbana, Illinois, 1950), p. 45: 'It would seem . . . *Venus and Adonis* was written no long time before its entry for publication.'

10 For the festival of the Pui, see my *Shakespeare the Craftsman* (London, 1969), pp. 31–2.

IV.

Shakespeare and the Use of
Disguise in Elizabethan Drama

Today disguise is a living part of the drama. Sir Francis Crewe of *The Dog beneath The Skin*, the mysterious stranger at *The Cocktail Party*, the intrusive little girls of Giraudoux's *Electra* do not bear the limited significance which naturalism and the set characters of the nineteenth century imposed. Disguise was then reduced to a subterfuge, restricted to the Scarlet Pimpernel, the hero of *The Only Way* or the heroine of *East Lynne* ('Dead! and he never called me mother!'). Ibsen and Chekhov transformed it. Those implications of self-deception and fantasy which are the stuff of *A Doll's House* and *The Cherry Orchard* lurk in a masquerade dress, or a few conjuring tricks at a ball. Yet even in its revival, disguise has not attained the manifold significance which it enjoyed in the Elizabethan theatre and which Shakespeare alone fully revealed.

A study of the subject was provided by V. O. Freeburg as long ago as 1915 and has not been superseded (*Disguise Plots in Elizabethan Drama*, Columbia University Press, New York). Dr Freeburg's conception of disguise belongs, however, to the nineteenth century: 'Dramatic disguise ... means a change of personal appearance which leads to mistaken identity. There is a double test, change and confusion.' He eliminates the mere confusion of *The Comedy of Errors* and the substitution of Mariana for Isabella in *Measure for Measure*, where, as in the similar situation of *All's Well*, Shakespeare himself actually uses the word:

> So disguise shall, by the disguised,
> Pay with falsehood false exacting,
> And perform an old contracting.

> Only in this disguise I think't no sin
> To cosen him that would unjustly win.

I should prefer to define disguise as the substitution, overlaying or metamorphosis of dramatic identity, whereby one character sustains two roles. This may involve deliberate or involuntary masquerade, mistaken or concealed identity, madness or possession. Disguise ranges from the simple fun of the quick-change artist (*The Blind Beggar of Alexandria*) to the antic disposition of Edgar or Hamlet: it may need a cloak and false beard, or it may be better translated for the modern age by such terms as 'alternating personality'.

Dr Freeburg distinguishes five main types of disguise, all of which Shakespeare employs. These are the girl-page (Julia, Rosalind, Viola, Imogen), the boy-bride (*Taming of the Shrew* and *The Merry Wives*), the rogue in a variety of disguises (Autolycus) the spy in disguise (Vincentio) and the lover in disguise (Lucentio in *The Taming of the Shrew*). All go back to classical comedy, and except for the girl-pages they do not represent important aspects for Shakespeare. The boy-bride and the rogue are bound to lead to farce, and are handled better by Jonson in *Epicoene*, *Every Man In His Humour* and *The Alchemist*.

For the Elizabethans, 'disguise' still retained its primary sense of strange apparel, and 'disguising' was still the name for amateur plays. In Jonson's *Masque of Augurs* one player uses 'disguised' in the slang sense (to be drunk, as in *Antony and Cleopatra*, ii vii 131) and is told 'Disguise was the old English word for a masque'. But it also carried the senses of 'concealment', and of 'deformity' ('Here in this bush disguised will I stand'; 'Her cheeks with chaps and wrinkles were disguised') from which the transition was easy to 'dissembling' ('disguise not with me in words'). The word thus retained a strong literal meaning yet also carried moral implications.

> Disguise, I see thou art an wickedness
> Wherein the pregnant enemy does much

says Viola, in the accents of Malvolio. New Guise and Nowadays, the tempters of *Mankind*, had been named from a dislike both of innovations and of that elaboration of dress which was so feelingly denounced by moralists from Chaucer to Tourneur.

The two archetypes were the disguise of the serpent and the disguise of the Incarnation. The devil's power of deceit furnished plots for many moralities. In Medwall's *Nature*, in *Republica* and in Skelton's *Magnifycence*, the vices take the virtues' names: in the last, Counterfeit Countenance becomes Good Demeanance, Crafty Conveyance becomes Sure Surveyance, Courtly Abusion becomes Lusty Pleasure and Cloaked Collusion becomes Sober Sadness. The two fools, Fancy and Folly, become Largesse and Conceit. The very

names of such vices as Ambidexter and Hardy-dardy signify their
power to juggle with appearance as they juggle with words. Slippery
speech belongs with disguise:

> Thus like the formal Vice, Iniquity,
> I moralize two meanings in one word.

Both are combined in the great figure of the Marlovian Mephistopheles, disguised as a Franciscan friar. It is this tradition which
lends such strength to Shakespeare's concept of the false appearance
or *seeming*. There is no direct disguise in Angelo, Claudius, Iago,
Iachimo or Wolsey, but an assumed personality. Miss Spurgeon has
shown the force of the image of borrowed robes in *Macbeth*. The
witches' invocation, recalling an important passage from Spenser on
the fall of man, first states the theme: 'Fair is foul and foul is fair.'
Lady Macbeth counsels her husband to look like the innocent flower
but be the serpent under it. Macbeth himself speaks of 'making our
faces vizards to our hearts, / Disguising what they are.' The clearest
dramatic presentation of the theme occurs when the porter of Hell
gate assumes a role which is no more than the mere truth. Here direct
and planned concealment stirs pity and terror less than the disguise
which is rooted in poetry and action, and perhaps not outwardly
signified at all.

The diabolical villains, Richard III, Iago and the rest were, of
course, not derived from any single original. Conscienceless
Machievels such as Barabas, and Lorenzo of *The Spanish Tragedy*
were behind them, as well as the Father of Lies; yet Donne's *Ignatius
his Conclave* may serve as evidence that the old diabolism and new
Machievellianism were linked in the popular mind.

Opposing infernal deceit was the heavenly humility of the Incarnation. The ruler of the world, concealed in humble garb, ministering to
the needy, and secretly controlling every event is reflected in the
disguised rulers (God's vicegerants), who wander among their subjects, living with them, and in the end distributing rewards and
punishments in a judgement scene. Heavenly disguise enables Vincentio to test the virtue of his subjects, Henry to learn the secrets of
his soldiers' feelings before Agincourt. Each of these roles has a long
stage ancestry, but Shakespeare has strengthened the force of the
disguise, which is in each case his own addition to the play. *Measure
for Measure* contains a number of pronouncements upon disguising,
and a wide variety of instances. The bride and the condemned
prisoner have each their substitutes, 'Death's a great disguiser', as the
supposed Franciscan says to the Provost. Lucio, a direct descendant

of the old Vice is 'uncased' in his own act of 'uncasing' the Duke. This is Shakespeare's fulle.t study of disguise.

Disguises generally mean a drop in social status (except in farce) and in comical histories came a whole series of rulers who wooed milkmaids, learnt home-truths from honest countrymen, stood a buffet with their subjects and finally revealed themselves with all graciousness. The exploits of King Edward in *George-a-Greene*, King Edward IV in Heywood's play, and King Henry VIII in *When You See Me You Know Me* foreshadow Henry V's jest with Williams. These jovial revellers seem related to the stories of Robin Hood and the King: Robin himself appears in some of the plays. Noble wooers in disguise often played a rustic part (as in *Friar Bacon*, *Mucidorus*, *The Shoemakers' Holiday* and *Fair Em*), and in his wooing, King Henry V again slips back into a rustic role, which, though it is not a disguise, is certainly an assumed part, and recalls such popular songs as:

> To marry I would have thy consent,
> But faith I never could compliment;
> I can say nought but 'Hoy, gee ho!'
> Words that belong to the cart and the plough.
>   Oh, say, my Joan, will not that do?
>   I cannot come every day to woo.

In the old chronicle play of *King Leir*, France wooed Cordella in such disguise. In his adaptation of this story, Shakespeare used another old tradition, that of the disguised protector. The tenderness and devotion of Kent to Lear, and Edgar to Gloucester are however but faintly suggested by Flowerdale of *The London Prodigal* or Friscobaldo of *The Honest Whore*, who in the guise of servants tend their erring children. In these plays, the disguise is comic as well as pathetic; yet the father who pities his children, like the husband who pities and succours his erring wife, must have had a biblical origin, and Shakespeare recalled this old tradition to its first significance.

Different aspects of the same disguise could be played upon (even Kent has his moments of comedy) because there was an 'open' or unresolved view of individuality behind Elizabethan character-drawing, which corresponded to the open use of words in Elizabethan poetry. Fixed denotation, which is encouraged by a standardised spelling and pronunciation, a dictionary definition, and controlling prose usage was still unknown. The great key-words had a radiant nimbus of association; they were charged with life, so that a writer could allow their significance to reverberate through a whole play. The meaning of poetry is not to be extracted but to be explored;

and the creative uses of the pun, as illustrated in recent articles in this journal, are analogous to the use of multiple personality or disguise. Characters are fluid, and the role may vary from a specific or strictly individual one to something nearer the function of the Greek chorus. The antic disposition of Hamlet, or Edgar as Poor Tom, create an extra dimension for these plays as well as giving depth and fullness to the parts. Hamlet's coarseness and Edgar's wildness are parts of themselves, but they are more than merely that. Madness is a protective ruse, deriving in part at least from the disguise of Hieronimo, and of Antonio's disguise as a fool in Marston's *Antonio's Revenge*. Through this mask Hamlet penetrates the disguises of Polonius, Rosencrantz and Guildenstern, and Claudius. Edgar as madman has something of the insight of

> the eternal eye
> That sees through flesh and all.

The revengers, Hamlet and Vindice, have x-ray eyesight; their double roles of revenger and commentator correspond to the antinomy of their characters. Here again there is an easy gradation from the choric to the individual. The Revenger was also both good *and* evil; for revenge was deadly sin, yet also the inevitable result of the greater sins which the hero so pitilessly anatomised. Such double roles had not only a verbal correspondence in the pun but a structural parallel in the 'shadowing' of mainplot by subplot, most fully developed in *King Lear*. As Poor Tom, Edgar describes as his own the sins of Oswald and Edmund: his sinister disguise helps finally to turn the wits of the old king: he talks of the devils that inhabit him, till at Dover Cliff they are exorcised; finally he appears vizarded, the unknown challenger who executes a just vengeance, and forgives his dying enemy.

The Elizabethan theatre included a wide range of representation. Ghosts, spirits and visions appeared, or could even be used as disguise (as in *The Atheist's Tragedy*, where the hero dresses as a ghost). The appearance of Caesar's or Banquo's ghost also adds an extra dimension to the dramatist's world. Unearthly and almost unbearably poignant is Paulina's revival of the ghostly Hermione from dead marble to flesh and blood:

> I'll fill your grave up: stir, nay come away,
> To death bequeath your numbness, for from him
> Dear life redeems you.

Leontes has but three words 'Oh, she's warm', and Hermione, save to Perdita, has none. It is the dream of all bereaved, handled with a sureness and delicacy that could come only from long mastery. In his last plays, Shakespeare makes disguise an essentially poetic conception, and varies the level of it more subtly than ever before. It is necessary only to think of Imogen, her brothers and Belarius, Posthumus as the poor soldier, Cloten in Posthumus' garments, the false seeming of the Queen and the vision of the ghosts and the gods; or of Perdita's contrast with Florizel, both of them with the more conventional muffling of his father and Camillo, and the many disguises of Autolycus. Perdita is seemingly a shepherdess, pranked up as a goddess for the May sports: Florizel is obscured as a swain. As they dance together, the disguised Camillo says:

> He tells her something
> That makes her blood look out: good sooth, she is
> The queen of curds and cream.

Truly it is royal blood that rises, even as Florizel's youth shows 'the true blood which fairly peeps through it.' Here the threefold meaning of 'blood' – passion, descent, blushing – corresponds with the complex function of the disguises. Like those of Imogen and her brothers, they isolate the innocence and truth of the young, they are vestures of humility which disclose true worth; and yet they give the action a masque- or pageant-like quality which sets it apart from the rest of the play. In *The Tempest*, the varying of shapes belongs principally to Ariel, to Prospero, who can go invisible, and to the spirits of the masques. Yet Ferdinand and Miranda are in some sense obscured, and the anti-masque of Trinculo and Stephano with their frippery adds at least a further visual pattern.

The physical basis of disguise remained indeed of great importance. When the actors were so well known to the audience, it must have been easy for the spectators, like the playwright, to translate 'Enter Dogberry and Verges' into 'Enter Kempe and Cowley'. Costumes had to produce the stage atmosphere now given by scenery, lighting and make-up, and changes of costume must therefore have been valuable. Apparel was not thought of as concealing but as revealing the personality of the wearer. 'The apparel oft proclaims the man', and some of the most bitter and prolonged religious quarrelling of the age centred in the Vestarian controversy. Sumptuous clothing was a subject for satirists both off and on the stage; the Puritans attacked the theatre with the plea, based on the Mosaic injunction that for a man to put on the garments of a woman was an abomination. Hence there could be no such thing as a mere physical transformation. As the body revealed the soul, so appearance should reveal the truth of identity. A character could be really changed by the assumption of a disguise. The modern woman who restores her self-confidence with an expensive hat, the soldier who salutes the Queen's Commission and not the drunkard who happens to be wearing its insignia act in a manner familiar to Elizabethans. Hence Prospero's discarding of his magic robe symbolised most adequately his transformation from Magician back to Duke of Milan.

Such deepened power of guise and disguise did not prevent Shakespeare from using it in a practical and even thoroughly stagey fashion upon other occasions. His earliest plays are full of disguisings of a superficial kind: the complexities emerge in *The Merchant of Venice*, where he builds up a scale of contrast between Jessica's purely formal disguise, Nerissa's imitative one, and the significant robing of Portia. Viola's disguise, complicated by her likeness to her twin, is also contrasted with the literal dis-guise of Malvolio in yellow stockings and cross garters, and with the clown's assumption of Sir Thopas's part. Shakespeare on occasion used all the conventional tricks, as in *The Taming of the Shrew*, *The Merry Wives*, or Margaret's disguise as Hero, which leads to Claudio's pretended unmasking of the false semblant in the church scene, and to the final comedy of the masks.

The girl-pages, who would perhaps occur most readily to the mind as Shakespeare's favourite line in disguise, were already familiar from earlier narrative and drama. In comedy, there is less open characterisation than in tragedy: instead, the roles become stereotyped, based on sets of 'characteristics'. When the heroine is disguised as a boy, her two roles may be sharply contrasted, giving an effect as of shot silk, as the boyish wit or the feminine sensibility predominates. Shakespeare allows some very stagey jests, such as the broad farce of Viola's duel with Sir Andrew: yet such parts as hers, with their obvious advantages for the boy-actors, also allowed Shakespeare to depict the relationship of men and women with a new ease and frankness. Rosalind enjoys her disguise and frankly exploits its possibilities, but even the most demure of the heroines is given a chance by indirection to find directions out. In spite of the clear contrast between appearance and reality, the disguised heroines owe the peculiar delicacy and felicity of their depiction largely to masquerade.

This particular convention remained popular, long after Shakespeare's day; Fletcher, in Bellario and Aspatia, drew a new and sophisticated version. Bellario's true sex is not revealed till the end, though by this time any theatrical page might be assumed to be a woman in disguise. In the later seventeenth and eighteenth centuries, 'breeches parts' were as popular with the actresses as they had been with the boys, and from the stage they re-entered the Romantic poem. Sir Walter Scott has two such characters, one the heroine of *The Lord of the Isles*, the other in *Harold the Dauntless*, where an utterly incredible Viking is attended for years by a devoted page, whose sex is finally revealed to the imperceptive warrior by no less a personage than Odin himself.

The deeper implications of disguise, however, did not long survive Shakespeare's day. Writers of today have rediscovered its possibilities for tragedy as well as comedy, and are no longer limited to the presuppositions governing *Charley's Aunt*, *Vice Versa*, or even *The Happy Hypocrite*. Yet the triple flexibility of language, characters and plotting which give the Elizabethans so strong and delicate a weapon belongs to them alone. Only occasionally in lyric verse, as in Yeats's sequence of *The Three Bushes* – where the old trick of *Measure for Measure*, the false bride, is put to new uses – disguise provides a statement of philosophic themes. The antithesis of Body and Soul, even of the One and the Many is symbolised in this folk story, written in ballad style and set to a popular tune. (Yeats's source, however, is actually a Provençal *tenzon*, which he may have learnt of from Ezra Pound; hence the mixture of courtly love convention with reminiscences of *Fair Margaret and Sweet William*.)

It may be that Shakespeare too drew some of his inspiration from popular literature, especially from ballads, where disguises of all kinds are of primary importance, both for comedy and for tragedy. Whilst disguise has been used in the drama, the pathos and depth of feeling in the ballads, dramatic in form as many of them are, far exceeds that of the pre-Shakespearean stage in general. Tom a Bedlam, Hind Horn, Fair Annie may have been the seed-plots for Edgar, Hamlet and Imogen, as the Robin Hood ballads were for the comical history plays. Shakespeare turned to the popular ballad in moments of deepest pathos for Ophelia and Desdemona, he turned to old wives' tales and riddles for the visionary horror of *Macbeth* and the visionary beauty of *The Winter's Tale*, as many times he drew his purest poetry from the diction of common life.

V.

Shakespeare's Hybrid:
All's Well that Ends Well

All's Well that Ends Well might have as its sub-title 'Two Plays in One'. In this chapter I shall be concerned with one of the plays only – the play that is revealed by the structure and the plot. Such a partial and one-sided approach is justified because, I believe, it reveals the governing idea[1] of the whole composition. This is perhaps a danger-ous assumption, for 'in attempting to isolate the idea that governs a play we run the risk of fixing it and deadening it, especially when the idea discerned is expressed as a philosophical proposition and stated in a sentence or two.'[2]

The governing idea of this particular play is one which I believe belongs rather to Shakespeare's age than to all time. To display it therefore requires what may seem a humourless and over-detailed study of the background of ideas. The method by which the idea is presented is not quite Shakespeare's usual one, though not unlike that discerned by modern critics elsewhere in his work.[3] No one could dare to suggest that Shakespeare took a moral idea and dressed it up in human terms; yet the allegorical mode of thought and the conception that literature should promote good actions were still very much alive in his day. They were not secure.[4] Shakespeare himself, in that period of the mid-1590s when he more or less has the stage to himself – the period between the death of Marlowe and the arrival of Jonson – transformed the conception of dramatic art and produced those ripe and humane works which for ever made im-possible such plays as Robert Wilson's.

The modern reader of *All's Well* may feel that the play contains one superb character study, that of Bertram; and at least one speech of great poetic power, Helena's confession to the Countess. Seen through Helena's eyes Bertram is handsome, brave, 'the glass of fashion and the mould of form': seen through the eyes of the older characters he is a degenerate son, an undutiful subject, a silly boy. The two images blend in the action, as we see him sinking from irresponsibility to deceit, but making a name for himself in the wars. He ends in an abject position, yet Helena's devotion continues undiminished. Her medieval counterpart, patient Griselda, whose virtues are passive, is not called on for more than obedience,[5] and the audience need not stop to wonder what kind of a person the Marquis could be, whether such barbarity could be justified as an assay of virtue, and how the final revelation could leave his wife with any palate for his company. As a character, he exists only to demonstrate Griselda's patience. But Bertram is not 'blacked out' in this way. The connection of his character and Helena's feelings with the general theme can be explained, but they are not identified with it.

In *All's Well* the juxtaposition of the social problem of high birth versus native merit and the human problem of unrequited love recalls the story of the Sonnets; the speeches of Helena contain echoes from the sonnets,[6] but the story to which her great speeches are loosely tied does not suit their dramatic expression. It illustrates the nature of social distinctions, of which the personal situation serves only as example. It might be hazarded that this first tempted Shakespeare, who then found himself saying more, or saying other, than his purely structural purpose could justify. Helena's speech to the Countess is the poetic centre of the play, but the structural centre is the King's judgement on virtue and nobility. For once, the dramatist and the poet in Shakespeare were pulling different ways. *All's Well that Ends Well* expresses in its title a hope that is not fulfilled; all did not end well, and it is not a successful play.

My contention is that *All's Well* fails because Shakespeare was trying to write a moral play, a play which he proposed to treat with the gravity proper, for example, to 'a moral history'.[7] He was not writing allegorically, but his characters have a symbolic and extra-personal significance. To write such a play the writer must be detached and in complete control of his material; and Shakespeare was not happy when he was theorising. Here he is not driven to bitter or cynical or despairing comment on the filth that lies below the surface of life. Instead of the stews of Vienna, the activities of Pandarus and Thersites, we have the highly moral comments of the young Lords on Bertram. Yet compared with *Measure for Measure* — to which it is most closely linked by similarities of plot[8] — the play appears more confused in purpose, more drab and depressing, if less squalid. Both are concerned with what Bacon called Great Place; the one with the nature and use of power, the other with the nature and grounds of true nobility. The characters are occasionally stiffened into types: the King becomes *Vox Dei*, which means that he is merely a voice. Yet at other times, but chiefly in soliloquy, deep personal feeling breaks through. Angelo's temptations and Helena's love are not completely adjusted to the stories which contain them. These feelings burst out irrepressibly, and in a sense irrelevantly, though they are the best things in the plays.

To compare *Measure for Measure* with its source play, *Promos and Cassandra*, is to see the shaping process of imagination at work: to compare *All's Well* with Painter's translation of Boccaccio is at least revealing.[9] The alterations are perfectly consistent, tending to greater dependence, humility, and enslavement on Helena's part and greater weakness and falsehood on Bertram's. New characters are added to voice Helena's claims to virtue and dignity – this is the chief purpose of the Countess, Lafeu, and the additions to the King's part – while others are created to stigmatise Bertram. An outline of Painter will make this clear.

Giletta of Narbonne is brought up with Beltramo and several other children; though not noble she is rich, and refuses many suitors for love of him. After his departure she waits some time (years are implied) before following him, and she sees him before she seeks the King. The conditions of her bargain are that she cures the King in eight days or she offers to be burnt, the King spontaneously adding that he will give her a husband if she succeeds. She asks the right to choose and, somewhat to the royal chagrin, names Beltramo. The King almost apologises to the firmly protesting Count, but pleads that he has given his royal word. After the wedding Giletta goes to Rossiglione, puts the estate in order, tells the people the whole story and goes away openly with a kinsman and a good deal of treasure. She reaches Florence, ferrets out Beltramo's mistress, plans the substitution and eventually gives birth to twin sons. At her leisure she returns, and entering on a day of feast, presents her two sons; Beltramo, to honour his word, and to please his subjects and the ladies, his guests who make suit to him, receives her as his wife.

These shrewd, unsentimental, vigorous Italians, who come to terms after a brisk skirmish, resemble Benedick and Beatrice rather than their own Shakespearian descendants. Two principal characters, the Countess and Parolles, have been added by Shakespeare, and two lesser ones, Lafeu and the Fool. The climaxes are heightened, and in the last scene Bertram is in danger of the law.[10] Shakespeare's hero is a very young man, highly conscious of his birth. He is handsome, courageous in battle, winning in manners: he is also an inveterate liar.

The Elizabethan code of honour supposed a gentleman to be absolutely incapable of a lie. In law his word without an oath was in some places held to be sufficient.[11] To give the lie was the deadliest of all insults and could not be wiped out except in blood. Honour was irretrievably lost only by lies or cowardice. These were more disgraceful than any crimes of violence. Alone among Shakespeare's heroes Bertram is guilty of the lie. Claudio, in *Much Ado,* is clear, and Bassanio, though he thinks of a lie to get himself out of an awkward situation at the end of the play, does not utter it. By such conduct Bertram forfeits his claims to gentility: a gentleman, as Touchstone remembered, swore by his troth, as a knight by his honour.[12] For this he is shamed and rebuked openly, not only by his elders but by his contemporaries and even by his inferiors.[13] The feelings of a modern audience towards Claudio or Bassanio may be due to a change in social standards, but Bertram is roundly condemned.

The fault, however, is not entirely his, for like Richard II, Prince Hal, and all other great ones in search of an excuse, he can shelter behind ill company. Parolles, or Wordy, a character of Shakespeare's own invention, is perceived in the end by Bertram himself to be the Lie incarnate. From the beginning the Countess had known him as

> a verie tainted fellow, and full of wickednesse,
> My sonne corrupts a well-derived nature
> With his inducement
>
> (III ii 90–2)

whilst Helena describes him before he appears as 'a notorious Liar', 'a great way foole, solie a coward'. It is not till the final scene that Bertram too acknowledges him

> a most perfidious slave . . .
> Whose nature sickens: but to speake a truth.
>
> (V iii 207–9)

In the earlier part of the play he is completely gulled by Parolles, who gains his ends by flattery. To the Elizabethan, the flatterer was the chief danger of noble youth, and his ways were exposed in most of the manuals of conduct. In Stefano Guazzo's *Civile Conversation,* a book of manners designed for the lesser nobility, much of Book II is taken up with the subject. Shakespeare in his comedy makes little use of the figure of the flatterer, and this differentiates him from Chapman, Jonson and Middleton, who took the parasite of ancient comedy and furnished him with the latest tricks of the coney-catcher. Falstaff is in some sense a flatterer, but he is never more deceived than when he thinks to govern his sweet Hal.[14]

Flattery thrives on detraction, and Parolles' evil speaking, which finally exposes him, has been anticipated by his double-dealing with

Helena and Lafeu. His cowardice is of no power to infect Bertram, but his lying is contagious, and in the last scene the Count shows how deeply he is tainted. The unmasking of Bertram re-echoes the unmasking of Parolles.

Shakespeare is unlikely to have felt deeply about the minutiae of social procedure, the punctilio of a modern and Frenchified fashion like the duel, or the niceties of address. Saviolo's discourse on the lie is put into the mouth of Touchstone, Segar's observations on Adam *armigero* are given to the First Gravedigger, and Falstaff has the longest if not the last word on Honour. But the question 'Wherein lies true honour and nobility?' was older than the new and fantastic codes of honour, or the new ideas of what constituted a gentleman. It is the theme of the first English secular drama, *Fulgens and Lucres* (*c.* 1490), where Medwall gave the lady's verdict for the worthy commoner against the unworthy nobleman, thereby proving his independence of his original, Buonaccorso, who in *De Vere Nobilitate* had left the matter open. In 1525, Rastell, *Of Gentylnes & Nobylyte*, treated the same subject, and it was an obvious theme for secular moralities. The question of blood and descent had been touched on by Shakespeare in *King John* in the triple contrast of Arthur, the legal successor, John the King *de facto*, and Richard the Bastard, whose royalty of nature makes him the natural leader. Civil nobility seen in relation to courtly life was a different aspect of the same problem and it is with this that Shakespeare is concerned in *All's Well*.

When at the turn of the fifteenth century, the ruling caste had ceased also to be a fighting caste, there remained for the elder and wiser the role of statesman or politician and for the younger sort that of courtier. The feudal tenant-in-chief had derived his standing from his military prowess and his local territorial responsibilities of delegated rule. Although the military profession was no longer paramount, the young noble was trained in war. The perfect courtier was required to be witty, full of counsel and of jests, skilled in music and poetry, a horseman, a patron of all noble science. Such arts of living could be learnt only at the court. He should be ambitious of honour – like Hotspur and Prince Hal – truthful and loyal, kindly and modest. His life was devoted to glory, and his reward was good fame. Such employments as the professions afforded – of which that of physician was held least worthy, as too close to the barber and the potecary – were the refuge of impoverished families and of younger sons. As the king was the fount of honour, the young noble's place was at court; but the vanity and corruption of court life were especially dangerous for the young. In actuality, the scramble for preferment was a dangerous game in which the player might lose his all.[15] Warnings against the court had been set forth in literature for more than a century. Spenser's *Colin Clout's Come Home Again* depicts both the glories and miseries of the court. A sick or ageing ruler left the courtiers exposed to all the natural dangers of the place without restraint. Such a situation is depicted at the beginning of *All's Well*. The metaphor of the sick king was always something more than a metaphor for Shakespeare. The Countess bids farewell to her 'unseason'd courtier' with open misgivings, and Helena, too, is openly afraid of the influence of the court on Bertram: Parolles' description is not inviting, and even the clown is not improved by it.[16] When the court is reached, all the virtuous characters turn out to be elderly. The King describes the perfect courtier in the person of Bertram's father, recalled to his mind by the young man's likeness (a resemblance already twice commented on):[17]

> Youth, thou bear'st thy Father's face,
> Franke Nature rather curious then in hast
> Hath well compos'd thee: Thy Father's morall parts
> Maist thou inherit too.
>
> (I ii 18–21)

The elder Rousillon is but lately dead when the play opens. In an extensive picture or mirror of his father, the King sets up to Bertram that model which had already been recommended to him by his mother. It constitutes one of the main statements of the play, embodying the idea of true nobility.

> He did look farre
> Into the service of the time, and was
> Discipled of the bravest . . . in his youth
> He had the wit, which I can well observe
> To day in our yong Lords: but they may iest
> Till their owne scorne returne to them unnoted
> Ere they can hide their levitie in honour:
> So like a Courtier, contempt nor bitternesse
> Were in his pride, or sharpnesse; if they were,
> His equall had awak'd them, and his honour
> Clocke to it selfe, knew the true minute when
> Exception bid him speake: and at this time
> His tongue obeyd his hand. Who were below him,
> He us'd as creatures of another place,
> And bow'd his eminent top to their low rankes,
> Making them proud of his humilitie,
> In their poor praise he humbled. . . .
>
> (I ii 26ff.)

The model which Bertram actually takes is the very antithesis of

this. Parolles claims to be both courtier and soldier, but his court-
liness is entirely speech, as his soldiership is entirely dress. Even the
clown calls Parolles knave and fool to his face (II iv). He is ready to
play the pander and to tempt Bertram ('a filthy Officer he is in those
suggestions for the young Earle', III v 17–18), yet at the end he crawls
to the protection of old Lafeu, who had been the first to meet with
provocative insults the challenge of the 'counterfeit'.

Affability to inferiors was indeed not always recommended: Elyot
held that courtesy consisted in giving every man his due, whilst
Guazzo thought 'to be too popular and plausible, were to make
largesse of the treasures of his courtesie, to abase himself, and to
shew a sign of folly or flatterie'.[18] Yet on the other hand, Theseus's
gracious kindness to the tradesmen, or Hamlet's sharp answer to
Polonius's 'I will use them according to their desert':

> Gods bodykins, man better. Use everie man after his desert, and who
> should scape whipping: use them after your own Honor and Dignity. The
> lesse they deserve, the more merit is in your bountie

illustrate the same virtue which the King praised in the elder Rousillon.

The arts of speech were indeed in themselves the very stuff of
which a courtier was made. Guazzo describes first of all the speech
and bearing to be cultivated, and then the truthfulnesss, fair speaking, and modesty which should characterise the matter of discourse.
Hence the ungraciousness of Bertram's petulance. 'A poore Physician's daughter my wife?' did not perhaps sound quite so outrageous
as it does now, for marriage out of one's degree was a debasing of the
blood which blemished successive heirs. But Helena is of gentle,
though not of noble blood, and all the other young nobles who have
been offered to her have been ready to accept her.

The question that is raised by Bertram's pride and the King's act is
one central to all discussion on the nature of nobility. 'One standard
commonplace on nobility took shape: that lineage alone was not
enough, but that the son of a noble family should increase and not
degrade the glory of his ancestors.'[19]

Aristotle had said that Nobility consisted in virtue and ancient
riches:[20] Lord Burghley, a potent authority in his day, lopped the
phrase down: 'Nobility is nothing but ancient riches.' Whilst it was
admitted that the King could confer nobility upon anyone, gentility
was sometimes held to be conferred only by descent, hence the
saying, 'The King cannot make a gentleman.' At the court of
Elizabeth, herself the granddaughter of a London citizen and surrounded by new nobility, the more rigid views were not likely to

prevail. Nevertheless 'nobility native' was inevitably preferable to 'nobility dative'.[21] Through inheritance it conferred a disposition to virtue, and even the degenerate were shielded in some manner by their descent, 'the fame and wealth of their ancestors serves to cover them as long as it can, as a thing once gilded, though it be copper within, till the gilt be worn away.'[22] Education and the example of his ancestors would also help the nobleman, though a bad education might corrupt him entirely.[23] The debate on old and new titles in Osorio's *Discourse of Civil and Christian Nobility* went in favour of blood, while Nenna's *Il Nennio* supported the lowly born. But all would agree with Mulcaster: 'The well-born and virtuous doth well deserve double honour among men ... where desert for virtue is coupled with descent in blood.'[24]

Desert for virtue is Helena's claim, and the two words echo significantly throughout the play. The causes for ennobling the simple were headed by 'virtue public', in other words, some great public service, and this it is which ennobles her. Learning and riches were other causes. Elyot declared that nobility is 'only the prayse and surname of virtue' and set forth the eleven moral virtues of Aristotle as the model for his Governor.[25] The essentially competitive nature of honour, while it was recognised, was not stressed.

In Helena and Bertram, the true and the false nobility are in contest. Helena seeks recognition: Bertram denies it. The King, with the Countess and Lafeu whom Shakespeare created to act as arbiters, are all doubly ennobled by birth and virtue and therefore judge dispassionately. By these three judges the young people are compared at intervals throughout the play, to the increasing disadvantage of Bertram. In the first scene, the Countess introduces Helena as inheriting virtue and yet improving on it. The technical terms of honour emphasise her point:

> I have those hopes of her good, that her education promises: her dispositions shee inherits, which makes faire gifts fairer ... she derives her honestie, and atcheeves her goodnesse (1 i 47ff.).

Of Bertram she cherished hopes less assured, but wishes that his blood and virtue may contend for precedence, and his goodness share with his birthright.

By making his social climber a woman, Shakespeare took a good deal of the sting out of the situation. Helena's virtues were derived from her father and from Heaven, to whose intervention she ascribes all her power to cure the King. She protests she is richest in being simply a maid, and the King offers her to Bertram with the words

> Vertue and shee
> Is her owne dower: Honour and wealth, from mee.

The promotion of a modest but dignified young woman is far from arousing jealousy.[26] Helena had been conscious of her lowliness and in her first soliloquy she almost despairs:

> Twere all one,
> That I should love a bright particuler starre,
> And think to wed it, he is so above me.
>
> (I i 97–9)

To the Countess, before making her confession, she says:

> I am from humble, he from honored name:
> No note upon my Parents, his all noble,
> My Master, my deere Lorde he is, and I
> His servant live, and will his vassall die.
>
> (I iii 164–7)

These words are not retracted by her confession for she protests that she does not follow him by any token of presumptuous suit: 'Nor would I have him till I doe deserve him' (I iii 199). At her first encounter with the King, Helena is almost driven off by her first rebuff. In stately couplets which mark out the solemnity of the moment she suddenly returns and offers herself as 'the weakest minister' of Heaven. She frankly claims 'inspired Merit' and warns the King that it is presumption to think Heaven cannot work through the humble. 'Of heaven, not me, make an experiment.' The King recognises the power of something greater than herself in Helena's voice and he submits. She is 'undoubted blest'.

Such claims shift the ground of Helena's nobility. To fail to recognise her as already ennobled in a superior way by the choice of Heaven is an aggravation of Bertram's offence in refusing the consummation of the marriage – itself a religious duty as Diana reminds him (IV ii 12–13). The Countess feels nothing but indignation with the 'rash and unbridled boy', for

> the misprising of a Maide too vertuous
> For the contempt of Empire.
>
> (III ii 27–8)

Even before the journey to court she had loved Helena as her own child (I iii 98, 143–4) and now she prefers her, disclaiming her proper son (III ii 68–9), who in rejecting such a wife has lost more honour than he can ever win with his sword. Helena's penitential pilgrimage raises her yet higher in the Countess's estimation, and finally, with the report of her death, she becomes 'the most vertuous gentlewoman, that ever Nature had praise for creating' (IV v 9–10).

In bestowing a wife on one of the royal wards, the King was certainly doing no more than Elizabeth and James had done. Much lesser persons regarded their wards as legitimate matrimonial prizes. The customary formula (which the King uses): 'Can you like of this man?' 'Can you like of this maid?' did not imply love but only the ability to live harmoniously together. Bertram, who is succinctly described by Lafeu as an 'asse', has, it is clear from the first scene, no dislike of Helena, but he knows her as his mother's servant and 'I cannot *love* her, nor will strive to doo't.' Only later does the brilliant idea occur to him that he was really in love with Lafeu's daughter.[27] His seduction of Diana 'contrives against his owne Nobilitie', and his responsibility for the death of Helena means that 'the great dignitie that his valour hath here acquir'd for him [i.e. in Florence], shal at home be encountered with a shame as ample' (IV iii 25–30, 79–82).

Bertram's 'folly', though excused as the fault of Parolles' ill-counsel (IV ii 1), and as 'Naturall rebellion, done i' th blaze of youth' (V iii 6), remains in the eyes of Lafeu a blot upon his honour. However much Bertram wronged his King, his mother, and his wife, he wronged himself much more (V iii 12–19). Lafeu champions Helena's memory rather in the way in which Paulina champions Hermione's, and the rapidity with which the King jumps to thoughts of murder when he sees the royal gem offered as 'an amorous token for fair *Maudlin*' is a proof of his feeling for Helena no less than of his well-merited distrust of Bertram. Like the rings of Bassanio and Portia, the jewels which are bandied about in the last scene are symbolic of a contract and an estate of life. The King's gem derived from him to Helena, and Bertram neither knows nor cares what it is. His own monumental ring symbolises all that he has thrown away.[28]

> an honour longing to our house,
> Bequeathed downe from manie Ancestors,
> Which were the greatest obloquie i' th world,
> In me to loose.
>
> (IV ii 42–5)

This jewel, with which he had taunted Helena, is found at the end in her keeping.

Nevertheless, though Helena is wise and Bertram foolish, though she is humble and he is proud, his final acknowledgement of her would constitute a strong ending. When Brachiano marries Vittoria,

or when in *A Woman Killed with Kindness*, Sir Francis marries
Susan, the condescension of the noble partner is matter for astonish-
ment. Even in realistic comedy, such as *Eastward Ho!*, the marriage
of court and city provides grounds for satire and for farce. Helena's
success would lose all point if it were not a great exception. If this
suggests that social theory enabled the judicious spectator both to eat
his cake and have it, the answer is that the same dilemma lies at the
centre of the play, and is expounded by the King in a full account of
the nature of title and dignity – a speech which had tradition behind
it, but which is sharply at variance with the nigglers who measured
whether honour came with the first or third generation of a new title.

> Tis onely title thou disdainst in her, the which
> I can build up: strange is it that our bloods
> Of colour, waight and heat, pour'd all together,
> Would quite confound distinction: yet stands off
> In differences so mightie. If she bee
> All that is vertuous (save what thou dislikst),
> A poore Phisitian's daughter, thou dislikst
> Of vertue for the name: but doe not so:
> From lowest place, whence vertuous things proceed,
> The place is dignified by th' doers' deede.
> When great additions swells, and vertue none,
> It is a dropsied honour. Good alone,
> Is good without a name. Vilenesse is so:
> The propertie by what it is, should go,
> Not by the title. She is young, wise, faire,
> In these, to Nature shee 's immediate heire:
> And these breed honour: that is honour's scorne,
> Which challenges it selfe as honour's borne,
> And is not like the sire: Honours thrive
> When rather from our acts we them derive
> Then our fore-goers: the meere words, a slave
> Deboshed on everie tombe, on everie grave:
> A lying Trophee, and as ofte is dumbe,
> Where dust, and damn'd oblivion is the Tombe
> Of honour'd bones indeed. . . .
>
> (II iii 124ff.)

Helena already possesses the essential attributes and therefore the
potentiality of honour, which the King by his recognition of her
claims will bestow. 'The name and not the thing' is vanity.[29]

Medieval tradition recognised three classes of nobility:[30] Christian, natural and civil. Pre-eminence must be given to sanctity, but the
saints included poor fishers, even slaves. Natural nobility or perfec-
tion of kind might be ascribed to animals, and a noble falcon justly so

termed. The writers of books of honour often mentioned these two classes, but pointed out that they could not discuss them. One of the fullest treatments of the subject is by Dante in his *Convivio*. He denies civil nobility any real value.[31] Nobility, he says, cannot be defined by riches, which in themselves are vile,[32] or by time, because all men ultimately derive from a common stock, but only by its effects. The necessary outcome or effect of Nobility is Virtue: where Virtue exists, Nobility must therefore exist as its cause. Nobility descends upon an individual by the grace of God (*Convivio*, IV xv) and is 'the seed of blessedness dropped by God into a rightly placed soul.' Dante goes on to expound the eleven moral virtues (much like Elyot). The claim to nobility by descent is then refuted, natural and Christian nobility identified, and civil nobility wiped out. Dante's Third Ode, upon which this section of the *Convivio* provides a commentary, is addressed to Beatrice, who, like Helena, is an example of active virtue, received by a direct infusion of grace. The language of religion is used with particular frequency by Shakespeare in this play,[33] and the gravest words of all are spoken by the Clown (IV v 50–9) when he describes how 'the Prince of this world' entices nobility 'into his court'.

> I am for the house with the narrow gate, which I take to be too little for pompe to enter: some that humble themselves may, but the manie will be too chill and tender, and theyll bee for the flowrie way that leads to the broad gate, and the great fire.

Helena is 'a Jewell' (v iii 1) which Bertram throws away. His rejection of her must be seen not in isolation but as linked with his choice of Parolles.[34] The first dialogue of Helena and Parolles, the Liar and Vertue as she herself has labelled them, must be seen as the encounter of Bertram's good and evil angels, who, if this were a morality, would contend for his soul in open debate.[35] In the final scene Parolles turns the tables on Bertram, and though the King dismisses the informer with contempt, an elaborate and inexorable shaming of the now utterly silenced young man proceeds. This last scene, in which Shakespeare completely forsakes his original, has the closest affinities with *Measure for Measure*. It is a judgement scene with charge and countercharge piled up in bewildering contradiction till they are resolved as if by miracle in the sudden appearance of the central figure. In this scene the King appears as the fount of justice: he deprives Bertram of all honour (v iii 184–6), though the revenges with which he threatens the young man should not be taken in any personal sense. Such a finale, with a royal judgement, and a distribution of rewards and punishments, was a well-established comic convention,[36] though it is difficult to resist the thought that in offering Diana a husband, the King shows some inability to profit by experience. The riddles with which Diana led up to the *dénouement* recall those in which Portia swore she lay with Doctor Balthazar to obtain the ring, and they are not to modern taste.

Bertram's conversion must be reckoned among Helena's miracles. What is well ended is her struggle for recognition, which he concedes her. Her devotion, tinged for the first time with bitterness, requires another mode of expression than the last dozen lines allow. She has been acknowledged by her lord: that her personal happiness is simply irrelevant, and the ending therefore neither hypocritical nor cynical, can be granted only if the play is seen as a study of the question of 'Wherein lies true honour and nobility?'

Notes

1 See Nevill Coghill, 'The Governing Idea, Essays in the Interpretation of Shakespeare – I', *Shakespeare Quarterly*, i (1948), pp. 9–16.
2 Ibid.
3 Two excellent modern editions appeared after this article was written, by G. K. Hunter (Arden, 1959) and Barbara Everett (New Penguin, 1970), see also Joseph Price, *The Unfortunate Comedy*, 1968.
4 Cf. Rosemary Freeman, *English Emblem Books* (London, 1948), pp. 19–22.
5 Helena shows herself similarly passive in her two scenes as wife (II iv; v). Unlike Parolles, she calls Bertram her 'master', both before and after marriage (I iii 166; III iv 9).
6 Helena's three great speeches (I i 91–110; I iv 199–225; III ii 102–32) have a number of parallels with the Sonnets, especially the second of the three. Cf. Sonnets xxvi, lvii, lviii, lxxxvii. The way in which Bertram is condemned recalls also the plain speaking which is so unusual a feature of the Sonnets (e.g. xxxv, lxvii, lxxxii, lxxxiv, xcv, xcvi).
7 A term defined by A. P. Rossiter in his edition of *Woodstock* (London, 1948): roughly, a chronicle history built on a moral theme.
8 e.g. the rejection of a devoted bride for insufficiency, and a compelled marriage ordered by the ruler: the substitution of one woman for another: the false self-accusation of the chaste woman, followed by prolonged lying from the culprit, culminating in his exposure through the arrival of an absent person: the slanderer who speaks ill of his lord and is unmasked in public.
9 William Painter, *The Palace of Pleasure* (1566), contains as the xxxviii novel the story of 'Giletta a phisition's daughter of Narbon', the original being Boccaccio, *Il Decamerone*, III ix. The subject of the relations of

All's Well to its sources is, I understand, being considered in detail by Professor H. G. Wright. See *Modern Language Review*, XLVI (1951), 431–5; and (1955) 45–8. Cf. Hunter, ed. cit., XXV–IX.

10 Bertram's own lies cause this, and the exposure of his treatment of Diana. Her use in this scene is entirely Shakespeare's own invention, and much increases the melodrama. Helena in Act II also increases the tension by offering to have her name traduced as a strumpet if she fails to cure the King, and by cutting down the period required from eight days to two.

11 R. Kelso, *The Doctrine of the English Gentleman* (Urbana, 1929), p. 78.

12 *As You Like It*, I ii. Cf. Mulcaster, *Positions* (reprinted London, 1898), p. 198.

13 e.g. IV ii 11–30 where Diana, who is perhaps his social equal, being descended from the ancient Capilet, rebukes him; IV iii 1–30, where the young Lords criticise him. Parolles' sonnet contains some nasty home truths: in the last scene the King and Lafeu are quite uncompromising. Bertram's word is not to be trusted (V iii 184–6).

14 Hamlet's discrimination between Polonius, his two schoolfellows, and Osric is a mark of the wise prince: Timon's failure to discriminate is his downfall.

15 See Lawrence Stone, 'The Anatomy of the Elizabethan Aristocracy', *Economic History Review*, xviii (1948).

16 I i 71, 80–2; 182–93, 224: III ii 13–29. See Kelso, op. cit., pp. 50–2, for a comparison between the English and Italian courtly traditions, which suggests that English courtiers were more frequently employed in administration and that mere attendance at court was in England not considered an occupation in itself. Yet in spite of this, Sidney, like Bertram, stole away to the wars, though 'with a copy of Castiglione in his pocket'.

17 I i 1, 71–2.

18 S. Guazzo, trans. Pettie, *Civile Conversation* (reprinted London, 1925), i 158.

19 John E. Mason, *Gentlefolk in the Making* (Philadelphia, 1935), p. 8.

20 *Politics*, IV viii 9.

21 Kelso, op. cit., p. 22.

22 Sir Thomas Smith, *De Repub. Anglorum* (reprinted London, 1906), p. 38.

23 Kelso, op. cit., p. 24, quotes La Perrière, *Mirour of Policie* (translated 1598): 'If he be evilly instructed in his young years, he will as long as he liveth have such manners as are barbarous, strange, and full of villainy.' The education of a prince or noble was the subject of constant discussion.

24 Mulcaster, *Positions*, p. 199; quoted by Kelso, op. cit., p. 30.

25 *The Governor*, ed. Croft, ii 38; quoted by Mason, op. cit., p. 26.

26 Her many hesitations, her disclaimer of any aspiration to a royal match, show Helena's decorum. No Elizabethan could, like a modern writer, have called it 'canny'.

27 The King had long ago arranged the match, in the young people's childhood, and Bertram's affection may be assumed to be politic; but his

readiness to accept the plan undermines his claim to freedom of choice in his first marriage.

28 In Painter's story the ring is not an heirloom, but prized by Beltramo 'for a certain vertue that he knew it had'. Bertram's use of Diana's ring as a love-token should not be pressed as a point against him, though it is hardly suitable: but his lying repudiation and slander of Diana is ignoble.

29 So, when she has fulfilled Bertram's conditions, Helena turns to seek not her lord, but the King (IV iv), because public recognition of her right is essential.

30 Kelso, op. cit., p. 21, where it is mentioned that later writers tended to ignore these divisions, or to pay them lip-service only.

31 *Convivio*, Fourth Treatise.

32 *Nobile* is derived by Dante from *not vile* (IV xvi).

33 e.g. I i 109–10, 239–40; I ii 57–8, 65–7; I iii 20–i, 212–13, 253; II i 139–44, 151–7, 163, 178–9; II iii 1–7, 28–9, 69; III iv 28–9; IV ii 21–9, 66–8; IV iii 55–63.

34 The pride of Parolles and the humility of Helena have been contrasted in their use of the term 'master': they are shown at the beginning as more or less social equals.

35 Bertram's ultimate rejection of Parolles, though well-deserved, is expressed with a wilful petulance, not with shame: 'I could endure anything but a Cat, and now he's a Cat to me' (IV iii 242–3).

36 e.g. *Friar Bacon and Friar Bungay, The Shoemaker's Holiday, An Humorous Day's Mirth.*

VI.

The Origins of *Macbeth*

A very broad definition of 'sources' must be my excuse for considering so familiar a topic as the origins of *Macbeth*. In this, the most concentrated of the tragedies, a particularly wide diversity of material was fused into unity. 'In the quick forge and working-house of thought', Shakespeare wrought at white heat. The material to be considered falls into three classes. First, the Scottish and English Chronicles supplied the facts, and one important scene; secondly, various works on witchcraft and demonology, including those of King James, gave some material for the witches' scenes (but here the interest lies rather in Shakespeare's innovations than in his borrowings); thirdly, earlier works by Shakespeare himself present in a simpler form some of the ingredients of this play, and an examination of what might be called the internal sources elucidates its inward structure. The repetitions, echoes and restatements which are to be detected in Shakespeare offer more than mere opportunity for pedantic correlation; they are alternative statements, varied embodiments of those deep-seated and permanent impulses which underlie all his work and make it, in spite of its variety, a vast and comprehensive whole – a single structure, though of Gothic design.

In reading through Holinshed's voluminous Scottish Chronicles, Shakespeare would come, about a third of the way through, upon the story of Duncan, the eighty-fourth king according to that account, and the narrative with which we are all familiar. The Chronicle gives a brief and bald summary of reign after reign, describing the same round of violence, murder, rebellion and general turbulence. It is as monotonous as the series of apocryphal portraits of these early kings to be seen in Holyrood Palace; and the power of its monotony is considerable. The picture of a strange, bleak, haunted world emerges, where savage beings fulfil the passionate cycle of their dreadful lives as if under enchanted compulsion.[1] But why, in reading through these legendary stories, did Shakespeare stop where he did?

The story of Duncan and Macbeth glorified the ancestors of King James, both the ancient house of Macalpine, and in Banquo, an imaginary figure invented by Hector Boece during the fifteenth century, the later Stewart line. It also introduced the weird sisters, whose prophecies might be adapted to foretell the happy future rule of King James himself, and who were at the same time akin to the North Berwick witches whose practices against him had provided one of the most celebrated witch-trials of the age. Moreover, Malcolm Canmore, husband of the English princess Margaret and initiator of many new customs, stood at the beginning of one new age in Scottish history, as James, heir to the united crowns of Scotland and England, stood at the beginning of another. A royal command performance was clearly in view from the very inception of the play.

In the Chronicle, the history of Macbeth is briefly told, but Shakespeare shaped it both by expansion and compression. He crammed into a single act of war the rebellion of Macdonwald, two Danish invasions and the revolt of Cawdor — which happened only *after* the prophecy in Holinshed. The whole account of how Duncan was murdered he took from elsewhere, the murder of King Duff; though Macbeth's stratagem to send into the Danish camp supplies of drugged food and surprise them 'so amazed that they were unable to make any defence' might have suggested the drugging of the grooms. In the Chronicle, Macbeth slew Duncan in open revolt, and no indications of remorse are given either before or after the event. The long reign of Macbeth Shakespeare shortens into a few weeks; the wizard who prophesied to Macbeth about Birnam Wood merges with the weird sisters; Macbeth's death takes place before Dunsinane, and not at the end of an inglorious flight. In sum, the debt to the Chronicle is of the slightest; so bald a narrative gave Shakespeare the merest skeleton of a plot. There is, however, one scene, that between Malcolm and Macduff in England, which is reported in very great detail. Indeed, it is out of all focus in the Chronicle and occupies almost as much space as the whole of the rest of the reign. This scene represents Shakespeare's greatest debt to Holinshed; clearly it took his eye, and here perhaps is the germ of how he first conceived the play.

Malcolm's self-accusations are much more convincing to the present age than they were to the nineteenth century, when this scene was generally disliked. It was usual to cut it for stage performance. Yet an exile trying to evade the trap of his totalitarian enemy might plausibly test the reactions of his promised supporters. In a world still full of displaced persons and *agents provocateurs*, this scene can be harrowing. In Holinshed, the whole incident is weakened by the fact that both Malcolm and Macduff know of the murder of Macduff's family before the dialogue begins, so that it is hardly conceivable that Macduff could at this time be Macbeth's agent. Shakespeare, on the other hand, makes his leaving of the defenceless 'wife and child' a reasonable cause of suspicion to the young prince. Macduff does not answer Malcolm's query on this point. It is the silence of a man embittered and mature, deeply mortified by such incomprehension of the depths of sacrifice for which his loyalty prepared him.

Here again the modern reader may add his personal endorsement. In 1942 I had the honour to meet in London one of the highest officers of the French Navy, who had escaped from France after the German occupation to fight from this country. He too left his wife and child exposed to the retaliation of the enemy. In those days no one asked him why.

In Holinshed, Malcolm accuses himself of licentiousness, avarice and promise-breaking, and it is only the last which drives Macduff to renounce him. Promise-keeping is so essential to the ruler that although as all treatises on government declared – and particularly King James's[2] – it is the bounden duty of the subject to conceal the ill deeds of rulers and not even to let his *thoughts* harbour any treasonable reproof of them, yet this particular crime is indefensible. Holinshed makes the rather subtle point that while Malcolm is diffident about his other crimes, he seems to expect Macduff to conceal the last. Shakespeare omits the irony, but he was engaged in adding to the list of crimes, mentioning especially contentiousness, which, as Dover Wilson points out,[3] would be particularly obnoxious to the pacifist James. Malcolm's final speech constitutes almost a definition by contraries of the perfect ruler.

Such ingenious dissimulation would appear to the royal auditor a proof of his wisdom, more striking that it was precocious – and the more likely to foreshadow that of his illustrious descendant. Might not James also remember those ten painful months following the Ruthven Raid in 1582, when as a boy of eighteen he had to practise dissimulation with the gang who kidnapped him and forced him to govern in accordance with their faction? 'Better bairns greet nor bearded men,' exclaimed Lord Ruthven, when James at his first capture burst into tears. The King never forgot, and years later he contrived Lord Ruthven's death should pay for it. Such memories might well have recurred and given to the scene of Malcolm's exile a deep personal significance.

The ruler was always allowed to practise extraordinary stratagems

in view of his extra responsibilities, as the Duke of Vienna did in
Measure for Measure. Malcolm was showing himself fit to rule –
cleverer than his father, who knew no art to find the mind's construction in the face, and did not probe below a fair appearance.

In his book on Shakespeare,[4] Hardin Craig has classed *Macbeth*
among the political tragedies, and there is no doubt that it was more
than a personal tragedy which happened to be about princes. The
natures of an ill-governed and a well-governed kingdom are contrasted throughout the latter half of the play. Here Shakespeare
moved away from the Chronicle, and relied partly on other works,
including those of King James, and partly on those views which had
formed in his own mind during the writing of his English histories.

The relation between the King and the body politic is a sympathetic one. When the King is sick or disordered, the land is disordered
too. First we are given the picture of a happy kingdom, in which
Duncan and his thanes support and respect each other. Duncan
plants honours, and labours to make them full of growing. His
subjects return to him all the bounties with which he nourishes them,
in duty and service. In her welcome Lady Macbeth falsely strikes this
note of devotion, which Duncan repays with an old man's gallant
politeness.

After his coronation, Macbeth tries vainly at his feast to recreate
the atmosphere of close-knit amity. But 'honour, love, obedience,
troops of friends' he must not look to have. His thanes look forward
to the time when they may 'do faithful homage, and receive free
honours', but the Scotland they inhabit is disordered, sick, a dis-
tracted body swollen with evil humours. This picture of the dis-
tracted kingdom is familiar from the plays of *Richard II*, *Henry IV*
and *Richard III*, where it is described at more length. Even Macbeth
sees that his land is diseased (v iii). He himself is haunted with the
sleeplessness that tormented the usurper Bolingbroke, and to read
the opening of the third act of *Henry IV Part II* is like listening to an
overture to *Macbeth*:

> O sleep, O gentle sleep,
> Nature's soft nurse, how have I frighted thee,
> That thou no more wilt weigh my eye-lids down,
> And steep my senses in forgetfulness? . . .
> Then you perceive the body of our kingdom,
> How foul it is; what rank diseases grow,
> And with what danger, near the heart of it?
>   (III i 6–9, 38–40)

Malcolm is 'the medicine of the sickly weal', the 'sovereign flower' who comes with the blessing and aid of the saintly Edward. The reference in IV i to the Confessor's sacred powers of healing was an especial compliment to James who prided himself on the inherited gift of 'the healing benediction'; but it was also necessary as a counterweight to the picture of Macbeth's unholy rule; as such, Shakespeare took it from the English Chronicle and inserted it in his main political scene.

Further, into Macduff's reproaches of the supposedly vicious Malcolm, Shakespeare inserts an account of the forebears from whom he has degenerated; his father Duncan was 'a most sainted king', and his mother one who 'Oftener upon her knees, than on her feet, died every day she lived.' This is Shakespeare's Duncan, not Holinshed's; while of Malcolm's mother nothing is known. Shakespeare has borrowed the saintliness from the description of Malcolm's wife, the English princess, St Margaret, who transmitted the blood of the Saxon line to the Scottish royal house, and whose little chapel still stands within the walls of Edinburgh Castle. It was she and Malcolm himself who rivalled each other in pious practices and holy living. But by putting this picture a generation earlier, Shakespeare has brought into the play yet another contrast with Macbeth and his fiend-like Queen, whose land is described in terms of the plague:

> where nothing
> But who knows nothing, is once seen to smile:
> Where sighs, and groans, and shrieks that rend the air
> Are made, not mark'd: where violent sorrow seems
> A modern ecstasy: the dead man's knell,
> Is there scarce ask'd for who, and good men's lives
> Expire before the flowers in their caps,
> Dying, or ere they sicken.
>
> (IV iii 166–73)

As rightful heir Malcolm alone has the power to depose an anointed king, usurper though he be; but the conquest is almost unopposed. 'The time is free.' An immense feeling of relief surges up as Macduff appears on the battlements with these words. Malcolm, encompassed with his kingdom's pearl,[5] proceeds to inaugurate a new era by bestowing new honours. He thus fulfils his father's words that 'signs of nobleness, like stars shall shine on all deservers.' He also introduces the principle of feudal monarchy, with hereditary succession, and tenancy of the crown, which in fact Malcolm Canmore did institute in Scotland, following the unsuccessful attempts of his great-grandfather and grandfather, Kenneth II and Malcolm II.[6]

This particular theme, however, Shakespeare does not emphasise, and for good reason. The ancient succession of Scotland had been by tanistry, that is, the monarchy was elective within a small group of kinsmen, the descendants of Macalpine. In consequence, the King was almost as a matter of course assassinated by his successor, who chose the moment most favourable to himself to 'mak siccar' an inheritance that could never be regarded as assured. In spite of earlier attempts to make it hereditary, elective monarchy still persisted; by tanist law Macbeth had as good a claim as Duncan, and his wife a rather better one. By nominating Malcolm as his heir, the historic Duncan committed a provocative act which Macbeth might not unreasonably resent, and in Holinshed his real notions of murder are formed only at this point. Shakespeare did not wish Macbeth to have any such excuse for his deed. It must be unprovoked to give the full measure of pity and terror. Therefore by suppressing the conflict between tanistry and the hereditary principle, he was bound to slur over the full nature of Malcolm Canmore's innovations.[7]

On the contrary, the principle of hereditary succession is firmly emphasised by the prominence given to Banquo and his descendants, and in the cauldron scene Shakespeare has gratified the family pride of his royal patron by a pageant of his ancestors. Henry Paul has pointed out[8] that the Stewart line presented the striking picture of nine successive sovereigns in *lineal* descent the one from the other. This direct lineal descent of the crown was a matter of pride to James, who referred to it in his speeches to Parliament and in his writings. Shakespeare's interest in genealogy had been amply shown in his English histories. Edward's seven sons, seven branches growing from one root, are recalled to mind by the family tree which has Banquo as its root – he so describes himself.

Banquo was a purely imaginary character, inserted into the Chronicle by Hector Boece to provide a proper ancestry for the Stewarts. Fleance's escape to Wales and his marriage with a Welsh princess 'explained' why the Stewarts did in fact come from the Welsh borders. But after 1603 the original expansion of the weird sisters' prophecy, whereby Banquo was hailed as father to a line of kings, was expanded still further, so that they also prophesied that his descendants should unite the kingdoms of England and Scotland. In the pageant of the three sybils given at St John's College, Oxford, in 1605, James and his family were greeted in this fashion, and moreover an endless progeny was promised him.[9] The show of the eight kings was an apotheosis of the Stewart line, and must have been staged with great grandeur. To a Jacobean audience it symbolised all the stability and order which they hoped from a settled succession. A family which had produced nine kings in lineal descent offered a fair hope of escape from those dynastic difficulties which Elizabeth's reign had made familiar. The eight phantoms are all 'too like the spirit of Banquo'. They are physical replicas of him, but in the last Henry Paul would see the person of Mary Queen of Scots, the eighth Stewart to wear the crown. At all events this scene would have a very powerful topical significance.

These two scenes, then, the cauldron scene and the scene in England, are the *political* highlights of the play. They are the scenes in which Shakespeare relied most heavily on his immediate sources – those he would start from. And they are the two scenes which would most particularly appeal to King James. They are also the least tragic in tone. One is spectacular, and the other, although, as I have said, it is much more poignant to the present age than to the previous one, is still in rather a different manner from the rest of the play. What have the theoretically well-justified dissimulations of this canny young man, this perfect looking-glass for princes, to do with the agonised visions of Inverness and Dunsinane? How do they fit one who has a father murdered as well as revenges to execute on the tyrant who popped in between the election and his hopes? Malcolm is own brother to that other canny young man, Harry Monmouth, who is likewise justified by all the textbooks on government, including *Basilikon Doron*; but we are not moved. He is impersonal. The man is lost in the ruler. He may be *Vox Dei*; it means that he is merely *vox*.

Because of the close relation to source material, the impersonal subject and the specific appeal to royal interest, it seems to me that these two scenes are probably the earliest to be written. I do not believe that Shakespeare, or any original writer, starts inevitably with Act I and ends with Act v. Nor do I think that, once submerged in his tragedy and well away from his sources, he would suddenly curb himself in mid-career and begin to treat these cooler matters. At the same time these scenes are too well articulated with the main plot to be additions, though small additions may have been made to them. The cauldron scene and the English scene are both in a quite laudatory, or at least a quite neutral sense, superficial. They belong to the top layer of the play.

The character of Lady Macbeth owes nothing to the Chronicle; it has been suggested that Shakespeare might have seen the MS. of William Stewart's *Buik of the Chroniclis of Scotland*, a metrical and expanded translation of Boece finished in 1535 which contains a few very crude hints on the behaviour of Donwald's wife during the murder of King Duff.[10] The resemblances seem to me negligible and unconvincing.

But a passage from the *Description of Scotland* which is prefixed to Holinshed's Chronicle and which to my knowledge has not hitherto been noted seems to be relevant. It is from chapter XIII:

> each woman would take intolerable pains to bring up and nourish her own children. They thought them furthermore not to be kindly fostered, except they were so well nourished after their births with the milk of their breasts as they were before they were born with the blood of their own bellies: nay, they feared lest they should degenerate and grow out of kind, except they gave them suck themselves, and eschewed strange milk, therefore in labour and painfulness they were equal [i.e. with the fighting men]. . . . In these days also the women of our country were of no less courage than the men, for all stout maids and wives (if they were not with child) marched as well into the field as did the men, and so soon as the army did set forward, they slew the first living creature that they found, in whose blood they not only bathed their swords, but also tasted thereof with their mouths, with no less religion and assurance conceived, than if they had already been sure of some notable and fortunate victory.[11]

The intimate relation between tenderness and barbarity, suckling and bloodshed in this passage seems to me to give the fundamental character of Lady Macbeth as it is embodied in the most frightful of her speeches, that in which she invokes the spirits of murder to suck her breasts, and that in which she finally goads Macbeth:

> I have given suck, and know
> How tender 'tis to love the babe that milks me,
> I would, while it was smiling in my face,
> Have pluck'd my nipple from his boneless gums,
> And dash'd the brains out, had I so sworn
> As you have done to this.
>
> (I vii 54–9)

Lady Macbeth is siren as well as fury. The tenderness of Macbeth for her is reciprocated; they are indeed one flesh. There are a number of parallels between her part and that of Webster's *White Divel*[12] which suggest that her seduction of Macbeth should not be too far removed from Vittoria's seduction of Brachiano in the manner of its playing. When Macbeth comes out of the death chamber she says two words: 'My husband?' The usual form of address is 'My thane' or 'My lord', but in this supreme moment she uses the more intimate, and for an Elizabethan the more unusual form.

The double crime of treason and murder is also deadly sin. In 1604 William Willymat, the translator of *Basilikon Doron* under the title of *A Prince's Looking-Glass*, followed it with an original work, *A Loyal Subject's Looking-Glass*, in which he described the prime causes of rebellion as pride, ambition and envy. All three animate

Macbeth. 'Pride can in no wise brook to be at command, and to submit himself willingly . . . to the obedience of magistrates, rulers and governors . . . be they never so well worthy of their place.' Macbeth cannot brook 'the boy Malcolm', who has only been saved from captivity by the sergeant, should be nominated heir. Almost his last words are 'I will not yield / To kiss the ground before young Malcolm's feet.' The stripling – he should be of an age with his cousin, young Siward – provokes his pride; the weird sisters have stirred up ambition, always thought of as evil; and his very hunger for golden opinions makes him envy imperial dignity and the graces of kingship which he discerns in Duncan, and which he so vainly tries to reproduce. By the end of the play, Macbeth is accused of the other deadly sins also (IV iii 55–7) – in fact he is equated with the devil:

> Not in the legions
> Of horrid hell, can come a devil more damn'd
> In evils, to top Macbeth.

He is 'this fiend of Scotland', a 'hell-kite' and a 'hell-hound'.

In its treatment of the supernatural, the play shows the same subtle blending of a variety of material which is seen in the political theme; and it was again especially calculated to interest James, hero of *Newes from Scotland* and author of *Daemonologie*.

There was no real scepticism about witches. *Macbeth* comes at the end of a decade when the convictions for witchcraft in the Middlesex circuit reached their highest point. New statutes had been passed in 1604 reinforcing those of 1580, which made the consulting and feeding of spirits, the use of dead bodies as charms, and even unsuccessful efforts to harm by enchantment into indictable offences.[13]

It is rather surprising that before *Macbeth*, witches had appeared on the stage only in such harmless forms as Mother Bombie or the Wise Woman of Hogsdon. *Faustus* had been the only great tragedy to be based on the supernatural. The magician is a magnificent and powerful figure, a man of intellect. He enters into a formal pact with the devil and consciously chooses damnation; in return for the sale of his soul he obtains supernatural powers (*Daemonologie*, Book I, chapter VI). Henceforth, though still free to repent, the devil coaxes and bullies him out of such wishes. The equal poise of Heaven and Hell that characterised the moralities is not maintained; the scales are weighed for Hell, dramatically speaking. The emissaries of Hell are more active, numerous and powerful than the emissaries of Heaven. The sinner, however, is led to will and choose his own damnation. He is never *possessed*.

Macbeth was the first play to introduce to the stage in a serious manner the rites and practices of contemporary witchcraft. The witch differed sharply from the magician, as King James observed (*Daemonologie*, Book I, chapter III). William West of the Inner Temple thus distinguishes them in his *Symbolaeographie* (1594):

> *Soothsaying Wizards.* Of this kind . . . be all those . . . which divine and foretell things to come and raise up evil spirits by certain superstitious and conceived forms of words. And unto such questions as be demanded of them do answer by voice, or else set before their eyes in glass, crystal stones, or rings, the pictures or images of things sought for.
>
> [Witches] . . . shake the air with lightnings and thunder, to cause hail and tempests, to remove green corn or trees to an other place, to be carried of her familiar which hath taken upon him the deceitful shape of a goat, swine, or calf etc. into some mountain. . . . And sometimes to fly upon a staff or fork, or some other instrument. . . .[14]

Whilst Dee or Forman consorted with kings and princes, the witch was generally a poor, solitary, ignorant old woman. King James points out that magicians were learned and sought public glory; witches were unlearned and sought revenge. They blighted man and crops, were ugly and bearded, and went accompanied by a familiar. The more lurid practices of the continental sabbat are not recorded of English witches; though in *Daemonologie* and in the record of the North Berwick case, elaborate rituals are described, blasphemous as well as mischievous.

Shakespeare's play, though the first to deal with this topic seriously, was quickly followed by others. *Sophonisba* (1606) and *The Divil's Charter* (1607) were succeeded by a number of Chapman's plays introducing spirits, and in 1615 by Middleton's *Witch*, a song from which was incorporated in *Macbeth*. Jonson's *Masque of Queens*, with its celebrated anti-masque of hags, was produced in 1609. As in *A Midsummer Night's Dream*, and later in *The Tempest*, Shakespeare created a new kind of supernatural drama and one which was very widely and generally imitated.

In all these plays, however, witches are used for spectacular and intermittent effects, and the marvellous elbows out the sinister. Marston and Jonson drew largely on classical sources. Hecate, in *The Witch*, is used to supply love charms and is surrounded by familiars but her influence is not decisive. Barnabe Barnes in *The Divil's Charter* is mainly indebted to *Faustus*, but the crimes of Alexander Borgia and Lucretia occasionally parallel those of Macbeth and Lady Macbeth, and the conjuring scene especially seems modelled on the cauldron scene, whilst Alexander is cheated by a riddle at the end, in much the same way as Macbeth.

In *Macbeth* Shakespeare combines many different traditions, so
that the weird sisters, or Three Destinies of Holinshed become
assimilated with the North Berwick coven in their malevolent rites,
yet they also acquire something of the magician's power to raise and
command spirits and to foretell the future. Shakespeare's witches,
like those of North Berwick, appear capable of flying 'through the
fog and filthy air'. They are able to sail in a sieve, to assume animal
forms, and control the weather. All this Agnes Sampson and her
coven claimed to do in their attempts to destroy the ship carrying
King James from Denmark.[15] But Shakespeare's hags also have
marks of the English witch – their beards, their animal familiars and
their acts of petty revenge against the sailor and his wife. These were
the things charged against many a poor old woman at the sessions.
Their gift of prophecy expressed in riddles – the riddling form of
words is not found in Holinshed – links them with such characters as
Mother Bombie, or Erestus, the 'white bear of England's wood' in
The Old Wives' Tale. Incidentally, Rosalind, in the last Act of *As
You Like It*, makes her promises to the lovers in the riddling form
proper to the Magician which she professes herself to be:

> I will marry you, if ever I marry woman, and I'll be married tomorrow: I
> will satisfy you, if ever I satisfied man, and you shall be married tomor-
> row. I will content you, if what pleases you contents you, and you shall be
> married tomorrow. (v ii 122–6)

The prophecies of the witches about Birnam Wood and the man
not born of woman are sprigs of folklore which also recall the earlier
comedies; for instance, Erestus's prophecy that Eumenides is to be
released from enchantment by a dead man.[16]

On the other hand, they have powers superior to those of common
witches. Bishop John Leslie called them devils disguised as women
(*De Origine, Moribus et Rebus Gestis Scotorum*, Rome 1578). They
can vanish instantly like bubbles, which suggests a demonic power
assuming and discarding human shape. They have no trace of any
fear of or subjection to higher demonic forces; though the spirits
raised in the cauldron scene are called 'our masters', yet the witches
conjure them up and speak to them with authority, such authority as
belongs to the magician like Faustus, the friar in *Bussy d'Ambois* and
Owen Glendower. Macbeth, who sells his eternal jewel to the
common enemy of man, is himself in Faustus's position, but he
makes no formal compact, nor is he given any supernatural powers.
He is tempted by rousing of his own worse instincts and led to
natural crimes; but, on the other hand, he never renounces God and
his baptism, as both witches and magicians were compelled to do.

After the murder of Duncan there is no possibility of his going back. He has crossed the invisible boundary which cuts him off from his kind. His hand is against every man. He is no longer a member of the human community, and finally he sinks to the level of a hunted rogue animal.

Yet although Macbeth's career recalls a descent into Hell, it is not presented openly as a descent into Hell. In the end he finds himself deceived in the witches, as the witch or magician was so often deceived by the Devil.[17] 'Be these juggling fiends no more believ'd,' he cries. In murdering Duncan, he committed mortal sin – the sin against the Holy Ghost as James called it in *Daemonologie* (Book I, chapter II) – that is, he consciously and deliberately did that which he knew to be evil, and which he detested even as he did it. The act brings the punishment which he foresaw, he loses this clear sight, wades in blood so far that he is blinded and becomes in the end insensible even to the death of his wife.[18] But the overt theological issue is never bluntly put. Hence H. B. Charlton can deny any religious significance to *Macbeth*, while W. C. Curry, Helen Gardner and Hardin Craig, not to mention Roy Walker,[19] see the play as 'essentially medieval and Christian'. The Prince of Darkness is present only through the acts of his emissaries, but they, while in many ways recalling the realistic witch, are 'creatures of another sort'. I would not be prepared to say whether they are human or not; they are more recognisable as human in Act I than in the later scenes, where they replace Holinshed's 'wizard', and have something of the Devil's power of deceit.

Lady Macbeth's relation with the dark powers is more mysterious. Women were thought far more susceptible to demons than men, and were far more frequently accused of evil practices. King James put the proportion as high as twenty women to one man (*Daemonologie*, Book II, chapter V). In her invocation to the spirits 'that tend on mortal thoughts' Lady Macbeth offers them her breasts to be sucked and invites them to take possession of her body; this was as much as any witch could do by way of self-dedication. Professor Curry considers the sleep-walking scene to be evidence of possession, and if she did lay 'self and violent hands' upon herself, Lady Macbeth committed the final act of despair.

Neither Macbeth nor his wife has any defences. Though his conscience at first speaks clearly, he has no Good Angel as Faustus has. Banquo may pray to the merciful powers to restrain his cursed thoughts, Malcolm and Macduff appeal to Heaven, old Siward commit his dead son to the soldiery of God, but Macbeth lives in an amoral world of old wives' tales and riddles – except for that one vision of the pleading angels with their trumpet tongues, and

Heaven's cherubim horsed upon the sightless couriers of the air, which recalls Faustus's vision of Christ's blood streaming in the firmament.

The portents which accompany the death of Duncan, and fore-shadow that of Banquo, are such as on the stage always appeared with the death of princes. The strange screams in the air and the horses that ate each other are developed from hints in Holinshed, but they are distinguished from other portents by the tone and colour of the language in which they are described. The thick darkness which hangs over the sky, the raven, owl and cricket's note are much less distinct than the fiery warriors who fought above the clouds in *Julius Caesar*. It is the thick night, the fog and filthy air, the smoke of Hell which create the peculiar horror of this play, and the omens are chosen to accord. How quickly it rolls down on the sunlit battlements where the martlet flits, as a Scotch mist will roll from a mountain! Just as the witches are more horrible because we do not know what they are – it would be a relief to meet Mephistopheles – so the whole treatment of the supernatural in *Macbeth* is characterised by a potent and delicately controlled imprecision. Hell is murky. The creatures of *Macbeth*, like the ghost in *Hamlet*, are not susceptible of any one theoretical explan-ation, religious or natural.

Yet in the end justice, whether God's or Nature's, prevails. There is no direct intervention, but in the final vengeance the ingredients of the poisoned chalice are commended to the sinner's own lips. (This happens literally in *The Divil's Charter*, where Borgia is poisoned with his own wine: it also happens, of course, in *Hamlet*.) Macbeth, who had begun as Bellona's bridegroom, ends in the same role as Macdonwald, his head hacked off and put on a pole. (Did Macdon-wald's head appear in the early scenes? According to Holinshed it was cut off.) The early description of Macbeth in battle which is given by the sergeant seems to me indubitably Shakespeare's. By the violence of it we are made unforgettably aware that bloodshed of itself is familiar to Macbeth – that his trade is hand-to-hand fighting. The physical side of Duncan's murder can cause him no qualms at all. Lady Macbeth, on the other hand, is not quite Holinshed's Valkyrie; perhaps she had not smelt blood before, and though she goes through the scene unflinchingly, she is haunted by the physical atrocity of it. To Macbeth, we may believe that the dastardly act of stabbing a sleeping old man was as instinctively repugnant as stabbing a kneeling man in the back was to Hamlet: 'Look on't again, I dare not,' he cries – he, who had unseamed men from the nave to the chaps.

It is here that we approach the deepest levels of the play and that we must leave external sources and seek within Shakespeare's own earlier work the foreshadowing of the terror and the pity which we feel. In the speeches of Macbeth, especially his five great speeches,[20] lies the heart of the mystery. They embody the experience which fundamentally gives rise to the play; and there are no sub-plots, no digressions to modify it.

Macbeth acts, according to Bradley, under a horrible compulsion; Dover Wilson imagines him following the air-drawn dagger in 'a horrible smiling trance'. The murder fascinates him as damnation fascinates Faustus. It is the inevitable, the irrevocable deed, after which he too dies in some sense:

> Had I but died an hour before this chance,
> I had liv'd a blessed time: for from this instant,
> There's nothing serious in mortality:
> All is but toys: renown and grace is dead,
> The wine of life is drawn. . . .
>
> (II iii 40–53)[21]

A period of intense and almost delirious anticipation is followed by complete collapse. There is one earlier picture of an 'expense of spirit in a waste of shame', one earlier picture of conscious guilt calling in night and the creatures of night for aid, one act of physical violence followed by as swift a repentance, one equally dishonourable breach of hospitality and trust. It is the one to which Macbeth himself refers;

> Now o'er the one half-world
> Nature seems dead, and wicked dreams abuse
> The curtain'd sleep: witchcraft celebrates
> Pale Hecate's offerings: and wither'd murder,
> Alarum'd by his sentinel, the wolf,
> Whose howl's his watch, thus with his stealthy pace,
> With Tarquin's ravishing strides, towards his design
> Moves like a ghost.
>
> (II i 49–56)[22]

What is to be learnt by turning back to the sententious *Rape of Lucrece*, with its emblematic description of the heroine, its lengthy complaints and testament, its studied ornament and its formal indictment of Night, Time and Opportunity? Here, I think, are the emotional components (as distinct from the narrative components) of *Macbeth* lying separate, isolated, and more crudely and simply expressed. Tarquin's feelings before the deed, and Lucrece's feelings after it, are identical with the central core of feeling in *Macbeth*.

Night, Opportunity and a deceitful appearance are accessories to the deed. In her lament, Lucrece indicts these three. An atmosphere of tragic gloom and murk is diffused in the description of Tarquin's rising and stalking through the darkened house towards his victim. Like Macbeth, he tries to pray in the very act of entering her chamber and is startled to find that he cannot do it. There is a remote likeness to the physical horror of Duncan's corpse in the sight of Lucrece's body at the end, so ghastly inert in its great pool of blood

> Who like a late sack'd island vastly stood
> Bare and unpeopled, in this fearful flood.
>   (1740–1)

But it is, above all, in the opening soliloquies of Tarquin that the likeness is apparent. Tarquin foresees the emptiness of his satisfaction, which Macbeth does not fully understand till after the deed; but the comment with which Tarquin's inward debate is introduced might serve as prologue to the later story.

> Those that much covet are with gain so fond,
> That what they have not, that which they possess
> They scatter and unloose it from their bond,
> And so by hoping more they have but less,
> Or gaining more, the profit of excess
>   Is but to surfeit, and such griefs sustain,
>   That they prove bankrupt in this poor-rich gain.
>
> The aim of all is but to nurse the life,
> With honour, wealth, and ease in waning age;
> And in this aim there is such thwarting strife,
> That one for all, or all for one we gage:
> As life for honour, in fell battles rage,
>   Honour for wealth, and oft that wealth doth cost
>   The death of all, and altogether lost.
>
> So that in venturing ill, we leave to be
> The things we are, for that which we expect,
> And this ambitious foul infirmity,
> In having much torments us with defect
> Of that we have: so then we do neglect
>   The thing we have, and all for want of wit,
>   Make something nothing, by augmenting it.
>   (134–54)

In his protracted debate with himself, Tarquin points out the shame to his family, his blood and his posterity, the transient nature of the gain (and here Macbeth echoes him):

> Who buys a minute's mirth to wail a week?
> *Or sells eternity to get a toy?*
>
> (213–14)

He dreads the vengeance of Collatine even while he recognises the ties of kinship and hospitality which bind them:

> But as he is my kinsman, my dear friend,
> The shame and fault finds no excuse nor end.
>
> (237–8)

Finally he rejects the counsel of reason in words which anticipate Lady Macbeth's 'tis the eye of child-hood, That fears a painted devil':

> Who fears a sentence or an old man's saw,
> Shall by a painted cloth be kept in awe.
>
> (244–5)

The crime which Tarquin commits, even more clearly, though not more truly, than Macbeth's, destroys the natural ties between him and the rest of the community. It is a sort of suicide. Both Macbeth and he commit a violence upon themselves from which they cannot recover. Examples have been known in the modern world where acts of sufficient violence will destroy the personality of the perpetrator; and even periods of acute nervous strain and danger, such as those to which combatants were subjected, will issue in nervous prostration and a feeling of complete emptiness of being. It is this identity between violence and self-violence (though in *The Rape of Lucrece*, the effects of the crime are given in the soliloquies of the victim) which a comparison of the two works reinforces as the central idea, the germ of the play. Macbeth's real victim is himself. Both *The Rape of Lucrece* and Macbeth reflect with very different degrees of skill a deep-seated and permanent experience; and the difference serves only to emphasise the unity of Shakespeare's art, the modifying and shaping power which his work as a whole seems to exert upon each of its parts. I think it is not fancy to say that *Macbeth* is the greater for being demonstrably by the hand that wrote *Othello*, or even the hand that wrote *Lucrece*; since the likeness which is discernible within such variety is proof that the play was written from the very depths of his mind and heart, and together with the multiplicity of sources which have furnished the subject of this paper, it gives a measure of the power, the intellectual and spiritual strength and pressure required, to weld them into one.

Notes

1   The atmospheric strength of the Chronicle is noted by Dover Wilson in
the New Cambridge edition of *Macbeth* (Cambridge, 1947), p. xii. He
quotes the earlier edition of Sir Herbert Grierson and J. C. Smith at this
point in support of the Celtic atmosphere of the story. In a paper read at
Cambridge in November 1950, Mrs N. K. Chadwick suggested that the
earliest chronicle, Wyntoun's, incorporates material from lost Celtic
sagas on Macbeth, particularly in the parts relating to the supernatural.
She bases this on changes in the style, indicating a Celtic original. There
is an independent Norse saga of Macbeth.

2   *Basilikon Doron*, and *The true lawe of free monarchies* (Edinburgh,
1597, 1598).

3   Wilson, op. cit. pp. xxxi-xxxii.

4   Hardin Craig, *An Interpretation of Shakespeare* (New York, 1948).

5   Henry Paul points out in his article, 'The Imperial Theme in *Macbeth*'
(*Adams Memorial Studies*, ed. J. G. McManaway et al., Washington,
1948, pp. 253–68), that the *pearls* set in the base of an imperial diadem
represented the several dependent fiefs (*loc. cit.* p. 264). What follows in
my text is indebted to this valuable article.

6   St Margaret, Malcolm's wife, and a strong influence in the shaping of his
policy, obtained from the Pope the privilege that Scottish kings should be
anointed (i.e. hallowed) at their coronation.

7   It is melancholy to note that Donalbain returned from Ireland to the Isles
and (after Malcolm's death) slew his nephew, David, but was in turn
succeeded by another of Malcolm's sons. With this one interval, the line
of Malcolm Canmore retained the throne.

8   Paul, 'The Imperial Theme', p. 258.

9   It has been much disputed whether Shakespeare knew this pageant or
not. Paul thinks he did.

10   See Dover Wilson, *Macbeth*, p. xvii, for a summary of the material.

11   *The Description of Scotland*, chapter XIII (translated from the Latin of
Hector Boethius by William Harison, and prefixed to Holinshed's
Historie of Scotland, 1577). As in the other quotations the spelling has
been modernised.

12   Vittoria's 'Terrify babes, my Lord, with painted devils' and the words of
Flamineo about her, 'If woman do breed man, She ought to teach him
manhood', recall respectively 'tis the eye of child-hood / That fears a
painted devil' and 'Bring forth men-children only.' The figure of the
great lady, great in wickedness, was popular on the Jacobean stage.
Lucrezia Borgia in *The Devil's Charter* also recalls Lady Macbeth in her
laments and swoon over the husband she has slain, her invocation of the
furies and her careful concealment of the murder by staging a mock
suicide.

13   C. H. L. Ewen, *Witch Hunting and Witch Trials* (London, 1929), pp.
19–21, 31. I am indebted for this reference and for much general
information on the subject of demonology to Mrs Florence Trefethan.

14   Ibid., p. 23.

15 See *Newes from Scotland*, 1591 (reprinted with King James's *Daemon-
    ologie* in the Bodley Head Quartos, London, 1924).
16 *The Old Wives' Tale* (*The Dramatic Works of George Peele*, ed. C. T.
    Prouty, vol. 3, 1970, p. 402).
17 In the words of King James (*Daemonologie*, Book I, chapter v) – which
    seem to be recalled by Banquo in I iii – the Devil tries 'to make himself so
    to be trusted in these little things, that he may have the better commodity
    thereafter, to deceive in the end with a trick once for all; I mean the
    everlasting perdition of their soul and body.' Cf. the deception of
    Alexander Borgia, unmasked at the end of *The Divil's Charter*.
18 This insensibility is contrasted with the Christian stoicism of Macduff
    and old Siward, who endure their bereavements courageously, not
    barbarously.
19 H. B. Charlton, *Shakespearian Tragedy* (Cambridge, 1948); W. C.
    Curry, *Shakespeare's Philosophical Patterns* (Baton Rouge, 1937);
    Helen Gardner, 'Milton and the Tragedy of Damnation', in *English
    Studies*, 1948, ed. F. P. Wilson (London, 1948); Hardin Craig, 'Motiva-
    tion in Shakespeare's Choice of Materials', *Shakespeare Survey* 4 (1951)
    pp. 31–2; Roy Walker, *The Time is Free* (London, 1949).
20 *Macbeth*, I vii 1–28; II i 31–64; III ii, 13–26, 46–53; V iii 40–53; V v
    17–28.
21 Cf. the line below, from *Lucrece*: 'Who . . . sells eternity to get a toy?'
    and the lassitude of Cleopatra at Antony's death:

> The odds is gone,
> And there is nothing left remarkable
> Beneath the visiting moon.
>
> (IV xv 66–8)

22 It may be noted that this atmosphere is recalled again in Iachimo's
    speech over the sleeping Imogen: night, 'our *Tarquin*' with his stealthy
    tread, the crickets' cry (*Cymbeline*, II ii 11–14).

VII.

Fate and Chance in
The Duchess of Malfi

In the second prison scene of *The Duchess of Malfi* there is a significant echo of the most terrible chapter in the Pentateuch, which seems hitherto not to have been recognised:

> I'll tell thee a miracle –
> I am not mad yet, to my cause of sorrow.
> Th' heaven ore my head, seemes made of molten brasse
> The earth of flaming sulphure yet I am not mad:
>
> (IV ii 25–8)

But it shal come to passe if thou wilt not hearken unto the voyce of the Lord thy God, to observe to do all his Commandments and his Statutes which I command thee this day, that all these curses shall come upon thee and overtake thee.

Cursed shalt thou be in the city and cursed shalt thou be in the field.

Cursed shall be thy basket and thy store.

Cursed shall be the fruit of thy body and the fruit of thy land. . . .

And the heaven that is over thy head shall be brasse, and the earth that is under thee shal be yron. . . .

So that thou shalt be mad for the sight of thine eyes which thou shalt see. (Deuteronomy, xxviii 15–18, 23, 34)[1]

The Duchess both compares and distinguishes her plight from that depicted in the curse of Mount Ebal: the earth under her feet is not iron but the flaming sulphur of Hell; nor is she granted the oblivion of madness. But the original context is not irrelevant, as it is in so many of Webster's borrowings.

The power of a curse, though it may be related to a coherent belief, is more usually superstitious, that is, it involves the supernatural as part of the free energy, the undirected power of the universe. The horror of Webster's play depends upon a powerful sense of the supernatural combined with a scepticism far deeper than that of professed rebels like Marlowe. An intense capacity for feeling and suffering, within a clueless intellectual maze, springs from the deepened insight into character which was Webster's greatest strength as a dramatist.[2] Fear of the unseen and unapprehended encompasses all his characters: the world to come is even darker than the midnight in which all his greater scenes are laid.[3]

> In what a shadow, or deepe pit of darknesse,
> Doth (womanish, and fearfull) mankind live.
> (V v 125–6)

The curse which falls upon the Duchess of Malfi is potent but undefinable, like the whole atmosphere of the supernatural in this play. The malice of her brothers is the immediate cause of her sufferings, but even as the hidden vindictiveness of the Cardinal surpasses the savagery of Ferdinand, it is a power beyond these two which the Duchess curses first and foremost: no less than the 'stars' themselves, which include in themselves or by their influence the whole material universe, the frame of things entire.

> I could curse the Starres . . .
> And those three smyling seasons of the yeere
> Into a Russian winter: nay the world
> To its first Chaos.
> (IV i 113–19)

To which Bosola, the instrument of Fate, opposes an implacable calm: 'Look you, the Starres shine still.' (IV i 120) The Duchess's reply, though in itself a bitter jest, implies the contagious nature of a curse: 'Oh, but you must remember, my curse hath a great way to goe', and runs on without a stop into the curse of the plague itself which she wishes on her brothers.

There are roughly five types of curse:[4] curses upon wrongdoers, either by the sufferer (imprecation) or the Church (excommunication); curses as adjunct to an oath; malignant cursing of the innocent by witches and sorcerers; hereditary curses (blights) upon a family – usually an extension of cursing in the first sense; and general curses upon specific acts, by whomsoever committed, which are a form of primitive legislation and of which the Jewish curse pronounced by the Levites from Mount Ebal is a powerful example.

The curse which the Duchess lays on her brothers invokes the powers of God and is a religious imprecation. Such a curse is the last weapon left to the helpless and oppressed, and was frequently used in Elizabethan tragedy, notably by Titus in *Titus Andronicus*, by Anne and other victims in *King Richard III*, by Constance in *King John*, and pre-eminently by Timon and Lear. The power of such a curse was greatest in a parent or king, in whose outraged authority God saw an image of His own. Cornelia, therefore, when she utters her twofold curse upon Vittoria and Brachiano, is armed with this double power of authority and wrong.[5]

In the earlier scene where she first recognises the doom which is upon her, the Duchess realises that the hereditary curse lies upon her children, and says

> I intend, since they were born accurs'd;
> Curses shall be their first language
> (III v 137–8)

Indeed a curse, irrespective of the guilt or innocence of the individual, may well be hereditary in 'the royall blood of *Arragon*, and *Castile*' to which the Duchess and her brothers belong, the physical tie which twinned her with Ferdinand and which is the only cause of the tragedy.

> Damne her, that body of hers,
> While that my blood ran pure in't, was more worth
> Than that which thou wouldst comfort, (call'd a soule)
> (IV i 146–8)

he cries to Bosola, but the pure blood of her royal descent which it is her crime to have contaminated carried, as all would know, the curse of that madness which later overtook Ferdinand himself.[6]

The curses which Ferdinand so freely vents are spoken in a transport of rage, but the solemn act of banishment performed by the Cardinal and the States of Ancona, which must have been spectacularly one of the high lights of the play,[7] has the full weight of civil and ecclesiastical authority behind it. That this is misused authority the pilgrims who act as chorus to the scene bear witness; but the splendours of the shrine of Our Lady of Loretto had been used previously in drama as a background to Machiavellian 'policy'.[8]

In his earlier play Webster had used a good deal of merely furious cursing: Vittoria, Brachiano and Isabella (in her play-acting) are more violent than deadly,[9] the politicians do not curse, and Cornelia herself at the end says to Flamineo:

> The God of Heaven forgive thee. Do'st not wonder
> I pray for thee? Ile tell thee whats the reason,

> I have scarce breath to number twentie minutes,
> Ide not spend that in cursing.
>
> (*The White Divel*, v ii 52–5)

In *The Duchess of Malfi* the most potent curses are 'not loud but deep'. A vow spoken with imprecation may constitute a curse: such is Brachiano's vow 'by his wedding ring' not to lie with Isabella, which she calls a 'cursed vow'. Ferdinand's vow never to see his sister more, which he makes the opportunity for a cruel deception, rebounds upon himself – as an unjust vow was likely to do – for it is the sight of her supposed dead face which unnerves him and awakes the madness in him.

It is Ferdinand who refers most frequently to the practices of the Black Art. Thrice does he accuse the Duchess herself of witchcraft,[10] but when Bosola suggests that she is the victim of sorcery, he scorns the idea:

> Do you thinke that hearbes, or charms
> Can force the will? Some trialls have bin made
> In this foolish practise; but the ingredients
> Were lenative poysons, such as are of force
> To make the patient mad. . . .
> The witch-craft lies in her rancke blood.[11]
>
> (iii i 88–94)

Nevertheless, part of her torment was that she was watched, prevented from sleeping, a recognised method of dealing with those who were themselves witches. In presenting the wax figures of Antonio and his children 'appearing as if they were dead', Ferdinand practises directly upon her life by a method analogous, as the Duchess herself recognises, to the most famous and deadly of charms.

> It wastes me more,
> Than weren't my picture, fashion'd out of wax,
> Stucke with a magicall needle, and then buried
> In some fowle dung-hill
>
> (iv i 73–6)

At the same time Ferdinand leaves with her a dead man's hand bearing a ring, with the words 'Bury the print of it in your heart.' The Duchess, discovering it, cries:

> What witch-craft does he practise, that he hath left
> A dead-man's hand here?
>
> (iv i 65–6)

This is a powerful charm which was also used in the cure of madness,[12] but which as the 'Hand of Glory' or *main de gloire* was an essential ingredient in the more deadly practices of the Black Art. The ring, which the Duchess is meant to see as Antonio's, is her own wedding ring which the Cardinal had violently torn from her before the shrine of Our Lady of Loretto: and a wedding ring was itself a sacred object possessed of virtuous powers.[13]

These horrible properties do in fact so benumb the Duchess that she feels to live is 'the greatest torture soules feele in hell' (IV i 82) and the servant who wishes her long life has pronounced a most 'horrible curse' upon her (IV i 110). The executioners 'pull downe Heaven upon' her (IV ii 238), and Hell opens before her murderers, both Bosola (IV ii 269) and Ferdinand. The curse of her blood lies upon them and cries for vengeance.[14] The sight of her dead face enacts her silent revenge upon them. It was generally believed that in the presence of a murderer the wounds of a corpse would bleed, the eyes might open and fix him with a blighting look, or the dead hand might point to him in denunciation. The effect on Ferdinand is to awake remorse: he denounces the murder and his tool Bosola, saying that the deed is registered in Hell (IV ii 327). This is perhaps an echo of Othello to the dead Desdemona: 'That look of thine will hurl my soul from heaven . . .'

The form of madness which overtakes him, lycanthropy, was recognised as a diabolic possession:

> The devill, knowing the constitution of men, and the particular diseases whereunto they are inclined, takes the vantage of some and secondeth the nature of the disease by the concurrence of his own delusion, thereby corrupting the imagination and working in the mind a strong persuasion that they are become that which in truth they are not. This is apparent in that disease, which is termed *Lycanthropia*, where some, having their brains distempered with melancholy, have verily thought themselves to be wolves and so have behaved themselves. . . . For God in his just judgment may suffer some men to be bewitched by the devill, that to their conceite they may seeme to be like brute beasts, though in a deede they remaine the true men still. (William Perkins, *A Discourse of the Damned Art of Witchcraft, Works* (1618, III, 611)[15]

In the last Act Bosola and Antonio are haunted by the Duchess, whilst Ferdinand and the Cardinal are haunted by devils, and death overtakes all four.[16] The curse which has involved the whole family is worked out.

These wretched eminent things
Leave no more fame behind 'em, then should one

Fall in a frost, and leave his print in snow –
As soone as the sun shines, it ever melts,
Both forme, and matter

(v v 138–42)

The influence of the stars is the divine method of governing the world as Sir Kenelm Digby points out in a passage which, though some twenty years later than the date of *The Duchess of Malfi*, may be cited as a typical statement of the general belief:

> no accident can be so bad in this life but that the celestial bodies have power to change it to good . . . not chance but the heavens and stars govern the world which are the only books of fate: whose secret characters and influences but few, divinely inspired, can read in the true sense that their Creator gave them.

This is no way impugns the doctrine of free will, for God having framed the world upon the strife and counterpoise of contraries, such as hot and cold, poisons and antidotes, summer and winter, to human souls, His highest work, He gave 'an entire liberty together with a constrained necessity which no way hinder or impeach each other.' The highest faculty of knowledge is the contemplation of the Creator and this the human soul is free to accept or reject, subject only to God's unconstraining foreknowledge. This inner freedom being granted, in the course of the outer world God governs not by direct and miraculous intervention, but arranges that

> inferiors should be subaltern to and guided by their superiors: the heavens then and stars, being so in respect of us, not only in place but in dignity, duration, in quantity, in quality and in purity of substance . . . must of necessity be allowed by us to be the causes of all contingent accidents and the authors of our fortunes and actions whereby the liberty of the will doth not immediately and expressly repugn and wrestle against the disposition of the heavens . . . since to meaner lights we by daily experience attribute the ominous presages of the deaths of kings, of revolutions and of empires, wars, pestilence, famine, dearths, and such other effects, let us without difficulty acknowledge a nobler operation in these glorious bodies that are the efficient causes of the other: and having admitted them for causes, you will grant that who hath the knowledge of their natures may, by calculating their motions of time to come, prognosticate their effects.[17]

By their foreknowledge, prognosticators could attempt to avert evil influences, and strengthen good ones – to rule the stars. This, however, was considered impious,[18] and although the casting of horoscopes was common enough, Antonio's one attempt to read the stars brings disaster. The *Life* of Cardano makes plain the real discomforts of star-readers. Bosola, it would appear, does not believe in the power of the prognosticators; though he does not go so far, with Shakespeare's Edmund, as to deny the power of the stars themselves:[19]

> Bosola: Tis rumour'd she hath had three bastards, but
>   By whom, we may go read i' th' Starres.
> Ferd: Why some
>   Hold opinion, all things are written there.
> Bosola: Yes, if we could find Spectacles to read them.
>
> (III i 72–6)

The most extensive statement of this doctrine comes in the central scene of Chapman's *Conspiracy of Byron*, a play to which *The Duchess of Malfi* shows particular indebtedness.[20] The astrologer himself begins by foreseeing some danger to himself, which he feels unable to avert:

> O the strange difference 'twixt us and the stars;
> They work with inclinations strong and fatal,
> And nothing know; and we know all their working
> And nought can do, or nothing can prevent![21]
>
> (III iii 6–8)

When he has read the fatal horoscope of Byron in which a Caput Algol prognosticates that the Duke is to lose his head, Byron curses him, and defies the stars, because as a rational soul he is of nobler substance than they.

> I am a nobler substance than the stars,
> And shall the baser overrule the better? . . .
> I have a will and faculties of choice
> To do, or not to do: and reason why
> I do, or not do this: the stars have none:
> They know not why they shine, more than this taper,
> Nor how they work, nor what: I'll change my course,
> I'll piecemeal pull the frame of all my thoughts,
> And cast my will into another mould. . . .
> [I'll] kick at fate. Be free, all worthy spirits,
> And stretch yourselves for greatness and for height,
> Untruss your slaveries: you have height enough
> Beneath this steep heaven to use all your reaches;
> Tis too far off to let you, or respect you.
>
> (III iii 109–18, 130–4)

However, like other tragic heroes the Duke rushes on his ruin, disregarding all the omens and warnings which he receives, and in the end, his friends can only pray that he

> ope his breast and arms,
> To all the storms Necessity can breathe,
> And burst them all with his embraced death
> (*Byron's Tragedy*, v iii 212–14)

which he does in that fine image which is also echoed by the Duchess, that the body is 'A slave bound face to face with Death till death.'[22] (v vi 38) But Byron's triumphant defiance of death is no stoic acceptance of its pangs. He succeeds, finally, in facing it – only that, and no more. He accepts the fact that a life as passionate and heroic as his own must be extinguished, but he cannot tolerate the circumstances: he, a single man, defies the 'kingdom's doom' (v iv 217), and his death, like his life, is a clash of opposites, 'vice and virtue, corruption and eternesse' mixed (v iv 190–1). In this he is a true microcosm or little world of warring elements.

He cites, only to reject them, the conventional stoic maxims, not because he does not believe them, but because he will not accept them as platitudes from the lips of the bishop who attends him. 'Talk of knowledge! / It serves for inward use.' (v iv 50–1)

Chapman's perfect stoics, Clermont D'Ambois and Cato, whose tempers are so settled that no calamity can disturb them, are something less heroic, as well as less human. Though they claim to accept their fate 'freely', 'with a man's applause', the impression they give is rather one of indifference.[23] The Duchess, who submits to the chastisement of Heaven, though the instruments are tyrannous (III i 90–5), has a natural courage and nobility of spirit that rises at the scent of danger. When she turns, expecting to see her husband, and sees her brother behind her, her first words are: ' 'Tis welcome' (III ii 77). And again when she sees the troop of armed men making towards her across country: 'O, they are very welcome' (III v 111). Bosola says that she seems 'rather to welcome the end of misery' than shun it (IV i 5–6), and at the very nadir of her hopes, when she has reached the calm at the centre of the whirlpool, the Duchess, equating herself, like Edgar, with the 'lowest and most dejected thing' of nature, discovers the anaesthesia that lies beyond.

> I am acquainted with sad misery,
> As the tan'd galley slave is with his Oare,
> Necessity makes me suffer constantly,
> And custome makes it easie.
>
> (IV ii 29–32)

Her misery is *sad* because it is settled and established, because it is adult and mature, and because it is massive and heavy, like the oar, a physical burden.[24] *Necessity* may stand either for the situation or for the stern goddess, *saeva Necessitas*, who has created it: and *constantly* means both continuously, or incessantly, or steadfastly and heroically (which is the older sense). There are thus two meanings combined in this passage: the Duchess is inured to the pain which she cannot escape, but she has also learnt to suffer, and acquired strength from her sufferings. The first meaning is supported by the image of the galley slave: yet after all, it was only the strongest who could survive in the galleys.[25] Bosola survived.

When, finally, Bosola brings in the coffin with the words 'may it arrive welcome . . .' the Duchess turns to face the last present of her Princely brothers with the words:

> I have so much obedience, in my blood,
> I wish it in their veines to do them good.
> (IV ii 168–9)

This does not of course mean that she is obediently accepting death, but that her blood (i.e. her passions, all that Ferdinand meant by 'her rancke blood') is now entirely obedient to her will, and therefore she is not physically terrified, or transported with physical rage as was Byron: she wishes that the choleric blood of her brothers were as obedient as hers. She is Duchess of Malfi still.

To doubt the power of the stars was perhaps atheistic and impious,[26] but on the other hand, to accept it would seem to leave Man, for all practical purposes, dependent on these second causes, and his fate to be, in Bosola's phrase, the star's tennis balls. This phrase was used also, however, with a significant variant – Fortune's tennis.[27] Fortune, or 'blind chance' was one of the commonest figures in Elizabethan pageantry, emblem books and devices. With her wheel, upon which humanity was bound, 'her rolling restless stone'[28] and her blinded eyes, she might be presented in a favourable aspect as Chance or Opportunity, in which case she had a long forelock, to be seized by the active and aspiring man; but more frequently she personified the 'turning and inconstant and mutability and variation' of unregulated accident, which calls attention to itself only when the accident is unfavourable. It is in this aspect that Kent defies her when he is set in the stocks by Regan:

> Fortune, goodnight,
> Smile, once more turne thy wheele
> (*King Lear*, II ii 179–80)[29]

Blind Fortune plays so large a role in *The Duchess of Malfi* that her influence may almost be thought to challenge that of the stars. It is the name under which the Duchess gives herself to Antonio, perhaps in recollection of the courtly habit by which ladies assumed such allegorical roles.[30] Later Delio, fearing that he is betrayed, cries

> how fearfully
> Shewes his ambition now, (unfortunate Fortune)!
> (II iv 105–6)

And if the dreadful horoscope which does in fact betray Antonio illustrates the malignancy of the stars, the accident which makes him drop it in Bosola's path is a freak of chance. This accident has often been censured as undramatic, a flaw in Webster's construction; it is on the contrary, eminently dramatic, as the recent production of this play made clear: it is precisely the kind of odd, unpredictable coincidence which, when events are wrought up to a sufficiently high pitch, can almost be counted on to occur. In the late war, half the casualties resulted from some such accident – and half the miraculous escapes. Someone just happened to be called away before the bomb fell, or just happened to have gone into the cellar. It is of course only in times of violence that such accidents mean the difference between life and death.

The Duchess greets those who have come to apprehend her with a defiance of Fortune:

> O, they are very welcome;
> When Fortunes wheel is overcharg'd with Princes,
> The waight makes it move swift. I would have my ruine
> Be sudden.
> (III v 111–14)

And in prison she thinks that her tragedy is terrible enough to unmuffle blind Fortune (IV ii 37–8). Antonio goes to his fatal interview with the same contempt of what Fortune can do:

> Though in our miseries, Fortune have a part,
> Yet, in our noble suffrings, she hath none –
> Contempt of paine, that we may call our owne.
> (V iii 70–2)

In the last Act of *The Duchess of Malfi* mere ill-fortune directs the 'mistakes' by which Bosola and Antonio are killed: yet the Echo had bid Antonio fly his *Fate* (V iii 44), and when Delio begs him not to go to the Cardinal's that night, he replies with a bitter punning jest that suggests a stronger power than blind Chance at work: 'Necessitie compells me'[31] (v iii 41) The play is filled with little omens, such as the Duchess's dream that her coronet of diamonds was changed to pearls, Antonio's name being drowned in blood, the tangling of the Duchess's hair,[32] and as the Pilgrim says, on witnessing their banishment:

> Fortune makes this conclusion generall,
> 'All things do helpe th' unhappy man to fall.'
> (III iv 48–9)

The alternative views that Fate or Chance rule the world are never set in open opposition to each other, and the omens might be interpreted as the work either of the one or the other. It is precisely this uncertainty at the heart of the play which is the heart of its darkness: either explanation, if it could be accepted as an explanation, would give some relief. But the opposition of Fate and Chance was in fact a familiar one,[33] the problem would be obvious to Webster's audience, without any formal antithesis being propounded. The astounding and gratifying thing is that he should have been able to resist the temptation to state a case; it is a renunciation of which few Elizabethans were capable, and least of all perhaps his friend Chapman.[34] The spectator, like the Duchess, goes into a wilderness where there is neither path nor friendly clue to be his guide. The Cardinal and Ferdinand may die acknowledging the justice of their ends in the highly sententious manner which was expected at the end of a Revenge play, but Bosola, to the end of his final couplet adds four mysterious words which come from a state far on the other side of despair.

> Let worthy mindes nere stagger in distrust
> To suffer death, or shame, for what is just –
> Mine is another voyage.
> (v v 127–9)

This blank feeling of Lucretian chaos is as far removed from the Deistic 'atheism' of Marlowe as from the determinist stoicism of Ford. Bosola, the conscience-struck and bewildered slave of greatness, so dominates any presentation of the play that the loves and crimes of the House of Aragon seem but a background to his tragedy.[35] Ferdinand, the Cardinal and the Duchess are born to rule: their imperious tempers are innate. Ferdinand draws his dagger before his sister, even when he has no reason to suspect her of a second marriage:

> This was my Fathers ponyard: doe you see,
> I'll'd be loth to see't look rusty, 'cause 'twas his
> (I i 370–1)

The Duchess turns away, and almost her next words are:

> If all my royall kindred
> Lay in my way unto this marriage:
> I'll'd make them my low foote-steps.
> (I i 382–4)

Bosola, a silent figure, listens to these high words from the Prince to whom he has already sold himself in what he recognises as a diabolical bargain.[36] His sympathy for the Duchess in the discovery scene is far more deeply felt than the momentary flash of compunction which Brachiano's betrayers feel: and the shock of his final comment:

> What rests, but I reveale
> All to my Lord?
> (III ii 374–5)

is only deepened by his self-contempt. After her capture he essays to comfort the Duchess[37] without ever being able to defy Ferdinand who observes contemptuously: 'Thy pity is nothing of kin to thee' (IV i 166). The word echoes through the latter half of the play: pity, 'the miracle of pity', and having carried out the murder, Bosola retorts the word upon his master: 'But here begin your pitty' (IV ii 272). Remorse works in Ferdinand as madness: the Hell which he had foreseen when he accepted Ferdinand's gold engulfs Bosola, and wakens in him the same vengeful love which in the earlier play Ludovico had felt for the wronged Duchess Isabella. It is Bosola, not Antonio, who speaks the most passionate lines in the play:

> Returne (faire soule) from darknesse, and lead mine
> Out of this sencible Hell: She's warme, she breathes:
> Upon thy pale lips I will melt my heart
> To store them with fresh colour.
> (IV ii 368–71)

He weeps (IV ii 390) and later he is haunted by the memory of the scene:

> Still me thinkes the Dutchesse
> Haunts me: there, there. . . . Tis nothing but my mellancholy
> (V ii 381–2)

It is as the embodiment of that blind and bewildered pity which, striking with his bitterness, occasionally rises into a general disillusion, that Bosola dominates the play. His great speech on the vanity of life, addressed to the captive Duchess in preparation for her death, recalls in its function the great speech of the Duke to the captive and condemned Claudio in *Measure for Measure*, but its immediate source is the Book of Job. This speech, more than any other epitomises what the play is really concerned with.

> Thou art a box of worme-seede, at best, but a salvatory of greene mummey: what's this flesh? a little cruded milke, phantasticall puffe-paste: our bodies are weaker then those paper prisons boyes use to keepe flies in: more contemptible: since ours is to preserve earth-wormes: didst thou ever see a Larke in a cage? such is the soule in the body: this world is like her little turfe of grasse, and the Heaven ore our heades, like her looking glasse, onely gives us a miserable knowledge of the small compasse of our prison.[38] (IV ii 122–31)

Webster had a delicate balance to maintain between the theatrical and the doctrinal in this scene. There is no doubt that the 'scene of suffering' in a Senecal play included physical atrocities of a kind which could not be paralleled in Webster[39] and that in the plays of the Machiavellian villain parricide was a necessary ingredient. It was therefore necessary, if his subject were to be brought home to his audience, that the action should be violent. In such a case the natural compensating impulse of the Elizabethan dramatist was to indulge in extended monologue, such as Constance's apostrophe to Death in *King John*, the 'passions' of Marston's characters, or the great set speeches of Chapman's tragic heroes. But Webster successfully steers between this Scylla and Charybdis. The pageantry of madness and death, the waxen figures, the disguises of Bosola all suggest that the events are inadequate to express the nature of the sorrow in which the Duchess is enfolded. The quality of her endurance is as far removed from the stoic insensibility of the 'Senecal man' – Feliche, Clermont or Charlemont – as it is from the hysteric passions of Marston's Antonio. Her insensibility is the natural insensibility of extreme shock, and it passes. Through her 'sensible Hell' she moves as a human figure, whose delicate gradations of mood show that even at the end, it is life, vulnerable but unquenchable, which dazzles the eyes of Ferdinand and which he (and we) mistake for death.

Notes

1 From the Authorised Version (1611) which appeared some two years before the play.
2 Cf. Professor Hardin Craig, *The Enchanted Glass* (Oxford, 1936), pp. 226–7.
3 The bedroom scene, the two prison scenes and the final scene are all night scenes. Cf. that chapter of Job which Bosola quotes elsewhere, 'the land of darknes and the shadow of death, A land of darknes, as darknes it selfe, and of the shadow of death, without any order, and where the light is as darkenes' (Job, x 21–2). See below, pp. 84–5.
4 This classification is my own. I have been unable to find any systematic study of the variety of curse beyond Ernest Crawley's little book, *Oath, Curse and Blessing* (Watts, 1934).
5 *The White Divel*, I ii 288–93. Cornelia kneels to utter this curse, as was commonly done. In the first Act of *The Divel's Law Case*, the mother kneels and curses her daughter in the same way: and the daughter is aghast (I ii 112–14).
6 The story of Juana the Mad, sister of Katherine of Aragon, must have been known to the audience, and that of the children of Philip II.
7 It was described by an Italian traveller in 1618 (E. E. Stoll, *John Webster*, Boston, 1905, p. 29).
8 By Chapman, *Byron's Tragedy*, I ii 78–82.
9 Vittoria, *The White Divel*, III ii 286–91, IV ii 125–40; Brachiano, II i 190–4, IV ii 43–9; Isabella, II i 245–54. Primitive curses often depend on a formula, and on being spoken in due posture, at a favourable hour of day.
10 I i 344–6, II v 1, III ii 165.
11 When Byron says that he has been bewitched by La Fin into committing treason, his accusers point out that witchcraft cannot affect the will, which, being one of the faculties of the rational soul – the others were reason and memory – could not be enforced.
12 G. L. Kittredge, *Witchcraft in Old and New England* (Harvard, 1929), p. 142. cf. above.
13 The Duchess had proffered it to Antonio as sovereign for the eyesight, and Antonio had seen a saucy and ambitious devil dancing in the circle (I i 464–76).
14 IV ii 78–80. A subject fully treated by writers on Revenge tragedy.
15 It is perhaps fair to add that King James in *Daemonologie* denied the supernatural origin of this disease. Bodin, *Demonomanie* (1580), accepts it.
16 Bosola, V ii 380–1; Antonio, V iii; Ferdinand, V ii 32–4, V iv 25–6; Cardinal, V iv 30–2, V v 1–7. The origin of this last is indicated in T. B[ramhall], *A Treatise of Spectres* ... 58, p. 37: 'A stubborn obstinate fellow a little before he died (as report goes) said that looking into a Pond he saw a shadow in the water which with a drawn sword threatened death to him. Sabellicus, lib. I, cap. 4.'

17 *Private Memoirs of Sir Kenelm Digby*, ed. Sir N. H. Nicholas (1827), pp. 127–32.

18 Cf. Professor Hardin Craig, op. cit. p. 6. He quotes *Paradise Lost*, VIII, 83–4: 'Heaven is for thee too high / To know what passes there. Be lowly wise.' G. Cardano cast the horoscope of Christ.

19 D'Amville, in Tourneur's *Atheist's Tragedy*, denies 'him they call the Supreame of the Starres' (II iv 158), and consequently the influence of the stars also. In a later scene (v i) he identifies his gold as the 'Starres whose operations make. / The fortunes and the destinies of men' (v i 22–3).

20 See especially I i 112–17, II ii 66–81.

21 Cf. *Duchess of Malfi* III ii 90–2; 'O most imperfect light of human reason / That makes us so unhappy to foresee / What we can least prevent.'

22 Cf. *Duchess of Malfi*, IV i 76–80: 'yond's an excellent property / For a tyrant, which I would account mercy – . . . If they would bind me to that lifeles truncke, / And let me freeze to death.' These particular lines of Byron are also printed separately by Chapman in *Euthymiae Raptus* (*Poems*, ed. P. B. Barrett, Oxford, 1941, p. 195).

23 *Revenge of Bussy D'Ambois*, III iv 70; IV i 149; cf. I iv 132; IV v 6.

24 For these various meanings of *sad*, *necessity* and *constantly*, see *N.E.D.* s.v.

25 In *Believe as You List*, a play which once or twice echoes Webster, the deposed King Antiochus, whose stoic fortitude defies imprisonment and torture, is literally sent to the galleys, and appears as a galley slave in Act v.

26 Lipsius, *De Constantia*, lib. 4, restated the classic argument for reconciling Stellar influence and man's free will, originally popularised in Boethius.

27 'The Starres tennys balls', v iv 63. *Fortune's Tennis* was the title of a play by Dekker, now lost: and also of an anonymous fragment dated *c.* 1600 (Chambers, *Elizabethan Stage*, IV, 14).

28 Fluellen's description of Fortune, *Henry v*,III vi 20ff.

29 And – how typically – Cordelia: 'For thee, oppressed King am I cast downe, / Myself could else outfrowne false Fortunes frowne.'

30 E.g. in *Cynthia's Revels*, II i, Hedon says that he calls Lady Philautia, his Honour: and she calls him, her Ambition.

31 Necessity in the sense of *poverty*, and necessity in the sense of *fate*. For another vital play upon this word, see the words of the Duchess quoted above, p. 80.

32 III v 19–21; II iii 59–62; III ii 61. Antonio says of the second, that the superstitious would call it ominous, but he believes it chance, 'meere accedent'.

33 Perhaps the best example of this common-place is the frontispiece of R. Recorde, *The Castell of Knowledge (1556)* which shows a castle with Astrology on the top: on the left, Knowledge upholding the Sphere of Destiny, and on the right, blindfold Ignorance holds the cord of a crank which turns the Wheel of Fortune inscribed *Quomodo scandit, corruet statim*. The Motto runs: 'Though spiteful Fortune turned her wheele, /

To staye the Sphere of Uranye, / Yet dooth this Sphere resist that wheele / And fleeyth all fortunes villanye. / Though earth do honour Fortunes balle / And bytells blinde her wheele advaunce, / The heavens to fortune are not thralle, / These Spheres surmount al fortunes chance.'

34 Compare, for example, these lines from a work much quoted by Webster in this play: 'It argues more powre willingly to yeeld / To what by no repulse can be repel'd / Than to be victor of the greatest state / We can with any fortune subjugate.' *Petrarch's Seven Penitential Psalms* (*Poems*, ed. P. B. Barrett, Oxford 1941, p. 249).

35 He is far more frequently present than any other figure: he unites the two groups, and he is the first character to exhibit the symptoms of melancholy which afterwards appear in the Duchess, Antonio and the Cardinal, and which seem to emanate from him.

36 'It seemes you would create me / One of your familiars ... Take your Divels / Which Hell calls Angels: these curs'd gifts would make / You a corruptor, me an Impudent traitor, / And should I take them they'll'd take me to Hell.' (i i 285–94)

37 iv i 21, 95, 101, 148. *Pity*: iii v 128–30; iv i 103–6, 111; iv ii 36, 272, 292, 373; v ii 306, 365–6; v iv 61. The word is almost always used ironically. Lipsius, op. cit. lib. I, dismisses pity as a weakness of the mind, distinguishing it from mercy, or the impulse to give active help, as a passive, self-indulgent and unfruitful affection.

38 'Remember I beseech thee that thou hast made me as the clay and wilt thou bring me into dust againe? Hast thou not powred me out as milke and cruddled me like cheese? Thou hast cloathed me with skin and flesh and hast fenced me with bones and sinewes ... Hast thou with him spread out the sky, which is strong and as a molten looking glasse?' (Job, x 9–11; xxxvii 18.) The rest of ch. x is all highly relevant, e.g. the verses quoted on p. 86, n. 3, and also ix 22–4. The verse directly used here by Webster seems also to be behind one of the sonnets of G. M. Hopkins: 'Bones built in me, flesh filled, blood brimmed the curse' (*Poems*, no. 45).

39 E.g. in *Tancred and Gismunda* the father murders his daughter's lover, sends her his heart in a golden goblet, and when she poisons herself her father blinds himself on the stage and then kills himself. The date of this play is 1599. Massinger's *Virgin Martyr*, perhaps the most revolting of all Elizabethan plays, has even a larger variety of tortures.

VIII.

Beaumont, Fletcher and the Baroque

The fifty-two plays ascribed to Beaumont and Fletcher would not have represented an unduly large output for the working life of even one man; their contemporary, Thomas Heywood, claimed to have had a hand in 220. Only five years, however (1608–13), can be reckoned as the period of their collaboration, after which Beaumont retired from the stage. The work of these five years sufficed to establish a type of play which remained influential throughout the century, and which was long considered superior to Shakespeare's. In his *Essay of Dramatic Poesy*, Dryden observes that two of Beaumont and Fletcher's plays were acted for every one by Shakespeare or Jonson; later he recognised that 'Shakespeare had an universal mind, which comprehended all characters and passions; Fletcher a more confined and limited ... he was a limb of Shakespeare' (*Grounds of Criticism in Tragedy*, 1679).

This judgement, given in the year when the Second Folio of Beaumont and Fletcher's plays appeared, rightly mentions Fletcher alone; for not only had he much the larger share in the writing, but it is his characteristic tone and attitude that prevail. The problem of deciding which plays belong to Beaumont, which to Fletcher, which to both and which contain works by other men is hardly susceptible of final solution; however, the linguistic studies of Cyrus Hoy have brought out clearly Fletcher's share in the plays. Two plays in the present volume are entirely Fletcher's – *The Faithful Shepherdess* and *The Wild Goose Chase*; *Bonduca* is probably so. *The Knight of the Burning Pestle* is now ascribed to Beaumont, while *The Maid's Tragedy* and *A King and No King* remain collaborative, as they purport to be.

Some plays were written for the choristers' troupe, the Children of Blackfriars; others for Shakespeare's company, the King's Men, who in 1608 took over the small select theatre at the Blackfriars for their winter quarters. Fletcher became one of the leading writers for this company, and seems briefly to have collaborated with Shakespeare; *The Two Noble Kinsmen*, on the title-page of 1634, is claimed for 'the memorable Worthies of their time, Mr John Fletcher and Mr William Shakespeare, Gent'. They are also supposed to have shared the writing of the lost *Cardenio*, and of *King Henry VIII*.

Beaumont died in 1616, the same year as Shakespeare; Fletcher in 1625, the same year as King James I. The writings of the two dramatists, as distinct from all that has been ascribed to them, supply a characteristic example of the most important kind of Jacobean poetry, the baroque.

Baroque art, which in the early seventeenth century developed all over Europe, is an art of distortion. The term *barocco* was originally applied by Portuguese jewellers to pearls of irregular form. In baroque art, whether sculpture, painting or poetry, the human form is shown in violent emotion, while it is at the same time naturalistically displayed, and not formalised by convention. Baroque poetry has been defined as

> poetry in which, although the problems of the age are reflected, the perfect poise between intelligence and sensibility is either destroyed or not achieved or not attempted, with the result that the poet has a distorted view of life, distorted through imagination and sensibility, without any care for apparent proportion or balance. . . . The baroque poet thus depends on his power to carry his reader into his own world, which is often a sort of surreality, and to light up for him those strange vistas which such baroque sensibility can open up, both in the concrete world of nature and in the recesses of man's sensibility. (Odette de Mourgues, *Metaphysical, Baroque and Précieux Poetry* (Oxford, 1953), p. 74.)

In Fletcher's plays extraordinary situations provide distortion, while the easy simplicity of the language provides the naturalism which contrasts with it. The first description of these plays as baroque came from Sofia, in studies courageously begun by Marco Mincoff during the last war.[1] The more recent work of Eugene Waith in America and Clifford Leech in England develops this view. Leech speaks of

> a more relaxed drama, which in its character types mirrored a stable world, and yet in its language maintained and indeed further developed the informality of the earliest Jacobean years. The essential property of the new Beaumont and Fletcher drama consists in its dislocation. . . . There is no firm ground for reverence, or for a cosmic scheme, in the great majority of plays which deeply bear John Fletcher's impress. Neither Fletcher nor Beaumont was ever a declared revolutionary, yet few

dramatists can have written plays as fully destructive by implication. (Clifford Leech, *The John Fletcher Plays* (1962), p. 32.)

A little later he refers to this drama's 'inherent and largely non-explicit scepticism' (p. 40).

Beaumont and Fletcher, succeeding the greater dramatists, Shakespeare and Jonson, could most readily outdo their predecessors by blending sophistication with violence. In these plays of genuine power the still unspent force of the language is diverted to virtuoso display; in tragedy as inflated rhetoric that sweeps along torrentially, and is used to present the most extreme and most extraordinary situations. These are often taken from classical exercises in the law, especially from Seneca and Suetonius, whose works would be familiar to the most intelligent and lively part of the select audience at Blackfriars, the young students from the Inns of Court. To this gentlemanly group the playwrights themselves belonged; Beaumont was the son of a judge. To hold back the vital piece of evidence till the end, as the playwrights often do, would be to invite the young lawyers to exercise their wits upon the plot.

In comedy the gay irresponsibility of rakes and spendthrifts, anticipating the mood of the Restoration stage, might be expected to appeal in wit, sophistication and successful impudence to such young men. All surrender to feeling is mocked; the pleasures of fortune-hunting and the reckless baffling of fools supply the staple of many plays, of which *The Wild Goose Chase* is the best. Mirabel is the first of a line of heroes culminating in his namesake, the hero of Congreve's *The Way of the World* (1700). Like Don Juan, Mirabel carries round his catalogue of seductions, but is captured in the end by the witty huntress Oriana, after a series of stratagems which include a wooing by her own brother, a scene in which she feigns to be mad for love, and finally the disguise of a rich heiress which, after she has secured him, Mirabel claims to have penetrated. 'Baffling', the sportive torment of an eccentric, is often practised by Fletcher's ladies on their lovers; for though love figures so prominently as motive, it is always seen as a comic madness. This can lead to some very horsy language, when for instance, in *Bonduca*, a Roman captain falls madly in love with the memory of Bonduca's daughter because of the firm constancy of her death; such language is destructive of the sentiment it claims to portray.

> What do I ail, i' th' name of heaven? I did but see her,
> And see her die; she stinks by this time strongly,
> Abominably stinks. . . .
> A pox upon the bots, the love-bots! Hang me! . . .
>
> (v ii 1ff.)

Here can be heard the pounding, blustering tones of asseveration that belong to all Fletcher's noble boobies in love – beginning with Arbaces, hero of *A King and No King*, whose notions of honour are inflexible and simple as a schoolboy's, while his surrender to passions betray a depth of self-ignorance that almost puts him on a level with the comic coward of the play, Captain Bessus.

The theme is the incestuous love of Arbaces for his supposed sister, eventually found not to be his sister at all. Plentiful hints of a mystery are dropped – the title itself would supply one – but not till the end does the wise old counsellor tell his enraged offspring: 'If you kill me – know – you kill your father!' The design of this play has been strongly defended, and is indeed very ingenious; but the passions of Arbaces, which unking him before he is unkinged by Gobrias, reduce him to comic proportions, and with him the simple heroic virtues he stands for. Arbaces is a much better example than Othello of the critical devaluation of the simple soldierly hero; and those inclined to see Othello in the way suggested by T. S. Eliot and F. R. Leavis would do well to look first at Arbaces.

In *The Maid's Tragedy* the violent, amoral and ruthless Evadne, whose delicate air deceives even her lover the King, is a fitting sister for the ruthless if devoted Melantius; each despises and uses weaker creatures for a personal end. The play offers a series of brilliantly planned scenes, fast moving and lurid, built round the frozen grief of the betrayed Aspatia, who gives the play its title. In the lament, where she sees herself in a 'tapestry of woe', can be found for once the full maturity of tragic speech, at the dead and motionless centre of all the fury:

> Suppose I stand upon the sea-beach now,
> Mine arms thus, and my hair blown with the wind,
> Wild as that desert . . . and the trees about me
> Let them be dry and leafless; let the rocks
> Groan with continual surges; and behind me
> Make all a desolation. Look, look wenches!
>
> (II ii)

It is no accident that T. S. Eliot chose these lines to set before one of his own most controlled and yet violent poems, 'Sweeney Erect'.

At the centre of the pastoral, *The Faithful Shepherdess*, lies the unappeased grief of Clorin for her buried shepherd. Yet here, too, with characteristic 'dislocation', Clorin is allowed to play at being inconstant, and by this therapeutic device release from his love-sickness a shepherd who has fallen in love with her virtue. Varieties of love-sickness give the theme, and Clorin cures them all.

The play is set in old-fashioned pastoral style, with four 'places' shown together – Clorin's bower, the holy well, a dale and a hollow tree. Such scenes had been familiar thirty years before, in plays by Lyly or Peele; but here Fletcher, drawing on Guarini's *Pastor Fido*, aims at deliberate contrast with the old merriments of 'Whitsun ales and cream', of 'country hired shepherds . . . with curtailed dogs in strings, sometimes laughing together and sometimes killing one another.' Yet once again the central feeling is deeply ambiguous; Pan, the shepherd's god, protects chastity but seems to practise lust; the shape-changing by which lustful Amaryllis takes on the form of faithful Amoret, the comic lubricity of Chloe, and the chaste disgust of Thenot and Perigot make up a strange blend of libertine freedom and slightly mawkish virtue. Twice the hero stabs the heroine; this sexual violence, like the similar wounding of Aspatia and Arethusa, a perversity forced upon a highly moral character by circumstances, is typical of Fletcher's plays. Like other baroque writers, he explores the morbid, the macabre, the taboo; he loves to set a character in extremes, yet to keep familiarity by a natural turn of speech. *The Faithful Shepherdess* is a delicate piece of artifice; its fragility and limitations are part of its charm.

In *The Knight of the Burning Pestle*, Beaumont recalls older drama by the mode of burlesque. The historic perspective strengthens the perspective that separates the play world from reality – a perspective that the more innocent characters do not see. Ralph, the 'prentice who has 'played Jeronimo with a shoemaker for a wager', dies in a speech that echoes *The Spanish Tragedy*; he has been fired by reading old romances, full of people, 'sometimes laughing and sometimes killing one another', and he brings in the Whitsun-ale festivities of the City when he appears as a May Lord, decked in scarves and rings. His mistress interrupts the play to admonish or advise, calls for actors as readily as she calls for beer, and has never seen anything but fairground shows before. Ignoring the music provided (reputed among the best in Europe), her husband George proudly pays for 'the Waits of Southwark', asking particularly for that vulgar instrument, the shawm.

This burlesque, dedicated to Keysar, manager of the children's troupe and himself a Citizen and Goldsmith of London, does not seem to distinguish between the rant of Kyd's *Spanish Tragedy* and that of Hotspur in Shakespeare's *Henry IV*. The main butt was intended to be Thomas Heywood, whom Lamb called 'a prose Shakespeare', and his popular play *The Four Prentices of London*. Heywood really was very naïve, yet perhaps Beaumont did not realise how far, by this mockery, he was displaying his own disinheritance.

The printer finds it necessary to say that the play is 'elder above a year' to *Don Quixote*; but Cervantes' wry and tender story left the chivalric virtues as noble, if not quite as realistic as before; his irony brings an adjustment of view, not a change of values. Don Quixote, like Hotspur, may be rapt with visions; he is not subjected to indulgent belittlement, like Arbaces.

The irony of Jacobean baroque, however, should be comprehensible to the present age; for the 'sick' humour of comedy, the notion of 'l'absurde' in tragedy provide insights highly relevant to the deeply disturbed, powerful, yet seemingly light-hearted work of those who have been called 'entertainers to the Jacobean gentry'.

Notes

1 Marco Mincoff, *Verbal Repetition in Elizabethan Tragedy* (St Clement Okridsky University of Sofia, 1944), pp. 98–103. See his *Shakespeare, Fletcher and Baroque Tragedy* in *Shakespeare Survey* 20 (1967).

IX.

Bogeymen, Machiavels and Stoics

Blacking up for the stage, the Elizabethan equivalent of the tragic mask or buskin, enlarged and made more theatrical the role – released tempestuous passion. Something supernatural survived from medieval drama, when 'his face was as black as a devil in a play', a primitive magic like that of the blanched face of the Ghost. Such characters were not subject to divided aims: the Blackamoor thundered with voice and tread, his costume was gorgeous, his feathers tossed high, he brandished a scimitar.

This Bogeyman became imaginatively joined with the Pope and Machiavelli in an infernal Trinity – the Pope representing Antichrist, another figure from late medieval drama, Machiavelli his all-pervading Spirit. The infidel represented barbaric cruelty and vigour, the others perverted intellect; in his symbol of the man-beast, the Centaur, Machiavelli had distinguished in the bestial part of man the Lion and the Fox, force and fraud (*The Prince*, ch. xviii). The Centaur, half-beast half-man is the best tutor of princes, as was Chiron of Achilles, such was Machiavelli's unedifying analysis.

Marlowe, who may have read Machiavelli at Cambridge, caricatures him for stage purposes in the Prologue to *The Jew of Malta*; joined with earlier imagery from Senecal tyrants, this figure survived until the closing of the theatres in 1642. Since the rise of nation-states with their new codes of secular diplomacy, clashes between public and private codes of morals had become embodied in the man who in chapter xv of *The Prince* goes 'to the real truth of the matter . . . for how we live is so far from how we ought to live that he who abandons what is done for what ought to be done, will rather bring about his ruin than his preservation.' Machiavelli had dared to be explicit about practices that were in themselves no novelty; but 'politics', a new and very dirty word, was defined in terms of Machiavelli's counsel. Bacon, whose essay 'Of simulation and dissimulation' came out in 1597, praised Machiavelli for showing not what men ought to do, but what they did; whilst a witty jester like Donne in *Ignatius his Conclave* (1611) showed the whole infernal Trinity outdone by the Jesuits (his own uncle had belonged to that Order).

Tragedies set in remote exotic lands of barbarism and fabulous wealth roused equal wonder and horror, but also represented a popular attempt to cope with disturbing clashes of cultural interests. The Barbary pirates were not always remote; raiders landed on the east coast of England, and many churches supported funds for the ransom of captives.

Machiavelli, himself the author of a brilliant comedy, *Mandragola*, was much given to maxims; in the English drama a set of such maxims – some in fact derived from older, classical sources – encapsulated the hated doctrines of tyranny and treachery in a kind of creed or manifesto. This is set out in an opening speech of Greene's *Selimus* I ii (Queen's Men, 1592); Shakespeare's Aaron in *Titus Andronicus* ends with a creed palpably based on Barabas in *The Jew of Malta* (v i 125–51); in *Alphonsus of Germany*, the secretary Lorenzo de Cyprus dictates such maxims to his prince, and for his pains is poisoned. Jacobean plays like *The Devil's Charter* (1607) and *The Bloody Brother* (1619), both given by the King's Men, carry this Devil's Creed:

> The surest ground for kings to build upon
> Is to be loathed and feared of everyone
> > (*Selimus* (1592), 1393–4)

> Might first made kings . . .
> > (*The Jew of Malta* (1593), prologue)

> 'Tis more safety for a prince to be feared than loved
> > (*Alphonsus of Germany* (1594), I i 157)

> The prince who shames a tyrant's name to bear
> Shall never dare do anything but fear.
> > (*Sejanus* (1603), II ii 178–9)

> Who cannot bear with spite, he cannot rule
> > (*The Malcontent* (1604), v iii 77)

With this goes a parody of stoic *apathein*, suppression of feeling:

> I that have neither pity, love nor fear
> > (*3 King Henry VI* (1592), v vi 68)

> First be thou void of those affections,

Compassion, love, vain hope and heartless fear
(*The Jew of Malta* (1593), II iii 170–3)

A settled wisdom in itself
Which teacheth to be void of passion,
To be religious as the ravenous wolf
Which loves the lamb for hunger or for prey
(*Alphonsus of Germany* (1594), I i 43–5)

and an advocating of treachery:

O sir! I love the fruit that treason brings,
But those that are the traitors, them I hate.
(*Selimus*, 2122–3)

Great Men still must have such instruments
To bring about their purposes, which once done
The deed they love but do the doer hate.
(*Caesar's Revenge* (1592–6), II iv 641–3)

This principle is old but true as fate,
Kings may love treason but the traitor hate.
(*The Honest Whore, Pt 1* (1604), IV iv 49–50[1])

To which last, the victim interjects as he prepares to poison his poisoner:

Is't so; nay, then, Duke, your stale principle
With one as stale, the Doctor thus shall quit,
He falls himself that digs another's pit.
(IV iv 51–3)

The Machiavels of Revenge tragedy are headed by Lorenzo of *The Spanish Tragedy*, with his murderous manipulation of his agent Pedringano; they represent the power of the evil ruler. The Bogeyman, descended from Marlowe's Barabas rather than Kyd, was equally popular in the first half of the 1590s, especially with Alleyn at the Admiral's Men. The Children of the Revels revived him a decade later. He shared maxims with the princely Machiavels, especially the one about the Lion and the Fox, the proverbial 'Slaves are but nails to drive out one another', and one deriving from Seneca's *Hercules Furens* (251–2) which Cinthio had rendered

Ché quando tu acquista ha la potenza
Il vitio di vertù tiene sembienza
(*Euphania*, II ii)

succinctly rendered in *The Malcontent* 'Mischief that prospers, men do virtue call' (v iv 73), and by Sir John Harington turned into epigram

> Treason doth never prosper; what's the reason?
> For if it prosper, none dare call it treason.

Tamburlaine, who initiated many traditions, stood much nearer to the historic Machiavelli. He is a heathen, but white, and his love Zenocrate, though Egyptian, is 'fairer than whitest snow on Scythian hills', he opposes the Turkish Bajazet, but also massacres the virgins of Damascus. The response must be paradoxical. By contrast the Jew of Malta and his Moorish slave join in a kinship that partakes of the Lion and the Fox, with unbridled passions and many physical horrors. Such threatening alliances between Italian and Jew, Turk or Blackamoor, generally end in a masked fight; evil at last eats up itself. The comic-horrific energy of the medieval devil continues in the primitive elements of such alliances.[2] It reappears today in Edward Bond's plays.

Peele's *The Battle of Alcazar* (1589, Admiral's Men), supplied Alleyn with a magnificent Bogeyman part as Muly Mahomet, but in the year following the defeat of the Armada also provided Londoners with a portrait of the supreme Machiavel, Philip of Spain, whose treachery brought about the death of the misguided Sebastian, King of Portugal. Philip had thus seized the crown of Portugal for himself; the pretender to the crown of Portugal, Dom Antonio, was at this time a refugee in London.

The 'plot' or scenario of this play survives with Alleyn's papers at Dulwich and shows how spectacle blended with tirades. The first dumb shew summarises previous events, as Muly Mohamet kills his two young brothers in their beds (shades of Richard III!) and strangles his uncle:

> Black in his looks and bloody in his deeds,
> And in his shirt stained with a cloud of gore,
> Presents himself with naked sword in hand,
> Accompanied, as now you may behold,
> With devils coted in the shapes of men
>   (I 16–20)

When the three ghosts rise together later, crying 'Vindicta!' (Ben Jonson was to burlesque the scene in *Poetaster*, III 2) – the by now defeated Muly Mahomet brings the raw flesh of a lioness to his Queen, broached on his sword, in lines that gained the compliment of parody from Dekker, Marston, Heywood and Shakespeare (2 *King Henry IV*, II iv 169):

> Feed then, and faint not, fair Callipolis. . . .
> Feed, and be fat, that we may meet the foe
> (II iii 548–68)

Such repetitions, for which Peele is notorious, may have served to put across words through the noise of crowds and stage battle, representing not tautology so much as loud-hailing. Or, as Inga-Stina Ewbank thinks, they may impress the visual wonders by emphasis and underlining.[3] The dumb shews become more portentous, till finally the Portuguese who has acted as Presenter is replaced by 'Fame, like an Angel' introducing the Battle itself, with the spectacle of the Blazing Star and a tree with two crowns that fall from it, symbolising the death in battle both of Muly Mahomet and of King Sebastian. All, as Fame announces, on 'Monday the fourth of August, seventy-eight.'

The third to fall, had 'a spirit equal to a king'; Captain Thomas Stukeley, whose death is blazoned on the title page, had become a London legend and was to feature in at least one later play.[4] Here his long dying speech proclaims that he was born on London Bridge – which as he came of a Devonshire family, is not probable; but 'stout Stukeley', the hero of many ballads, had certainly married an Alderman's heiress, squandered her fortune, fought in Ireland and in Spain. His joining with Sebastian in the invasion of North Africa diverted him from leading a Papal expedition to Ireland; had he not died in Barbary, as a traitor after the Massacre of Smerwick, his head might have appeared on London Bridge. His reckless 'huffing' – as he himself terms it – established him in popular eyes as a 'mad' Englishman to whom ordinary rules of behaviour did not apply. Sebastian gives a big speech just before the battle glorifying Queen Elizabeth and prophesying the defeat of the Armada (although, as in Sheridan's *The Critic*, 'it is not yet in sight!') The dominant figure however remains Muly Mohamet, presiding over the dumb shew of a 'Bloody banquet' where dead men's bones, and their blood in skulls, are served up. He invokes death and hell for all men, curses nature who brought him forth:

> Damned let him be, damned and condemned to bear
> All torments, tortures, plagues and pains of hell
> (IV ii 1159–60)

> Thou mother of my life that brought me forth,
> Cursed be thou for such a cursed son,
> Cursed by thy son, with every curse thou hast
> (V i 1279–81)

He cries for a horse (again one thinks of Richard III), and after death suffers the gruesome horror of being flayed, his skin stuffed with straw, and paraded through the kingdom.

This tragedy openly challenges *Tamburlaine*; lacking Marlowe's egoistical sublimity, Peele evolves a form at the minimum remove from popular entertainment, satisfying to a London audience. Unlike Greene, whose staider and more academic quatrains in *Selimus* did not work on the stage, Peele does not import a clown, but relies on spectacle – including 'three vials of blood and a sheep's gather', something called 'the bells of Pluto' presumably an under-stage effect, and Alleyn, who evidently found in this verse exactly what he needed.

The Jew of Malta supplied the model for the Bogeyman plot. Courage and ambition drive Barabas onward in a rapid, sometimes incoherent series of stratagems until, as he seems triumphant, he is trapped by an intended victim. The action depends on pace, as the Bogeyman, increasing his duplicities in a series of tricks that display his ingenuity, becomes in turn the hunter's prey; yet, like an acrobat somersaulting round the arena, he gathers speed all the time. This is implied on the title page of the choristers' play *Mulleasses the Turk* (1607, Revels), which promises 'An excellent tragedy of Mulleasses the Turk and Borgias, Governor of Florence, full of interchangeable variety beyond expectation' – the Borgias are transplanted from Rome to Florence as the birthplace of Machiavelli. The author was a schoolmaster and a graduate of St Catharine's College, Cambridge, which had a strong acting tradition; Shakespeare's company met the challenge with Barnabe Barnes' *The Devil's Charter*, which also deals with the Borgias, and shares another feature – the theme of pederasty.

Parricide became a regular theme also; wife-murder occurs in *Mulleasses the Turk*, *Alphonsus of Germany* and *Lust's Dominion*. Barabas uses his black slave to kill his daughter and a whole convent of nuns; the unfilial Selimus exclaims of his father

> 'Twere good for him if he were pressed out,
> 'twould bring him rest and rid him of his gout
>
> (322–3)

and reincarnated many years later in *The Raging Turk*, the same Selimus drily mocks

> I love nim better than to let him dig
> Himself a grave while I may take the pains.
>
> (2856–7)

This ferocious play, which seems to contain a murder a minute, was acted some time before 1618 by the students of Christ Church, Oxford; its author, Thomas Goffe, also produced a sequel, *The Courageous Turk*.

The peak of popularity for Bogeymen seems in London to have come in the early 1590s with plays like the lost *Tamercham* in two parts (1588–96), and *The Turkish Mahomet and Hiren the Fair Greek*, of which Shakespeare's Pistol preserves one of the more operatic moments: 'Have we not Hiren here?' (2 *King Henry IV*, II iv 165). In these, and such revenge plays as *Soliman and Perseda* (1592), *Alphonsus of Germany* and the powerful hybrid of *Titus Andronicus*, atheism, parricide go with a frisky delight in evil for its own sake, which defined the role for the actors, aided the hasty collaboration of authors, and served as signal to the audience.[5] Atheism had been given a Machiavellian twist in the prologue to *The Jew of Malta*:

> I count religion but a childish toy,
> And hold there is no sin but ignorance
> (14–15)

a sentiment abbreviated in *The Massacre at Paris* by the aspiring Duke of Guise to:

> My policy hath framed religion.
> Religion! O diabole!
> (II, 65–6)

Aaron the Moor had cried 'If there be devils, would I were a devil' (*Titus Andronicus*, v i 147) and 'almost split his sides with extreme laughter' as Titus was tricked into cutting off his own right hand. Machiavellian atheism was to be echoed again and again (*Selimus*, 244–5; *Sejanus*, II ii 162; *Mulleasses the Turk*, 427–8; *The Jews' Tragedy* (1622–6) II ii 96–8) In *A Christian Turned Turk* (Revels, c. 1610) great emphasis is laid on the apostacy of Ward.

Lust's Dominion, generally dated round 1600, is from Henslowe's group[6] and its leading character Eleazer the Moor who seized the crown of Spain, is unremittingly termed a devil in such phrases as

> Truth to tell,
> Seeing your face, we thought of hell
> (II ii 122–3)

> Here hell must be, where the devil governs you
> (III ii 244)

> A Moor,
> That has damnation dyed upon his flesh
>
> (V ii 19–20)

He replies to his victims' curses with

> O sweet airs, sweet voices! . . . .
> Sweeter and sweeter still! O harmony,
> Why, there's no music like to misery
>
> (V ii 46, 52–3)

Mulleasses also was to 'crack his sides' at torment; in the late and feeble play of *The Rebellion*, the villain 'hugs himself'

> How subtle are my springes; they take all.
> With what swift flight unto my chaffy bait
> Do all fowl fly unto their hasty ruin.
> Clap, clap your wings and flutter, hasty fools.
>
> (III i)

In Lust's Dominion a wicked Queen plays a prominent role; in Jacobean times her part in intrigues was to increase. The political, camerist element was strengthened against open violence. The complicated masked fight was intensified by the example of Ben Jonson's *Sejanus* (1603) in the diabolic trio of Sejanus, the Emperor, and Macro, with the Empress Livia and her chilling discussions of poisons and cosmetics. Ben Jonson was well acquainted with Machiavelli and one of his objects – it had also been Machiavelli's – was the assimilation of ancient to modern history. For Jonson, Tacitus showed that Machiavelli *worked*: Machiavelli put forward his theory in discourses on Livy.

> Xenophon draws no other conclusion . . . than that a prince who wished to achieve great things must learn to deceive. . . . Nor do I believe that there was ever a man who from obscure condition arrived at great power merely by employing open force, but there are many who succeed by fraud alone. (*Discourses*, Book II, ch. 13)

The choristers' revival of the Bogeyman round 1607–10 produced tragical farces; perhaps they were played for kicks, in parody of Alleyn, now retired. The star of the Revels players was Nathan Field, kidnapped at thirteen in 1600. For the young lawyers, most probably, Shakespeare wrote *Troilus and Cressida*, with the malice of Thersites, the butchery and dishonouring of Hector's dead body. Through the folk elements of flyting and bogeys, the discerning might survey irrational evil within the body politic and the human mind. Such break-up of order and degree could hardly be faced directly. The most atrocious spectacle of the early drama is probably *An Alarum for London* representing the Sack of Antwerp by Spanish troops in 1576; Shakespeare's company put it on in 1599 – about the time that he showed the Roman mob in *Julius Caesar* tearing to pieces the poet Cinna. At the same time, in a mixture of stoicism and Calvinism, Fulk Greville in his closet dramas showed Turks in dramas where mental turmoil wracks passion-driven men.

The tradition persisted sporadically. Fletcher's *The Bloody Brother* (1619) uses the maxims; his *The False One* (1620) rests on the example of *Sejanus*. In 1633 Heywood published *The Jew of Malta* because Richard Perkins wanted to try Alleyn's famous role. Shirley made a Machiavel the hero of *The Politician* (1639); in the very late tragedy *The Sophy* (1641) Denham, though rejecting in his prologue any statecraft of Machiavelli, in the villainous counsellor Haly compounds Eleazer with Shakespeare's Iago, till the Sophy blinds his own son, and is himself finally poisoned. In *The Fatal Contract* (1639) William Heminges shows his virtuous heroine in disguise as a Moor, in which form she commits all kinds of crimes quite foreign to her 'real' self.

In *The Rebellion* it is said 'Raymond the Moor is the devil's cousin-german for he wears the same complexion; but there's a right devil . . . and that's the count Matchevil.' This was published in 1640.

In 1641 even Heywood was publishing a pamphlet against 'projectors' with the title *Machiavel, as he late appeared*.

The stoic hero, the learned dramatists' answer to the Moor and the Machiavel, was provided with a counterbalancing set of maxims, his creed or manifesto. Rather surprisingly, these plays also belong to the choristers' theatre of Jacobean time: the most notable authors were Marston and Chapman. Here perhaps the authors had more choice; they had not to meet the demands of actor-sharers. The stoical roles in Chapman's plays were sustained by the star Bogeyman Nathan Field, whom Chapman called his 'loved son'.

The stoic virtue of Fortitude was neither passive nor negative; as Seneca explains in his *Moral Epistles* (LXVII), it encouraged the exercise of all other virtues and was almost indistinguishable from courage.[7] To endure torture with contempt, as Hieronimo does at the end of *The Spanish Tragedy*, transforms victim into conqueror; the usual classical examples were Regulus and Scevola; yet after a few early figures, such as those in *The Wounds of Civil War* (1588) the drama seldom presented a complete stoic. The stoic consolations of his father are rejected by Shakespeare's Bolingbroke in

King Richard II; the stoics of *Julius Caesar* are placed in perspective.

Marston, who from the first had invested in pessimism, began with the unwavering stoicism of Andrugio, the banished Duke of Genoa, who in *Antonio and Mellida* (Paul's, 1600) boasts

> There's nothing left
> Unto Andrugio but Andrugio
> (III i 59–60)

Clad in full armour, as he had been throughout the play, he enters the court of his enemy to claim the ransom put as a price on his head:

> Piero, I am come
> To soil thy name with an eternal blot
> Of savage cruelty; strike, or bid me strike.
> (V ii 159–61)

The foe is overcome and reconciled – temporally. In the tragic sequel, *Antonio's Revenge*, Andrugio's funeral opens the play, for Piero has treacherously killed him; his son rejects stoicism.

> 'Tis reason's glory to command affects!
> Lies thy cold father dead, his glassed eyes
> New covered up by thy sad mother's hands? . . . .
> Comfort's a parasite, a flattering Jack,
> And melts resolved despair. O boundless woe. . . .
> (I ii 274–86)

Pandulpho Felice, father of Antonio's friend, whom Piero has also murdered, proves an imperfect stoic, who at first tries to maintain superiority:

> This heart in valour even Jove outgoes:
> Jove is without, but this 'bove sense of woes
> (I ii 335–6)

In hope of the future reversal of their fortunes, he defies the Machiavellian Piero:

> I tell thee, Duke,
> I have old Fortunatus' wishing cap,
> And can be where I list even in a trice.
> I'll skip from earth into the arms of heaven,
> And from triumphant arch of blessedness
> Spit on thy frothy breast.
> (II i 242–7)

Later, however, after Antonio has rejected the precepts of Seneca, Pandulpho joins him:

> Man will break out, despite philosophy.
> Why, all this while, I have but played a part
> Like to some boy that acts a tragedy,
> Speaks burly words and raves out passion,
> But when he thinks upon his infant weakness,
> He droops his eye. I spake more than a god,
> Yet am less than a man
>
> (IV ii 69–75)

A boy actor was speaking these words. Marston's consciously artifical tragedy is full of reversals. Contrary to usual practice, its plot is not historical but is set in Genoa, which was the birthplace of Marston's mother's family, the Guarsi; perhaps he was remembering some tale from childhood.

Chapman's stoical heroes begin with Strozza, in *The Gentleman Usher*, a tragi-comedy with a farcical treatment of the eponymous hero. He was more consistently given to stoicism than any other dramatist, and in his early Jacobean tragedies he showed the ruin of two passionate soldiers taken from modern French political history, Bussy D'Ambois and Marshal Byron; Byron had been executed only in 1602, five years before Chapman's play. In his next play he presented the most developed study of stoicism. *The Revenge of Bussy D'Ambois* (1610) is a subversive anti-play. No stoic could be more defiant than Chapman in flouting and inverting the facts of history – as depicted in his own previous play – and the conventions of Revenge tragedy. 'Excitation to virtue', 'deflection' from vice was his justification. This play presents an imaginary brother of the historic Bussy D'Ambois, surrounded by historic figures from that earlier tragedy. It shows the death of the Count Montsurry who was still alive when, in 1610, the play was shown at Whitefriars.[8] Other characters are inverted: King Henry III, previously shown as Bussy's patron, becomes a murderous Machiavel, working through his agent, Baligny, Clermont D'Ambois' brother-in-law, to assassinate the Duke of Guise, who is himself transformed from the Machiavel of the earlier play (and of Marlowe's *Massacre at Paris*) to Clermont's beloved lord and admirer. The anti-monarchical sentiments are particularly daring.

In the opening scene a Malcontent denounces the failure to punish Bussy's murder; it is made 'parallel with law', 'Since good arts fail, craft and deceit are used' (1 i 64), and an ignoble peace is blamed. But the sympathetic listener is actually a royal spy, who in soliloquy repudiates all he has feigned, in the manner of Webster's spy, Bosola. 'Treachery for kings is truest loyalty' (II i 32).

Honourable amends in a duel is the only revenge that Bussy's brother Clermont will seek of Montsurry, direct instigator of the crime. The Duke of Guise is not only exempted from his share in it, but is also exonerated in a set defence from guilt for the Massacre of St Bartholomew. This is in flat contradiction to Marlowe's tragedy *The Massacre at Paris* (and Chapman was deeply influenced by Marlowe). The Huguenot Gentillet in his influential *Contre Machiavel* had held the Italian by his doctrine responsible; Chapman blames the religious divisions, without which 'Religious Guise had never massacred'. Marlowe would have denied him that quality, with his contemptuous cry of 'Religion! O diabole!'

Chapman was the son of an ardently Protestant family, sworn servant of the fiercely anti-Catholic Henry Prince of Wales, whose hero was Henry IV of France. The Ghost of the murdered Bussy, withheld till the beginning of Act V, in his soliloquy laments

> The body of felicity, religion
> Set in the midst of Christendom, and her head
> Cleft to her bosom, one half one way swaying,
> Another th'other . . .
>
> (V i 18–21)

but declares that since every act carries ineluctably its own consequences, crimes entail retribution, through 'the joints and nerves sustaining Nature'.

Chapman had published separately as a lyric 'Pleased with thy place' Clermont's creed, taken from Epictetus.

> God hath the whole world perfect made and free,
> His parts to the use of the All: men then that be
> Parts of that All, must as the general sway
> Of that importeth, willingly obey
> In everything without their power to change.
>
> (III iv 58–62)
>
> In this one thing, all the discipline
> Of manners and of manhood, is contained:
> A man to join himself with the universe
> In his main sway and make (in all things fit)
> One with that All, and go on round as it
>
> (IV i 137–41)

In the interval between these two speeches Clermont has been treacherously ambushed through a plot of his brother-in-law and the

King. Though his resistance is heroic, he calmly accepts captivity, continuing his discourse, until Guise procures his release. But Guise's assassination exposes him to

> all the horrors of the vicious times,
> None favouring goodness.
>
> (v v 186–7)

He has no power to avenge an act royally sanctioned, but unwilling 'to feed thieves, beasts and be the slave of power' he exercises the supreme stoic choice of freedom, and dies by his own hand – not indeed as a Hamlet but a Horatio. He terms himself Guise's 'Creature'; is Guise his God?

Preferring a love 'chaste and masculine', a love of reason to that of blood, Clermont had refused to marry his devoted mistress, the Countess of Cambrai. To follow Guise, he will 'uncase his soul' from his body – an image obliquely sexual; Guise is more openly amatory to Clermont (v i 189–90). In the opening scene Clermont is termed by the two Machiavels his 'minion', who talks stoicism to him,

> Hangs upon the ear of Guise
> Like to his jewel.
>
> (I i 152–3)

The subversive powers of this play issue from the interlocking of all its contradictions. In very strange contexts, images of great violence appear against marriage to an insatiate woman (I ii 43–8; III i 30–8; IV i 60–75). These tortuously applied, 'conceited', strained images are given embodiment in the scene where the dead Bussy's mistress Tamyra lies on the ground where he fell, embracing as his memorial the bloody imprint of his corpse. At the end of the play, the three surviving women, who have each represented the powers of 'blood' and passion throughout, retire to a cloister. The third is the sister of the two D'Ambois, a virago who, impatient of her brother's stoicism, had herself disguised as a man to challenge Bussy's murderer.

Clermont's final accomplishment of honourable revenge is followed by a *danse macabre* in which the ghost of Bussy joins with those of the Guise, his brother the Cardinal, and the ghost of Admiral Coligny, Huguenot victim of the Massacre. This foreshadows the death of Clermont. Catholic legend asserted that the Elizabethan Lord Chamberlain Lord Hunsdon had been summoned, when dying, by six ghosts, moving in a dance chain, and led by Leicester!

The homosexual character of the court of Henry III of France was already notorious; the undertones of this play combine the stoicism of the previous tragi-comedy with its treatment of a homosexual infatuation (there treated farcically). Combined with the bold anti-monarchical sentiments, this might well come from the household of Prince Henry.

The question of whether a suicide is a noble expression of stoic freedom or the supreme and damnable act of despair, forbidden to every Christian, is left unresolved; it is the strongest of all ambiguities in this anti-play.[9]

The mystery deepens when the publication in 1613 was dedicated to the brother of the infamous Frances Howard, younger son of the Lord Chamberlain, the Earl of Suffolk, who in 1605 had rescued Chapman from jail after the scandal of *Eastward Ho!* Sir Thomas Howard was coupled with Henry Prince of Wales as Castor with Pollux in the last of the sonnets Chapman appended to his *Iliads* (1612),[10] Sir Thomas tilted in the wedding barriers that accompanied the marriage of Frances Howard to the King's homosexual favourite, Robert Carr, Earl of Somerset in December 1613. Carr was selected by Chapman for his patron-in-chief after the death of the Prince of Wales, although whilst Henry lived the two had been at emnity. When Somerset in 1616 fell from power, Chapman found new grounds for stoic doctrine. The *Odyssey* was offered to Somerset as an example of patience under adversity, and Somerset's fate is generally thought to be reflected in the last of Chapman's modern French tragedies *Chabot, Admiral of France*. When accused by a tribunal led by the Chancellor, the hero refuses to defend himself, except with

> My innocence, which is a conquering justice,
> And wears a shield that both defends and fights. . . .
> Death is the life of good men; let 'em come
>
> (II ii 56–64)

Chabot insists even to the King that his merits justify the royal bounty, but in spite of being cleared in law, he dies of a broken heart at the King's unkindness. His trial and that of the Machiavellian Chancellor, take up much of the play; Bacon, the prosecutor of Somerset at his trial for the murder of Sir Thomas Overbury, himself fell in 1621.

Caesar and Pompey, Chapman's last play, offers as maxim 'Only a just man is a free man'; Cato exemplifies stoic suicide, fortified by a most unstoic belief in the resurrection of the body.

To defend free will to this extent against the powers of earth might call in question the power of Heaven itself; predestination, like monarchical absolutism, was generally subscribed to. Chapman's courage in putting forward both sides of the question might interest young lawyers but might have imperilled himself and the young actors who presented his plays. He did not observe historic truth, as he explained in the dedication of *The Revenge of Bussy D'Ambois*; as the setting was so very modern, its implications must have been clear.

The link between *The Revenge of Bussy D'Ambois* and Cyril Tourneur's *The Atheist's Tragedy* has been several times observed;[11] this play, put on by the King's Men and written by a follower of the Cecils, could be seen as a 'correction', controverting Chapman. The youthful French soldier Charlemont, jailed by his villainous uncle, the atheist D'Amville, does not find that his 'reason' altogether commands his 'affects' (III i 1–26) but is bold in confronting an enemy:

> I have a heart above the reach
> Of thy most violent maliciousness,
> A fortitude in scorn of thy contempt
> (Since fate is pleased to have me suffer it)
> That can bear more than thou hast power t'inflict.
>
> (III iii 35–9)

The ghost of his murdered father appears explicitly to forbid Revenge as unchristian; on the scaffold Charlemont leaps up as in triumph and is followed by his faithful mistress Castabella. D'Amville seizes the executioner's axe and with it strikes out his own brains. Nothing could be more orthodox.

The stoic heroine had appeared in Marston's *Sophonisba* (1606), and was to reappear in Fletcher's *Bonduca* (1613) and *Valentinian* (1614), in Webster, where her role is much more subtle and is not 'doctrinal' – the Duchess of Malfi is no stoic – and traditionally in a Christian role in Massinger's *The Virgin Martyr* (1620). Martyrdom was the one profession open equally to both sexes.

Massinger also wrote for Nathan Field *The Fatal Dowry* (1619), with a French soldier and scholar Charlerois as hero. To redeem the body of his father who has died in debt, he submits to prison, and after a splendid funeral

> gladlier puts on this captivity
> Than virgins long in love their wedding weeds
>
> (II i)

At the end of a complex plot, he kills his adulterous wife and her lover, for which again he faces trial; treacherously stabbed, he dies averring his 'triumphant innocence' in a state 'constant and unmoved'. (This story was early in the next century to be adapted by Nicholas Rowe in a successful tragedy, *The Fair Penitent*.)

A dozen years later, in *Believe as You List* (1631), Massinger returned to King Sebastian of Portugal, who was widely believed to have survived the Battle of Alcazar, and have vainly sought to establish his identity. To meet the demands of the Censor, Massinger had to transfer the events to remote antiquity. The political relevance of such themes meant that even then it could not be staged; by chance, the author's text survives. Antiochus, whose constancy is based on his innate royalty, is sustained by a stoic philosopher in the beginning; at the end, he appears as a galley slave, but still undaunted.[12]

Achilles' shield depicted the whole organic world; the shield of Perseus enabled him to confront Medusa. The poets looked on sights intolerable except in the mirror of art. Directly experienced, they induced only turbulence or contradiction. Such plays reach from instinctive and unformulated dread, as far as the times would permit, towards definition and formulation of religious or political conflict not yet susceptible of theoretical formulation. In *The Revenge of Bussy D'Ambois*, the ghost of Bussy declares that a man should not always be bound by his own limits, and freely submit to the 'main sway'. There are circumstances in which the divine spark within him demands action:

> What corrupted law
> Leaves unperform'd in kings, do thou supply
> And be above them all in dignity.
>
> (v i 97–9)

If royal man in his native powers can rise above law, what relation has the 'All' to this situation? After the appearance of the ghosts, Clermont thinks perhaps all actions 'are done before all times in th' other life' (v v 132). This is not Christian but could be determinist, if hardly a kind acceptable to Augustine, or Calvin. (In the name of free will Byron denied all power of influence to the stars and defied his King.)

Art's irrecoverable dimension is what in sermons used to be termed their 'application'. In Peele it is clear enough; but what was meant by an attack on peace in a reign where the monarch claimed as his motto 'Beati pacifici' must remain an open question. These Jacobean stoic plays remain on the shelf – with Ben Jonson's eulogistic masques and his *Catiline*. Marston took Holy Orders and gave up plays; his old opponent in satire, Joseph Hall, became a famous preacher, known as 'The Christian Seneca'; Inigo Jones composed an epitaph for Chapman 'Christian poet'.

Notes

1 See also *The Malcontent* (1604) IV iii 148–50; *The Phoenix* (1604) II ii 232; *The Revenger's Tragedy* (1606) I ii 193; *Women Beware Women* (1622) II ii 444; and cf. *King Richard II* (1595) V vi 38 for this maxim.
2 A list of such plays is given in John Quincy Adams' edition of John Mason, *Mulleasses the Turk* (Bang's *Materialen*, XXXVII, 1913) including lost plays.
3 Inga-Stina Ewbank, 'What looks, what words, what wonders?' *Elizabethan Theatre V* ed. George Hibbard, (Macmillan, 1975).
4 See below, pp. 115–16.
5 For the friskiness, cf. 'Dr Faustus and the Eldritch Tradition', in Vol. I of these papers; cf. A. P. Rossiter, *Angel with Horns* (1961) and Willard Farnham, *The Shakespearean Grotesque* (1971).
6 See Cyrus Hoy, notes to Fredson Bowers' edition of Thomas Dekker vol. IV (1980).
7 See J. M. Rist, *Stoical Philosophy* (1969), especially the chapters on Fate, Necessity and Suicide. Antony Caputi, *John Marston Satirist* (1961), discusses stoicism briefly, pp. 52–8.
8 See R. J. Lordi's edition (Salzburg, 1975). *The Revenge of Bussy D'Ambois* was entered in the Stationers' Register 17 April 1613; but *The Atheist's Tragedy*, which appears derivative (see below) was published in 1611. See note 11 below.
9 Cf. Alexander Leggatt, 'The Tragedy of Clermont D'Ambois', *Modern Language Review* vol. 77, Part 3, July 1982, 524–36, for the notion of the anti-play; cf. Marion Trousdale, *Shakespeare and the Rhetoricians* (1982) 'Some conclusions', pp. 169–72.
10 This translation, dedicated to Henry Prince of Wales, on his death in November 1612 had hastily to be revised; a mourning frontispiece and frantic dedications to many noblemen were appended. Sir Thomas, as the youngest, was the last. *The Revenge of Bussy D'Ambois* may have carried special poignancy for Chapman in 1613, though the Prince of Wales would not have tolerated himself a comparison with Guise. Chapman was singularly maladroit in such matters.
11 I briefly dealt with this in *Themes and Conventions of Elizabethan Tragedy* (1934) in dealing with *The Atheist's Tragedy*; it was treated by Michael Higgins, *Review of English Studies*, vol. XIX, 1945, 255–62; and by Clifford Leech, *Journal of English and Germanic Philology*, vol. LII, 1953, 525–38. See note 8 above for implications; and for the themes of anti-monarchic sentiment and homosexual devotion cf. *The Maid's Tragedy* (1610).
12 See Philip Edwards, 'The Royal Pretenders', *Threshold of a Nation*, 1979.

X.

Thomas Heywood, Shakespeare's Shadow

'A description is only a shadow, received by the ear.' (*An apology for actors*)

Most conspicuously neglected of Renaissance dramatists, Thomas Heywood has not been edited since 1874, although Arthur Brown and Blakemore Evans both collected materials; his non-dramatic works remain uncollected to this day. A clue may be found in the strictures of critics:

> to inform the verse, there is no vision, none of the artist's power to give undefinable unity to the most various material. Of those of Heywood's plays which are worth reading, each is worth reading for itself, but none throws light upon any other. (T. S. Eliot, *Elizabethan Essays* (1934), p. 107)

> It is not – emphatically – a minor nuisance that a young man capable of an interest in literature should be stimulated to work up a feeling of enjoyment when reading the plays of Dekker and Heywood. (L. C. Knights, *Drama and Society in the Age of Jonson* (1937), p. 256)

Frederick Boas thought 'of course he wrote far too much', and Fredson Bowers stigmatised him as 'an assembly-line dramatist'. The most considerable modern study, that of Michel Grivelet (1957), whilst far more penetrating, points in its sub-title, *Thomas Heywood et le drama domestique Élizabethain*, to the works worth reading – his two marital dramas. In the quarter-century since Grivelet's essential study, a radical shift in the approach to dramatic texts has shown itself, chiefly in Shakespearean studies. Heywood has an important role, not yet recognised in this investigation, in supplying such a variety of 'Bad', corrupt texts.

In 1633, approaching sixty, Heywood, in a note to *The English Traveller* pointed out very explicitly that he did not *wish* to be read. His poetic *Troia Britannica*, yes; his huge folios, *The History of Women*, *The Hierarchy of the Blessed Angels*, yes; but of the 220 plays in which he claimed 'an entire hand or at least a main finger' only twenty, in battered texts, survive. He resembled Shakespeare in being a sharer in one of the leading London companies, a full professional actor, but his working life of fifty years more than doubled Shakespeare's. He said many plays had been lost by changing of companies, others withheld by their owners, the actors; but also, 'it was never any great ambition in me, to be in this kind voluminously read.' His dramatic achievement was not transmissable in print; the 'undefinible unity' given to 'the most various material' occurred in performance. Words alone represented a scenario, an operatic score for a collaborative cultural event, when actors and audience bestowed the final shaping. The ingredients were familiar, the mixture new – this is not 'assembly-line' activity. The notion of a fully collaborative, multiform rite, a *dromenon*, involving the Muses of Song and Dance, celebrating the community itself, is accepted for the Stuart masque. It is no less obviously true of the seven City pageants composed by Heywood in the 1630s and printed with the motto *Redeunt spectacula* on each. It is true of his most popular work, *The Four Ages* (1612), that secular craft cycle of five plays. (*The Iron Age* is a double play; not surprisingly since it covers the Trojan War from the rape of Hesione to the death of Agamemnon.)

Only recently have the implications of E. A. Honigmann's *The Stability of Shakespeare's Text* (1965) been applied, in the editing of the Oxford Shakespeare; the implications for Heywood are vital. Certain plays of Shakespeare – *Troilus and Cressida* and *King Lear* – surviving in Quarto and Folio texts are seen as representing two valid versions. Stanley Wells, general editor of the Oxford text, propounded at Stratford in 1982 that the Quarto of *King Lear* might be the 'authorised' copy, Shakespeare's draft before performance, the Folio, a later playhouse text incorporating later revisions, some by him, some by others, but in any case an independent version. Conflation of the two for an eclectic text becomes a major editorial act of interference. *Troilus and Cressida*, it is thought, exists in a Quarto based on Shakespeare's 'foul papers', and a Folio text on a late prompt book.[1] Harold Jenkins' Arden *Hamlet* curtly dismisses such ideas in a footnote, but this is perhaps the last monument to an old tradition for the modern interest in performance has now impinged upon the last stronghold of 'literary' scholars, the text itself. Many of the surviving texts of Heywood appeared years after their first performance when they were being given in theatres very different from their first venue. *The Fair Maid of the West*, published in 1631, but dated by one of its recent editors as early as 1602, feels as if it survives in a new version of an old scenario. The 'feel' of the dialogue to me is Caroline – here one must be content to be impressionistic – and the choruses suggest that some of the original action – the seafight might have been staged at the Boar's Head or the Red Bull – was cut out for the little Cockpit Theatre.

To reconstitute a dramatic text is an act of cultural archaeology – the recovery of a full context or at the worst a sense of what is now irrecoverable: Heywood repays such an approach.

Beginning to work as an actor bound to Henslowe from Lady Day 1598, he was already known as a dramatist. Had Henslowe hoped to get a second Shakespeare for the Boar's Head? In 1592–3 he worked with Shakespeare on the text of *Sir Thomas More*; it was in the section assigned to him (Hand B) that Shakespeare's famous speech was inserted.[2] Like Shakespeare, he remained with the one company, which became the Queen's Men in 1603; later the Lady Elizabeth's; finally in part Queen Henrietta Maria's. In 1606 the company moved from the Boar's Head to the newly-built Red Bull in Clerkenwell, where Heywood took up residence. In 1617 they migrated to the Cockpit, a small, indoor theatre in Drury Lane, the first to appear on that historic site.

Heywood's surviving marital dramas, *A Woman Killed with Kindness* (1603) and *The English Traveller* (1633) are worth reading; that is, they can be reactivated in the mind of an attentive reader. In the second, both the address to the Reader and the Prologue recognise special claims:

> A strange play you are like to have, for know
> We use no drum nor trumpet, nor dumb show;
> No combat, marriage, not so much today
> As song, dance, masque to bombast out a play
> Yet these all good and still in frequent use
> With our best poets; nor is this excuse
> Made by our author, as if want of skill
> Caused this defect; it's rather his self will. . .
> He only tries if once bare lines will bear it.

Condemnation of 'bombast', an attitude fashionable with those who scorned the Red Bull show, conflicts with a sense that it is a defect to trust to 'bare lines'. The play having accidentally fallen to the press, as Heywood explains, he took the opportunity to dedicate to a very respected friend of his much respected uncle, and to utter a defiance to Prynne's *Histriomastix*, recently published, and widely execrated.

Heywood's concern for family bonds is akin to his own sense of the familial ties within the band of players. His *Rape of Lucrece* was published 'by consent', for it was scarce honest to make 'double sale' first to the stage and then to the press. Better however than allowing 'corrupt and mangled' copies made by ear. Thirty years later he mused in a Prologue for his immensely popular drama on Queen Elizabeth, *If you know not me, you know nobody* (printed in *Pleasant Dialogues and Dramas*):

> Plays have a fate in their conception lent,
> Some so short-lived, no sooner shewn than spent:
> But born today, tomorrow buried, and
> Though taught to speak, neither to go nor stand.
> This (by what fate I know not) sure no merit –
> That it disclaims – may for the age inherit,
> Writing 'bove one and twenty; but ill nurst.
> And yet received as well performed at first. . . .
> So much that some by stenography drew
> The plot, put it in print (scarce one word true).

Nathaniel Butter, the 'pirate', when reprinting for the seventh time, coolly added this Prologue and an Epilogue, with a few amendments which may have been Heywood's!

This play, brought out soon after the Queen's death (like Dekker's on the same subject *The Whore of Babylon*) proved uncommonly durable as theatrical material. Heywood continued to be acted in the same way as Kyd's *The Spanish Tragedy*, or Marlowe's *Jew of Malta*. It was Heywood who recorded Kyd's authorship of the first, and who published the second forty years after Marlowe's death, with a special Prologue for his actor friend Richard Perkins, who wanted to revive it, to test himself in one of Alleyn's leading roles. In *The Hierarchy of the Blessed Angels* (1635) Heywood recalls his fellow-poets as Kit, Will, Ben, Jack and ends his list 'I hold he loves me best that calls me Tom.' He wrote a *General (though summary) description of all poets both foreign and modern*, which has perished. The catastrophe of his most famous drama involves what Grivelet termed 'l'horreur sacrée qui s'attache à la profanation du foyer' (p. 151), but Heywood's foyer was the foyer of the theatre.

The Prologue to *A Woman Killed with Kindness* (1603) apologises in a manner that success alone would justify for 'bareness', whilst the Epilogue suggests that opinion will differ; some will judge it 'too trivial' some 'too gross', just as wine will be judged 'new, old, flat, sharp, sweet and sour'. Clearly he had a modern theatrical sense of the value of debate in stimulating an audience.

One of his earliest surviving plays (in a ruinous text) is *The Famous*

History of the Life and Death of Captain Thomas Stukeley (1596, published 1605); the 'huffing' adventurer from George Peele's *Battle of Alcazar* (1589)[3] is shown in London, Ireland, Spain, Rome, Morocco; he is recalled again in the second part of *If you Know not me* as one who 'had a spirit equal to a king'. He had become one of London's own legends; and these were central to Heywood's communal or familial bonding.

Our Johannes Factotum probably remodelled an earlier *Godfrey of Bulloigne* for his notorious *Four Prentices of London* (1600), where not only this Christian member of the Nine Worthies but his three brothers are apprenticed in London, owing to the exile of their father, the Count of Bulloigne. Their adventures all over Europe are really quite impervious to the later burlesque of Beaumont in *The Knight of the Burning Pestle*; they are first in the line that leads to The Magnet and The Gem – to Billy Bunter and Harry Wharton.

If Heywood began with romance and chronicles, by the turn of the century he had learnt much about the art of playwriting. When in 1602 he was signing receipts for court payments of the Earl of Worcester's Men (later Queen Anne's Men) he had already joined the group whose outstanding feature was that it was always to be led by a clown. Kemp was succeeded by Thomas Greene, he by William Rowley, who wrote plays. Greene was thin and Rowley fat, but both had to have 'fat' parts in any play.

Heywood's characteristic lines are the sympathetic heroine, whether a 'fallen woman' like Jane Shore in *King Edward IV* and Mistress Frankford, or a martyr of constancy, like Princess Elizabeth; and the young prodigal, who appears in *Stukeley*, Sir Thomas Gresham's nephew in Part II of *If you Know Not me*, young Chartley in *The Wise Woman of Hogsdon* and Young Lionel in *The English Traveller*.

The Fair Maid of the West is in many ways a modern romance; it could be termed the first western. The sub-title 'A girl worth Gold' indicates that although virtue takes first place, riches are not neglected. The irresistible Bess Bridges of Plymouth is ensured a fortune whether running an English tavern, or leading her ship's crew (all enamoured to a man) to victory on the Spanish Main. She is plainly deputy for a greater Elizabeth; and when everyone is united at the court of Fez, the fortunate presence of a captive clergyman enables her to be joined with her long-lost lover, whilst the Clown, eager for honour, finds out just in time what is involved in being Chief Eunuch. Bess's charms both inflame and subdue the King. No one ever really gets hurt; in spite of its apparent artlessness, the artifice of the game is firm enough.

Young Chartley of *The Wise Woman of Hogsdon* outdoes most of the wild youth of this kind of comedy in pledging himself to three brides at once.[4] The final scene exposes each in turn, and he finds that he has apparently married a boy – who, however, is Bride No. 1 in disguise. Although he makes Bertram of Roussillon look like a model of restraint and self-control, young Chartley is allowed a sudden repentance at the end of a most skilfully contrived farce in the Feydeau style, the scene being what is fairly obviously the Wise Woman's brothel. Its permissiveness banishes finger-wagging at Prodigal Sons, and contrasts very notably with the near contemporary *Measure for Measure*, or the cynicism of Chapman's *The Widow's Tears*. The latest of such stories, the sub-plot of *The English Traveller*, gives names from beast fable to Young Lionel, his clever servant Reynard (the Fox). The fable is Plautine; and the old father, who has secretly witnessed his son's wildness, is crowned with a coxcomb before being recognised; but none the less forgives all.

Heywood was perfectly capable of neat and well-articulated joining of plot and sub-plot (as in *A Woman Killed with Kindness* which can be dated precisely, February 1603); in the later play, it is the contrast between youth and age in tragic main-plot and farcical sub-plot that gives a kind of bonding. Heywood knew better than most the art of *projection*. His plays are conceived for effect, for establishing *rapport*; there is something for an actor to give his audience. His most characteristic and most skilful use of control lies in the poignant reticence of grief in his wronged husbands or his constant women. A single repeated word perhaps represents a stage sob; Frankford's 'Oh, Nan, Nan!', Bess Bridges' address to her lover's picture:

> when none save the bright stars
> Were up and waking I remembered thee,
> But all, all to no purpose.

In a culture not illiterate but very largely oral, Heywood's plays are largely opaque to the present age. What now of course is most opaque is the spectacular element, the stage language of gesture, blocking, emblematic costume, the familiar appeals to a London scene. If playmakers relied on the marriage of image and speech (the 'device' of early Tudor shews) for Heywood there was no contest between poet and painter. In so far as he thought at all, he thought pictorially, in terms of spectacle, from *The Four Prentices of London* to his last great success, *Love's Mistress* (1634), where he enthusiastically acknowledged in his Dedication the collaboration of Inigo Jones. His more usual partner was Gerard Christmas, the Inigo Jones of the City, with whom he worked not only upon the Lord Mayor's pageants, but on the decoration of a warship, *Sovereign of the Seas*: for Christmas was official painter to the Royal Navy.

In *Popular Culture in Early Modern Europe* (1978) Peter Burke devotes a section to 'the Triumph of Lent over Carnival', or the 'petty bourgeois ethic' as he terms it, over a tradition 'harder to define because of generosity and spontaneity and a greater toleration of disorder' (p. 213). In Heywood the conflict seems to have been reconciled. He could not but give a leading role to Disorder in the person of Will Kemp, Thomas Greene or William Rowley, a fat clown who was also a dramatist, and with whom he collaborated, with the curious results seen in *The Rape of Lucrece*, where horn-pipes and funerals are bewilderingly alternated. The editor of *The Old English Drama* suggested that – like the poet of *Histriomastix* – Heywood wrote the play in drink; but it was widely successful, and in 1612 formed part of a double bill at court, with the story of Alcmene's innocent adultery (*The Silver Age*). For this performance the King's and Queen's companies joined; Shakespeare and Heywood may have played together.

Heywood's admiration for Shakespeare when he was twenty-one is attested in his earliest poem *Oenone and Paris*, registered 28 May 1594, a blatant imitation of *Venus and Adonis*. When he wrote his *Tragedy of Lucrece*, his printer friend Nicholas Okes had just reissued Shakespeare's poem *The Rape of Lucrece*. Heywood's admiration for Shakespeare the poet is made plain; his bashful serving-man, however, becomes Heywood's clown (Brutus *assumes* clowning). There are large debts to Lady Macbeth and to Goneril in Tullia's part; her 'There is no earth in me, I am all fire' is Cleopatra's. But the pith of the performance was the songs, which were constantly being increased; it is as though Lear's Fool were allowed to swamp the play. There is one about the taverns of Rome; one on 'The Cries of Rome', which include 'Bread and meat, bread and meat, for the tender mercy of God, to the poor prisoners of Newgate, four score and ten poor prisoners!', followed by 'Salt, salt, white Worcester-shire salt!' The three-man catch in which the clown betrays Lucrece's rape to Valerius and Horatius (he has sworn to say nothing) opens:

Valerius:	Did he take fair Lucrece by the toe?
Horatius:	Toe, man?
Valerius:	Ay, man
Clown:	Ha, ha, ha, ha man, fa derry derry down, ha fa derry dino!

The clown enjoys a particularly direct, electrical contact with his audience. It can be dangerous. It is stronger than the relation of any other player; the clown therefore challenges the playwright;

Heywood accepted the relationship. The outrageous catch immediately precedes the tragic death scene of Lucrece. It may be that Heywood was remembering the Porter's scene from *Macbeth*, without grasping what Shakespeare had done with his ironic clowning there.

It is extremely difficult to know how Heywood approached this story. Recently, critics have been concerned with Webster's use of 'clashing tones', with the 'horrid laughter' that reverberates in Revenge tragedy at this time.[5] Heywood's juxtapositions are far more discordant and shocking than anything in Tourneur or Webster. Yet these men were friends (their elegies for Prince Henry were to be bound up together and issued in a single volume when a tragic occasion in actual life called them to express unambiguous grief). Webster in my view imitated Heywood in his *Appius and Virginia*.[6] Collatine's advice to his friends in *The Rape of Lucrece* that under tyranny they should

> Wear out our hours in harmless sports . . .
> So shall we seem offenceless and live safe
>
> (IV iii)

may reflect upon the fate that had overtaken the choristers' theatres, mainly through the political implications of Chapman's plays.

Heywood's most spectacular success, *The Four Ages*, which dramatised his own verse history, *Troia Britannica*, also used many familiar dramatic stories; the Twelve Labours of Hercules had been cited twenty years earlier by the upstart player in Greene's *Groatsworth of Wit* (1593) as a part in which he 'thundered terribly'. Chapman's translation of Homer was also drawn on (Homer appeared as Presenter in the first play), but, even more freely, the dramatic stage successes of William Shakespeare (including Hector's treacherously contrived death). Two troupes were required to stage this gigantic series; the capital outlay must have been considerable, but success was assured. And at the end, all was related home to London once more, as the Ghost of Hector prophesied to Aeneas that his descendants should build a New Troy on the banks of the Thames. This work represented Heywood's crowning achievement to his contemporaries, until the advent of *Love's Mistress* in his later years. The Shakespearean lines must have been gleaned in the playhouse, since *Othello*, *Macbeth* and *The Tempest*, which are laid under contribution, were not in print. Saturn's wife, preparing to sacrifice the infant Jupiter at her husband's command exclaims 'I'll kiss thee ere I kill thee!' Medea invokes a

Goddess of witchcraft and dark ceremony,
To whom the elves of hills, of brooks, of groves,
Of standing lakes and caverns vaulted deep
Are ministers, three-headed Hecate. . . .
That by incantations can remove
Hills from their seats, and make huge mountains shake,
Darken the sun at noon, call from their graves
Ghosts long since dead. . . .

It may be seen from the edition by Arlene W. Weiner (1979) that *The Iron Age* is even more heavily endebted, with Clytemnestra echoing Gertrude, Thersites appearing from *Troilus and Cressida* (almost the only railing character in Heywood). Sinon's 'A horse, a horse' is capped by Pyrrhus with 'Ten kingdoms for a horse to enter Troy!', but the famous line from *King Richard* III was by then common property. The text of this, the last of the *Ages*, did not appear till 1631, by which time Homer as Presenter has disappeared. The ghost of Agamemnon appears as his son is about to kill Clytemnesta, who thinks her son is mad because she can see nothing. She is killed, Helen commits suicide, and Ulysses is left, with Aeneas, future founder of New Troy, as sole survivors.

In view of his Autolycus-like pickings from Shakespeare's repertory, Heywood's rebuke to the printer Jaggard at the end of *An Apology for Actors* is not without a touch of comedy. Two epistles from Heywood's poem *Troia Britannica*, were added to *The Passionate Pilgrim* in 1612, ascribed to William Shakespeare. It might be thought, Heywood protested, that *he* had stolen them from Shakespeare, who was taking them back! But he knew Shakespeare to be 'much offended with M. Jaggard, that altogether unknown to him made so bold with his name.' Various other well-known lyrics, including 'Come live with me and be my love', were included by Jaggard, who subsequently took Shakespeare's name off the title page.

Shakespeare continued to furnish Heywood with material; *The Captives* (1624) is based on Plautus, but the two chaste heroines immured in a brothel have a clear stage ancestry in *Pericles*, whilst the sub-plot comes from *The Jew of Malta*. Only once, I think, did Heywood improve a line of Shakespeare, when in *Troia Britannica* 'Tis double death to drown in ken of shore' (*Rape of Lucrece*, 1114) becomes 'Tis double death to drown in sight of shore.'

The Golden Age was pirated and printed in 1611 by William Bullinger; Nicholas Okes, Heywood's printer friend who specialised in play-books then printed two more of the series.

The two parts of *The Iron Age* were not printed till 1631 when Heywood observed:

I know not how they may be received in this age, where nothing but Satirica Dictaeria and Commedia Scommata are now in request; for my own part, I never affected either when they stretched to the abuse of any person, public or private.

He was happier to praise; and it was possibly the great success of his *Four Ages* which encouraged him to publish in 1612, again from the press of Nicholas Okes, his *Apology for Actors*. It would appear from the concluding rebuke to the choristers' companies for their scurrility that it was written before they disappeared; but here it is the energy generated by the sight of his own success that transports Heywood.

A description is only a shadow, received by the ear but not possessed by the eye; so lively portraiture is merely a form seen by the eye, but can neither show action, passion, motion, or any other gesture to move the spirits of the beholder to admiration; but to see a soldier shaped like a soldier, act like a soldier . . . to see, as I have seen, Hercules in his own shape hunting the Boar, knocking down the Bull, taming the Hart, fighting with Hydra murdering Geryon, slaughtering Diomede, wounding the Stimphalides, killing the Centaur, pashing the Lion, squeezing the Dragon, dragging Cerberus in chains, and lastly on his high Pyramides writing *Nil Ultra*, O these were sights to make an Alexander. (B3v–B4r)

His *Apology* does not tell later generations much about the form of the Jacobean theatre. It is itself a spectacular demonstration of the public role of actors; the great dignity and glorious ancestry of the profession is paraded. Webster supports his 'beloved friend'; the leading man of the Red Bull, dashing Richard Perkins, and Christopher Beeston also contribute praises, whilst Heywood commends the printer Nicholas Okes (Heywood's hand was almost illegible).

Although the *Apology* called forth an immediate refutation from a precisian, its appearance registers a modest confidence. Several actors by now were vestrymen, or churchwardens in their parishes. It may be that even Ben Jonson was not above noting Heywood's success; in January 1615 his court masque was entitled *The Golden Age Restored*. It is however Caroline Heywood who shows the most astonishing proofs of his theatrical competence; for he not only penned the seven mayoral triumphs which were probably the most directly influential of all his spectacles, he also wrote the courtly and sensitive drama of *The English Traveller*, a complete transformation of the theme of his earlier marital plays; and he achieved a court triumph in his sixty-second year with *Love's Mistress*, variously known as *Cupid and Psyche*, and *The Queen's Masque*.

Henrietta Maria offered the play as birthday entertainment for the

King at Denmark House on 17 November 1634; they had already seen it at the Cockpit, and saw it a third time within a few days. This remarkable fruit of forty years' playwriting has been fully discussed in its ritualist and neo-platonic aspects by Jackson Cope.[7]

Although it was spectacular, and the settings devised by Inigo Jones, Psyche's labours could not rival the labours of Hercules, nor perhaps even 'Medea hanging in the heavens with strange fiery works in the habit of a conjurer'; six different sorts of ass dance in an anti-masque; six contrary characters, victims of love, give the *corps de ballet* a second dance. Scenes in Vulcan's forge and at the infernal court of Pluto: a singing contest, lost by Apollo to the Clown, a final assembly of the Seven Planets to do homage to the King and Queen (in imitation of Carew's court masque of the parions February, *Coelum Britanicum*) decorate the story itself, which is expounded in entr'acte discussions of Apuleius with Midas (representing ignorance). This is Jonsonian, but the theme itself recalls the *Emblems* of Francis Quarles, published that year. Illustrations to Quarles, especially the Fool with childish winged Amor and Anima in Book II, Anima climbing the hill to the tower (Book IV, emblem II) or the repentent figures in garments of tears (Book V, emblem V), look forward to the plates Heywood was himself to use in his *Hierarchy of the Blessed Angels*, (which Cowley was later to link with Quarles!).[8] But the plot is light and airy; Psyche pardons her two wicked sisters instead of consigning them to a horrid death as in Apuleius. When the play was revived at the Restoration, Pepys saw it no less than five times, particularly praising its 'good variety' – full of 'variety and divertissements'. The Clown is as predominent as ever; a bastard son of Midas, first he defies Amor, is thrown in love with a hideous old hag (like Sir Tophas in Lyly's *Endymion*), then purloins a Box of Beauty (full of 'ugly painting') with which he spots his face like the clown's in the plays of Redford nearly a hundred years earlier. Pepys greatly enjoyed the 'jeer' with which he parodied Heywood's own Trojan tragedy:

> This Troy was a village of some twenty houses ... by this Troy, ran a small brook that one might stride over. On the other side, dwelt Menelaus, a farmer who had a light wench to his wife ... (II iii 40–55)

A little earlier he had seemed to recall Berowne's railing on Cupid (II iii 20–7; cf. *Love's Labours Lost* III ii 164–95). Psyche's cry as she sees the beauty of the sleeping Cupid 'Churl beauty, beauteous niggard' seems close to the language of the Sonnets. However the most considerable borrowing is from a lost play *Cupid and Psyche*, by Dekker, Chettle and Day, written in 1600 for the Admiral's Men,

and recorded in Henslowe's *Diary*. This would have gone quite
undetected but for the chance that a portion of the text has survived;
it is quoted by Raymond Shudy in his edition of Heywood's play.

In view of Heywood's strictures to Jaggard in 1612, about *The
Passionate Pilgrim* his practice in 1634 must seem to mark a total
distinction between speech and text.

Here is the passage signed Thomas Dekker, in *England's Parnas-
sus* (1600).

> Sacred Apollo, God of Archery,
> Of Arts, of pleasure and of Poetry,
> Jove's fair haired son, whose yellow tresses shine,
> Like curled flames; hurling a most divine
> And dazzling splendour, in those lesser fires
> Which from thy gilt beams (when thy Car retires)
> Kindle those tapers that lend eyes to night,
> O thou that art the Landlord of all light
> Bridegroom of morning, day's eternal king,
> To whom nine Muses (in a sacred ring)
> In dances spherical trip hand in hand,
> Whilst thy seven-stringed lute their feet command,
> Whose motion such proportioned measure bears,
> That to the music dance nine heavenly spheres.
> Great Delian priest, we to adore thy name,
> Have burnt fat thighs of bulls in hallowed flame,
> Whose savour wrapt in smoke and clouds of fire
> To thy star spangled palace did aspire.

And here is Heywood's adaptation *Love's Mistress* I ii 16–31
(1634):

> Sacred Apollo, God of Archery,
> Of arts, of *physic* and of poetry:
> Jove's *bright* haired son, whose yellow tresses shine
> Like curled flames, hurling a most divine
> And dazzling splendour *on* these lesser fires,
> Which from thy gilt beams, when thy Car retires,
> Kindle those tapers that lend eyes to night;
> O thou that art the landlord of all light,
> Bridegroom *to* morning, day's eternal king,
> To whom nine muses, in a sacred ring,
> In dances spherical, trip hand in hand,
> Whilst thy *well*-stringed *harp* their feet command:
> Great *Delphian* priest, we to adore thy name
> Have burnt fat thighs of bulls in hallowed flame,
> Whose savour, wrapped in clouds of smoke and fire,
> To thy star spangled palace *durst* aspire.

There is a shorter passage of five lines copied with the same literalness in II i 5–9:

> When many a weary step
> Had brought us to the top of yonder mount,
> Mild Zephirus embraced us in his arms,
> And in a cloud of rich and sweet perfumes.
> Cast us into the lap of that green mead.

> When many a weary step
> Had brought us to the top of younder *rock*
> Mild Zephirus embraced us in his arms
> And in a cloud of rich and *strong* perfumes.
> *Brought*'s unto the *skirts* of *this* green mead.

An actor must perforce have many lines in his power to recall; and how much came from this lost play we simply do not know. Theatre material was regarded, it seems, as common property within the theatre, however dishonest it might be to print it elsewhere; the text was burnt with the Admiral's plays in 1622. In a play originally commissioned by Henslowe in May 1600 from Dekker, Chettle and John Day, none of the original three could retain any strong sense of ownership. Does this signal the death of the author in theatrical terms? No, I think not. The two theatrical friends who edited Shakespeare's first Folio did their best for him; and, after all, behind that work is someone called William Shakespeare (in my view, it *was* William Shakespeare and not anyone else); behind Heywood's plays there is a consistent approach to the material; the same is true of other actor-dramatists, like Rowley and Brome.

One must remember too that Shakespeare's texts (with others) were adapted in the second half of the seventeenth century very freely, and these versions ought not to be looked on as debased Shakespeare, but as evidence of what the theatre of that time was like. The first edition of Dryden's *Troilus and Cressida or Truth found too Late* (1679) is prefixed by the following verses from one Richard Duke:

> . . . Shakespeare 'tis true this tale of Troy first told,
> But as with Ennius Virgil did of old,
> You found it dirt but you have left it gold.
> A dark and indigested heap it lay,
> Like Chaos ere the dawn of infant day,
> But you did first the cheerful light display.
> Confused it was as Epicurus' world
> Of atoms by blind chance together hurl'd,
> But you have made such order through it shine
> As loudly speaks the workmanship divine.

Dryden's essay prefixed to this work is the fullest statement of the new position in regard to tragedy; by making Cressida loyal, and killing everybody at the end ('they all die upon the place, Troilus last') he followed the model of his better-known version of *Antony and Cleopatra*, without quite reaching the extremes of *The Tempest* or *The Enchanted Island*.

Most ephemeral, though in their day not least influential of Heywood's plays, were the Lord Mayor's Triumphs of 1631–9, for which he devised a regular and simple form[9] – the water pageant, the opening speeches, the anti-masque, the main action and the conclusion. The last of the series, *London's Peaceable Estate* (1639), celebrates a Lord Mayor who had travelled to Greenland, Muscovy and Turkey. The City's plantations in Ireland, Virginia and the Bermudas testify that the adventurous spirit of the still-popular Fair Maid of the West passed to London merchants. The River Nile makes an appearance (allowing a long digression upon the habits of the crocodile) but the heart of the matter is a warning against domestic warfare; we should pray for peace

> Lest that too late (having stern war excited)
> We wish that peace which (while we had) we slighted.

John Okes, son of Nicholas, was now publishing Mayoral Triumphs, of which this was to prove the last; fortunately for Heywood, he was buried as 'Thomas Heywood, Poet' in his parish church of St James, Clerkenwell 16 August 1641, a year before the King raised his standard at Nottingham.

Heywood was at once fluent and adaptable in his response to pressure, his acceptance of convention providing a bulwark against dissent. His talent instantly answered the helm of public demand, whilst the wooden walls of his defensive orthodoxy in matters civic, moral or religious proved quite impregnable to any storms of controversy. He was uniquely qualified to adapt the pageant devices, the non-verbal theatrical language – always more conservative than speech – to the mood of the time, whilst preserving its continuity. He was as fluent as his friend Webster was slow, the shapeless profusion of some of his latest encyclopedic miscellanies taxing even that tolerant age. Outside drama he could not achieve a form; his works are either rigid or amorphous.

Much new information has recently come to light on Heywood's theatres, the Boar's Head, the Red Bull, the Cockpit; and much more detailed study has been made of the various printers, especially of Nicholas Okes.[10] If this were applied to the critical sifting of Heywood's texts, more especially those which have not appealed in terms of their literary qualities, the general relation of the theatre and the published texts might be clarified. It is possible that after the relative paucity of his output in the years 1614–24, Heywood achieved the status of print because of that wave of Caroline nostalgia for the times of Elizabeth which has been remarked in the later works of Ben Jonson.[11] Heywood was sixty in 1633, a Nestor of the stage. The one really serious revision he made when after thirty-five years he turned his attention to the pirated text of *If You Know not Me* was to improve the account of the Spanish Armada, and make it the climax (incidentally, the players were now *using* this bad text in the theatre, the original presumably being lost!).[12]

Shakespeare speaks to every part of the world; the art of Heywood, though his medium was complex, was nearly as ephemeral as the actor's. It may illuminate Shakespeare's later romances – plays of the gaps, especially *Pericles* with its theatrical power to raise corrupt and broken dialogue in the romance's combination of the exotic and the familiar, the extremes of intimacy and violence.

If a poet is a maker, Heywood merits the title, though his preference for performance leaves him but Shakespeare's shadow. The fact that in Eliot's terms, none of his plays throws light on any other – an overstatement, but understandable – depends on the exact adjustment of each moment of dramatic life by his sense of the theatre; for he was its servant, and not, like Shakespeare, its master.

To my uninstructed mind, the fifty years of his dramatic career offers an unexplored field for the modern, sophisticated resources of theatrical archaeology and sociology, knowledge of the techniques of Renaissance printing which computer research supplies and modern linguistic interests, to unite for a joint exploration in depth.

The Heywood of his own day was not the Heywood who meagrely shows himself among the lesser figures of the stage. Those enormous and very expensive folios, *Nine Books of Various History Concerning Women* (1624) were dedicated to his first patron, the Earl of Worcester[13] revised by Milton's nephew, Edward Philips, and reshaped by Heywood himself in 1640 as *The Exemplary Lives and Memorable Acts of Nine the Most Worthy Women of the World*. Each book was named after one of the Nine Muses. *The Hierarchy of the Blessed Angels* (1635), an even larger folio, was dedicated to the Queen. These works far outmeasure the printed remains of Shakespeare and Jonson combined. Yet Heywood clearly held sympathies with the City fathers who were to oppose the King in the next decade. Perhaps he would himself have justified limiting his interest in the words of Cicero that he quoted in his *Apology for Actors*: 'Content thee, Caesar, there be many heads busied and bewitched with their pastimes now in Rome, which otherwise would be inquisitive after thee and thy greatness.'

Notes

1 'The Once and Future King Lear' delivered by Stanley Wells at the bi-annual Shakespeare Conference, August 1982 will be published in *Shakespeare Survey*; see also the article by Gary Taylor in *Shakespeare Survey* 33 (1980). For *Troilus and Cressida*, see the new Oxford text, ed. Kenneth Muir (1982) – who, however, probably would dissent about *King Lear*.

2 See the edition by V. Gabrieli and G. Melchiori (Bari, 1981); they are preparing an edition for the Revels Plays.

3 The influence of Peele (son of a pageant writer, himself a deviser of London pageants) was such that he himself became a London legend, and appears in *The Puritan* (1606, Paul's) under the name of George Pyeboard (a peil being a baker's shovel). For *The Battle of Alcazar* see above pp. 98–100.

4 Cf. Matheo in *The Honest Whore*, young Flowerdale in *The London Prodigal*, various figures in *Westward Ho!* and *Northward Ho!*. Young Thornley in *The Witch of Edmonton* is a tragic variant.

5 See Nicholas Brooke, *Horrid Laughter in Jacobean Tragedy* (1979); Jacqueline Pearson, *Tragedy and Tragicomedy in the Plays of John Webster* (1979).

6 Webster here used an innocent story to make a political comment. See my *John Webster, Citizen and Dramatist* (1980), pp. 177–9.

7 Jackson I. Cope, *The Theater and the Dream, from Metaphor to Form in Renaissance Drama* (Baltimore, 1973). See also the edition by Raymond C. Shudy (Salzburg, 1977), and his article in *Elizabethan Theatre* VII, ed. G. R. Hibbard (Macmillan, 1979).

8 Instead of elevating poetry, Quarles and Heywood abuse its divinity.

9 Cf. my article, 'The Politics of Pageantry', in *Poetry and Drama 1570 –1700*, ed. A. Coleman and A. Hammond (1981), for earlier pageants In 1612 Heywood supplied verses in the first English Emblem Book, H. Peacham, *Minerva Britannia*.

10 See the work on the Quartos of *King Lear* by P. M. W. Blayney (Cambridge, 1982).

11 See Anne Barton, 'Harking back to Elizabeth; Ben Jonson and Caroline Nostalgia', *English Literary History* vol. 48, pp. 706–31 (Baltimore, 1981).

12 See the edition of Madeleine Doran in the Malone Society Reprints (1935).

13 Edward Somerset, Earl of Worcester (1553–1626) succeeded Essex as Queen Elizabeth's Master of the Horse, presided at the treason trial of

1605, and was Lord Great Chamberlain at Charles I's coronation. He was the father of the two brides celebrated in Spenser's *Prothalamion*; his wife was a daughter of the Earl of Huntingdon, and Heywood dedicated to him the work on good women as having been 'the happy husband and fortunate father of such'.

The Irish Renaissance

XI.

Yeats and the Elizabethans

For many people, Yeats was the greatest poet of our time – greater even than T. S. Eliot. Comparing these two poets, I would say that Yeats began with poetry of dreamy idealism and withdrawal, and moved always towards a greater astringency, a more sinewy verse, which included many of the negative emotions; whereas Eliot, who began with elliptical and violent studies of the negative feelings, ended with a mellow and reconciled valediction. Perhaps it does not greatly matter where the poet starts; he will have to learn to include the opposite view, what Yeats called the anti-self, in his poetry. And perhaps the pilgrimage of the poet is the pilgrimage in search of his deeper self.

I have thought to compare Yeats not with his contemporaries, but with the poets of our golden age, and this for a very simple reason; Yeats was primarily a love poet, and the poets of Elizabethan England were the first masters of this style (if you except Chaucer). By love poetry I mean poetry in which a basic human relationship is enlarged by wit and imagination. But there are several other good reasons why the poetry of Yeats should be looked at beside the poetry of the late sixteenth century. This was a period of the English plantation of Ireland and Anglo-Irish speech retains some flavour of popular Elizabethan English; in Yeats's youth, the village fiddler still lingered, old ballads and ballad tunes were sung, as in Shakespeare's day.

But Yeats was also a devoted student of the high and courtly Elizabethan love poetry from boyhood; in youth he edited Spenser's poems and wrote what is one of the best essays on Spenser. So one might begin again with the proposition that Yeats's early love poetry is close to the courtly verse of Elizabeth, because Yeats absorbed it; but that his last verse is close to the popular poetry of Elizabeth, because he was using a language and a tradition which went back, little modified, to the oral poetry of three and a half centuries before. I am thinking of the ballads of his *Last Poems*. In the first case, the debt is a poetic craftsman's and direct; in the second, it is indirect, one of idiom and approach and inheritance. Or again, one might suggest that the development of Yeats, which I have already compared with that of Eliot, follows the same course as the development of Elizabethan love poetry in the earlier time; first a high Petrarchan idealism, leading to a sharp and bitter poetry, which includes many of the same negative emotions as Jacobean lyric, or drama.

This brings me to the final reason why Yeats's poetry may be studied in the light of the Elizabethans'; like them, Yeats was constantly remaking his world in his love poetry (and also remaking his poems as the Variorum edition shows). Through one supreme relationship he worked out the changing relation to everything else. In this his love seems to me less Platonic than neoplatonic. As he wrote in a poem that for once was not addressed to the supreme lady, Maud Gonne; but to Olivia Shakespear, the second of his loves:

> Others because you did not keep
> That deep-sworn vow have been friends of mine;
> Yet always when I look death in the face,
> When I clamber to the heights of sleep,
> Or when I grow excited with wine,
> Suddenly I meet your face.
>
> ('A Deep-Sworn Vow')

In an early essay, speaking of love, Yeats said:

> Such love and hatred seek no mortal thing but their own infinity; and such love and hatred can become love and hatred of the idea . . . if your passion is but great enough, it leads you to a country where there are many cloisters.

The image of the beloved becomes an instrument of the primary imagination (as it was for Shakespeare in that great but neglected Sonnet 53: 'What is your substance, whereof are you made?'). Take another poem of Yeats from the same volume, *The Wild Swans at Coole* (1919):

> One had a lovely face,
> And two or three had charm,
> But charm and face were in vain
> Because the mountain grass
> Cannot but keep the form

Where the mountain hare has lain.
('Memory')

The sudden displacement of relations to the rest of the world, by relation to a person *through whom* all else is mediated is familiar in ordinary life to most of us. In the life of the poet, however, it produces a special sort of crisis, for the beloved then becomes an instrument of poetic interpretation. There is the theme of the poetry or what is taken into it; and the result of the poetry, or the new relation established by it; and the image which has passed through a poet's mind may emerge as something quite different, even in relation to himself, from what it was before. So, as T. S. Eliot said, relations that are important in living may be unimportant in poetry, and vice versa, because the poetic inheritance may fuse with some relations of daily life more readily than others. A single scene may imprint itself on the poet's mind and nourish him for years.

In his introduction to the *Poems of Spenser* (c. 1900) Yeats said that the 'Vision in the House of Busyrane' had this power for him; he had seen in his mind's eye this strange procession over and over again; 'and it was only last summer when I read the Fourth Book of the *Faerie Queene*, that I found I had been imagining over and over the enchanted procession of Amoret.' Yeats thought the *Epithalamion* the most beautiful of Spenser's poems (it was written for his Irish bride, Elizabeth Boyle) and condemned the 'intolerable artificial sonnets'.

> His genius was pictorial, and these pictures of happiness were more natural to it than any personal pride or joy or sorrow. . . . To no English poet, perhaps to no European poet before his day, had the natural expression of personal feeling been so impossible, the clear lineaments of the human character so difficult.

Yeats finds this human feeling only in the earliest verse, the hexameters and the *Shepherd's Calendar*. In his poetry about women, Yeats thought Spenser too deliberately a poet. He could express more personal joy and sorrow about men than women, and loved the landscape even more than man. In Yeats's pastoral early work, 'The Isle of Statues', he escaped to Arcadia and a Spenserian paradise. Yeats's early poetry, in so far as it is thin and unbodied, follows Spenser, yet he rebukes Spenser even then for a lack of feeling for the living pastoral poetry that was all about him. Spenser was iron-hard in his views about the Irish, and Yeats rebuked him also that he advised 'the harrying of all that keep flocks upon the hills', and of all 'the wandering companies that keep the wood'. Yeats says

'There are moments when one can read neither Spenser nor Milton, when one recollects nothing except that their flesh had been partly turned to stone,' but then he remembers Spenser's landscapes, his 'smooth pastoral places . . . the religion of the wilderness.'

The religion of the wilderness represents the best that the early Yeats drew from Spenser – the vision of the woodland full of wandering lights, of the wandering companies from the Land of Heart's Desire; or the strange misty remote islands of Oisin. By these means feeling is dissolved into its simplest, remotest mood. I think the rhythm of the lines he quotes from Spenser's hexameters have something of the Faery Child's spell in *The Land of Heart's Desire* – though Yeats said he could not scan Spenser.

> Unhappie verse, the witness of my unhappy state,
> Make thyself fluttering wings for thy fast flying
> Thought, and fly forth unto my love wheresoever she be
> Whether lying restless in her heavy bed or else
> Sitting so cheerless at the cheerful board, or else
> Playing alone careless on her heavenly virginals.
> If in bed, tell her that my eyes can take no rest,
> If at board, tell her that my mouth can eat no meat;
> If at her virginals, tell her that I can hear no mirth.

> The wind blows out of the gates of the day,
> The wind blows over the lonely of heart,
> And the lonely of heart is withered away . . .
> You shall go with me newly married bride . . .
> Where beauty has no ebb, decay no flood,
> But joy is wisdom, time an endless song . . .
> But I can lead you, newly married bride,
> Where nobody gets old and crafty and wise,
> Where nobody gets old and godly and grave,
> Where nobody gets old and bitter of tongue . . .
> Come to the woods and waters and pale lights.

It is incredible that this play was first performed as curtain raiser for *Arms and the Man* by Bernard Shaw! The struggle between religion and morality (represented in this play by the priest and the husband) and the 'beautiful sensuous world' of fairy is the struggle that Yeats discerned in Spenser; and what Spenser rejected in Ireland yet imaged in his own poetry was for Yeats 'all the kingdom of fairy, still unfaded'. In so far as Yeats in his own early poetry loved the landscape more than man (or woman) he was Spenserian. An example of such is the famous and lovely lyric 'Down by the Salley Gardens', where all the feeling is carried by the nostalgic memory of Sligo.

Down by the salley gardens my love and I did meet;
She passed the salley gardens with little snow-white feet.
She bid me take love easy as the leaves grow on the tree,
But I, being young and foolish, with her would not agree.

In a field by the river my love and I did stand,
And on my leaning shoulder she laid her snow-white hand.
She bid me take life easy, as the grass grows on the weirs;
But I was young and foolish, and now am full of tears.
(*Irish Monthly*, October 1886)

The woods and waters and pale lights, the delicate wavering rhythms of Spenser remained; occasionally a strong line that he remembered for years, such as he quoted from 'The Ruins of Time', Spenser's lament for Leicester, – which in old age Yeats was to apply to his own beloved dead:

No fox can foul the lair the badger swept –
(An image out of Spenser and the common tongue)
('The Municipal Gallery Revisited')

This is an adaptation of

Spite bites the dead that living never bayed.
He now is gone, the while the Fox is crept
Into the lair, the which the Badger swept.
('Ruins of time', ii 215–17)

So that some of the bitterness in Spenser, at first rejected, worked through and out by the end.

Shakespeare's influence on Yeats underwent, I think, a similar transformation. The most Shakespearean of his early plays is *The Shadowy Waters*, which is heavy with the mood of the last Act of *Antony and Cleopatra*. The echoes are not verbal, for a less Shakespearean style than that of the early Yeats could hardly be imagined, but of mood and act. The strange unearthly music in the air; the lovers' scorn and contempt for the world ('''Tis paltry to be Caesar'); the utter oblivion of all wrongs committed, even against the beloved, in the rapture that assumes the God and Goddess in death – the idea of Stellification; the bemused attendants. These visions of a world beyond the world are alike, and a great echo comes at the close, where death is near; Charmian's cry, 'O eastern star!' is answered.

Peace, peace!
Dost thou not see my baby at my breast,
That sucks the nurse asleep?

This is transmuted by Yeats to Dectora's words to Forgael:

> O flower of the branch, O bird among the leaves,
> O silver fish that my two hands have taken
> Out of the running stream, *O morning star*
> Trembling in the blue heavens like a white fawn
> Upon the misty border of the wood,
> Bend lower that I may cover you with my hair,
> For we will gaze upon this world no longer.

The baby has been transmuted to 'a white fawn upon the misty border of the wood' — what an image for a Viking warrior like Forgael, except that by this time the whole world has been drawn into the dream. This stately ceremony of death (to be revived in *Deirdre*, with the double image of the net and the harp) is the first way in which the interpretation and interpenetration of the whole world through the Beloved is begun in Yeats's poetry.

In Shakespeare, who approached poetry otherwise, this play of *Antony and Cleopatra* comes at the end of his tragic cycle, the fulfilment of the implications first set out in *Romeo and Juliet* (a play to which Yeats returned in *Last Poems* with the lyric 'Parting'). And although Yeats worked over and over *The Shadowy Waters* (there are four versions of it between 1900 and 1911) he did not alter this last scene which is the heart of the play.

One may say of this pseudo-Shakespearean poem, I think, that it is the least clearly focused of all Yeats's works. Neither the world which is renounced, nor the heavenly world of the wild birds to which the lovers aspire, nor the Beloved with whom and through whom this is achieved, have any clarity of outline; all is indeed misty and shadowy, at the very edge of the world, at the very edge of the Atlantic horizon, with these 'thoughts that dodge Conception to the very borne of heaven.' And precisely this shadowy, hazy, undramatic quality of the early poetry reveals its potential. It is like the wide unfocused stare of the infant.

This was Yeats's personal achievement; in a vulgar age, he succeeded in 'emptying' the language — helped by the Rhymers' Club and memories of William Morris. It was not so with the early Elizabethans. There the level of beautiful and accepted commonplace allowed any artist to construct a poem into which any man could pour his own interpretations, a transparent envelope of words for the courtly or popular audience to fill, as for instance in the first twenty sonnets of Shakespeare. But for Yeats, as for them, poetry was life; who examined poetry was dead; and his relations with the poets and their myths were as intimately part of himself as relations with people. The stuff of life was necessarily an amalgam of the two, for a craftsman – son of an artist, to whom art was as natural an environment as the air he breathed.

A simple early form, including a rejection of the world, is 'The White Birds' from the volume *The Rose* (1893). Also a little later, 'He wishes his Beloved were Dead' (*The Wind Among the Reeds*, 1899).

The great passion that unified Yeats's vision came when, on 30 January 1889, he met Maud Gonne. The part of Cathleen Ni Houlihan in Yeats's play was written for Maud Gonne to act. And his early poem 'He thinks of those who have Spoken Evil of his Beloved' is a piece of dreamy enchantment that turns abruptly to heady Elizabethan rhetoric:

> Half close your eyelids, loosen your hair,
> And dream about the great and their pride;
> They have spoken against you everywhere,
> But weigh this song with the great and their pride;
> I made it out of a mouthful of air,
> Their children's children shall say they have lied.

Published in 1898 this was first called 'Aedh to Dectora' (the heroine of *The Shadowy Waters*).

It was not till the image of the Beloved had been distanced and turned into a mask, like the image of some Japanese dancer, till the political issues became also more troubled, that a true fusion between the personal and the public love was won in Yeats's poetry. From about 1910 Maud Gonne really did turn into something like Cathleen Ni Houlihan for Yeats – she was the instrument by which he worked out his relations with his world. Hence the conflicts of those four volumes written between 1910 and 1921 – the period of the Irish Revolution, of Yeats's own marriage.

In the plays and poems of the previous decade Yeats had written of kings and crowns because they reminded him of Maud Gonne and her queenly beauty:

> Some may have blamed you that you took away
> The verses that could move them on the day
> When, the ears being deafened, the sight of the eyes blind
> With lightning, you went from me and I could find
> Nothing to make a song about but kings,
> Helmets, and swords, and half-forgotten things
> That were like memories of you . . .
> But, dear, cling close to me; since you were gone

My barren thoughts have chilled me to the bone.
('Reconciliation', *The Green Helmet And Other Poems*)

Yet simultaneously with this tender, human admission of failure and love, powerful images of a Phoenix and of Helen of Troy, images from literature of the past, rebuilt and dramatised the figure of the beloved in a remote and mythological era. Here the link with the present was not through her own life but through the poet's art. The Beloved as a mode of relationship, subjectively conceived, whether in politics or art, became more significant than the real-life aspect of the situation. This attitude, medieval in its origins (it is found in Dante and Petrarch), was transmitted to Yeats through the earliest modern poets who used it, those of the English Renaissance, especially Philip Sidney. Though Ezra Pound introduced Yeats to medieval poetry, a poet's task must be learned through his own language, and the Elizabethan poets had formulated their love poetry in language on which Yeats's own poems could be established. The clearest example of how Yeats remade his poetry can be seen in 'The Sorrow of Love', a poem which first appeared in *The Rose* (1893) and was finally redrafted as late as 1925. The different stages have been carefully analysed by Jon Stallworthy in his book *Between the Lines*.

Here, from a poem already addressed to the Beloved, and opposed to the World, the mythology of a Homeric tale fills and enlarges the image, till the whole world is focused through Helen of Troy, who is, as Walter Raleigh would have said, the 'image and form' that embodies 'love's ground, his essence and his empery'.

Shakespeare himself set out this doctrine whereby the Beloved, like a kind of burning glass, draws together the whole scattered rays of the universe, in *Love's Labour's Lost*:

> From women's eyes this doctrine I derive,
> They sparkle still the right Promethean fire,
> They are the ground, the books, the academes,
> That show, contain and nourish all the world.

But in Yeats's verse a counter-truth began to work its way out. Through contemplation of the Beloved, the poet begins to know more intimately different levels and distinctions of his own experience, while they still held together various aspects of *her*. Even as the high poetry separates out in images of Marlowe's Helen or Shakespeare's Phoenix (the height of his Platonic poetry) – even so, Yeats becomes more relaxed and familiar in handling of his personal love story, as in 'The People' (in which she defends the common people against his complaint; written February 1916, just before the

Easter Rising) or more objective and critical of the woman (as in
'Broken Dreams'). The initial stages of splitting up a unifying image
may be intensely difficult and painful, involving elements of rage and
frustration. In Shakespeare it can be seen in Sonnets 83 and 84 'I
never saw that you did painting need' and

> You to your beauteous blessings add a curse,
> Being fond on praise, which makes your praises worse.

If ambivalent or conflicting aspects become irreconcilable, the
position of the lover becomes unendurable, as in the agony of
Shakespeare's Troilus, when fact destroys vision:

> Within my soul, there doth conduce a fight
> Of this strange nature, that a thing inseparate
> Divides more wider than the sky and earth,
> And yet the spacious breadth of this division
> Admits no orifice for a point as subtle
> As Ariachne's broken woof to enter.

This second stage of conflict in Yeats lasted from the age of
forty-five to fifty-seven, (1910 to 1922) and can be traced through
The Green Helmet (1910), *Responsibilities* (1914), *Wild Swans at
Coole* (1919) and *Michael Robartes* (1921). The first opens with a
dream poem which seems to me like a recollection of the Death of
Elaine in Malory.

HIS DREAM

> I swayed upon the gaudy stern
> The butt-end of a steering-oar
> And saw wherever I could turn
> A crowd upon a shore.
>
> And though I would have hushed the crowd,
> There was no mother's son but said,
> 'What is the figure in a shroud
> Upon a gaudy bed?'
>
> And after running at the brim
> Cried out upon that thing beneath
> — It had such dignity of limb —
> But the sweet name of Death.
>
> Though I'd my finger on my lip,
> What could I but take up the song?
> And running crowd and gaudy ship
> Cried out the whole night long,

> Crying amid the glittering sea,
> Naming it with ecstatic breath,
> Because it had such dignity,
> By the sweet name of Death.

This was a real dream of Yeats, and he applied to it Blake's words 'The authors are in Eternity', but it seems to me symbolic of the death of the young and innocent aspect of his own love. Malory tells how when the barge reaches London with the corpse of the girl who died for love, the crowd throng down to the banks to see the silent steersman and his shrouded companion:

> And there they found the fairest corpse lying in a rich bed that ever I saw, and a poor man sitting in the bargette, and no word would he speak . . . and she lay as she had smiled. (Vinaver, *Works of Malory*, p. 1096.)

In three poems Maud Gonne is compared with 'a woman Homer sung' – heroic but archaic; the same image was to be repeated in the next volume. Or as it is more personally put in the poem 'Peace':

> Ah, but peace that comes at length,
> Came when Time had touched her form.

The doctrine of Platonic forms is expounded as consolation for a very human privation (the humanity comes out in the rhythm):

> Vague memories, nothing but memories,
> But in the grave all, all, shall be renewed.
> The certainty that I shall see that lady
> Leaning or standing or walking
> In the first loveliness of womanhood,
> And with the fervour of my youthful eyes,
> Has set me muttering like a fool.
>   ('Broken Dreams')

In the fourth and final volume of this group Yeats remakes himself and chooses the human and the temporal. In 'An Image from a Past Life' a fairy form is rejected (is she Fand or is she Maud Gonne?) and in 'Under Saturn' the poet writes to his wife:

> Do not because this day I have grown saturnine
> Imagine that lost love, inseparable from my thought
> Because I have no other youth, can make me pine;
> For how should I forget the wisdom that you brought,
> The comfort that you made?

Along with the Phoenix image, on the other hand, there appears an image of statues, one for himself and one for his love ('I have met in a man's house / A statue of solitude') and a man 'May turn from a statue / His too human breast.' There is a loveliness 'dragged into being' 'by toils of measurement' a superhuman beauty; but petrified. The image of a stone comes as the poet sees himself as 'a weather-worn, marble Triton among the streams,' for

> Too long a sacrifice
> Can make a stone of the heart
> ('Easter 1916')

This great image derives perhaps from *Othello*; 'my heart is turned to stone; I strike it and it hurts my hand' (IV i 179–80) as he says to Iago. In the play *The Only Jealousy of Emer*, the hero is turned by enchantment to a motionless form by the sea-witch Fand, but he is saved by the sacrificial love of his wife.

Later we have a new kind of Phoenix – a young child. There is Maud Gonne's daughter Iseult Gonne; there is the young girl whom Yeats married; and finally, in the 'Prayer for My Daughter', his own child, come to restore him to a human world. The child, like Perdita or Miranda, reopens for the ageing poet his communications with mankind.

The Elizabethan poet from whom Yeats could have gained most in this phase of his love was Spenser's friend and patron, who held great estates in Ireland, but came from the Celtic west of England, with all its melancholy and fire – Sir Walter Raleigh. In Raleigh, as Donald Davie observed in an acute essay,[1] there is a crucial ambiguity between love as object and love as energy; or between the person of the Beloved and the relation which *through* that person is established with a whole world:

> And though strong reason hold before mine eyes
> The images and forms of worlds past,
> Touching the cause why all those flames that rise
> From formes externall can no longer last
>
> Than that those seeming beauties hold in prime
> Love's ground, his essence, and his emperie,
> All slaves to age, and vassals unto time,
> Of which repentance writes the tragedy:
>
> But this my heart's desire could not conceive,
> Whose love outflew the fastest flying time,
> A beauty that can easily deceive
> Th' arrest of years, and creeping age outclimb.

> A spring of beauties which time ripeth not,
> Time that but works on frail mortality,
> A sweetness which woe's wrongs outwipeth not
> Whom love hath chose for his divinity;
>
> A vestal fire that burns but never wasteth,
> That loseth naught by giving light to all,
> That endless shines each where, and endless lasteth,
> Blossoms of pride than can nor fade nor fall.

In this 'lofty, insolent and passionate' verse, despair and rejection pound like the waves of a fast-flowing tide against the rock of 'love' – love for a person which was also love for a particular way of life (and a glorious one) which she embodied. The worship of Maud Gonne as Phoenix or Helen of Troy or as the Statue which in the last poems she becomes, may be not unreasonably compared with 'The Ocean's Love to Cynthia': Raleigh had long residence in Ireland and the blood of Cornish Celts to bring to his poetry this liquid flow and proud height of disdain, this mingling of fluctuating mood and haughty assurance (which however he did not reach before his fortieth year).

Once more and once only did Yeats return to the Elizabethan mode. He had said that Spenser wrote better of men than of women; in the elegy 'Shepherd and Goatherd' written at Glendalough in March 1918 within a few weeks of the death in war of Lady Gregory's only son, Yeats told Lady Gregory that he had modelled himself on 'what Spenser wrote of Sidney' (*Letters*, p. 648).

In another poem, 'In Memory of Major Robert Gregory', he called his dead friend 'Our Sidney and our perfect man'. The later elegy is the more intimate, and much better poetry than the Spenserian pastiche. In the first stiffness of grief and shock, Yeats took refuge in an Elizabethan convention which enabled him to write not about the dead man, but about the mourners – himself, and Lady Gregory. The poem does not celebrate the dead, it reconciles the living to their loss by its consolation of shared grief. As such, it uses an artifice that Yeats otherwise would not have yielded to; only in the final song of the old Goatherd 'He grows younger every second' does Yeats leave the convention and give fuller impersonality and warmer tenderness. 'Dreaming back', the dead man relives his life from end to beginning:

> He grows younger every second
> That were all his birthdays reckoned
> Much too solemn seemed . . .
> The outrageous war shall fade;
> At some old winding whitethorn root

He'll practise on the shepherd's flute,
Or on the close-cropped grass
Court his shepherd lass,
Or put his heart into some game,
Till daytime, playtime seem the same . . .
('Shepherd and Goatherd')

Like Yeats, Shakespeare in the bitterness and beauty of his last plays, *The Winter's Tale, The Tempest, Pericles*, is boldly adapting very simple forms from his youth to strive after something very delicate and difficult – country folk's tales of marvels and monsters. The scale of Yeats's poems is lesser than this, nearer to those adaptations of ballads by lesser seventeenth-century writers; for example, Raleigh's 'Walsingham' with its bold paradoxes.

I have loved her all my youth,
But now old, as you see,
Love likes not the falling fruit
From the withered tree . . .
But true love is a durable fire,
In the mind ever burning;
Never sick, never old, never dead,
From itself never turning.

or the great anonymous seventeenth-century song of Tom-a-Bedlam:

From the hagg and the hungry goblin
That into rags would rend ye,
The spirit that stands by the naked man
In the book of moons defend ye,
That of your five sound senses
Ye never be forsaken,
Nor wander from yourselves with Tom
Abroad to beg your bacon.
    While I do sing any food, any feeding,
    Feeding, drink or clothing:
    Come, dame or maid, be not afraid,
    Poor Tom will injure nothing . . .
With a host of furious fancies,
Whereof I am commander,
With a burning spear and a horse of air,
To the wilderness I wander.
By a knight of ghosts and shadows
I summon'd am to tourney,
Ten leagues beyond the wide world's end,
Methinks it is no journey;

or the more lightly bitter song of Bishop Corbet (written for a servant) 'Farewell Rewards and Fairies'.

> Lament, lament, old abbeys,
> The fairies' lost command . . .
> And all your children stol'n from thence
> Are thence grown Puritanes,
> Who live as changelings ever since
> For love of your domaines . . .
>
> A tell-tale in their company
> They never could endure,
> And who so kept not secretly
> Their mirth was punished sore.
> It was a just and Christian deed
> To pinch such black and blue;
> O how the Commonwealth doth need
> Such justices as you!

In the seventeenth century the learned could use ballad style in this skilful fashion, as Yeats did in 'Come gather round me Parnellites' and 'The Ghost of Roger Casement'. The same 'low' style is turned on to 'high' love mythology in the sequence of 'The Three Bushes'. The story comes from a medieval *tenzon*, a Provençal poem. In these verses there is pity for the body, in the absurdity of its erotic automatisms, and pity for the price exacted for a Platonic ideal. It bears something of the pity we find in the use of old ballads for Ophelia, and its strangeness of conceit would not be beyond a Jacobean poet's understanding (though I cannot think of any age between these two that could so have combined earthy directness and lofty vision). In this curious sequence I think Yeats found a way to define the nature of his love. The mistress and the maid represent two aspects of love, rarely to be combined in one person; but to the lover they appear as one. The daylight lady represents Platonic or Petrarchan love; the love for what is and must remain unobtainable. This is what as stellified and later as petrified love, Maud Gonne had represented. 'That love I best which flies beyond my reach' said one of Marlowe's heroes, but this idealised love no longer satisfies. The model and type was the love of Dante for Beatrice or Petrarch for Laura de Sade 'the exemplary Avignon housewife, chaste and gay, and on the whole rather bored with the poet who was to make her name a familiar symbol' (Bishop, *Petrarch and his World*, p. 70).

In 'The Three Bushes' love takes a body, but not the body of the Beloved; and because of this, in physical union 'all the labouring heavens sigh'; in the chaste greeting is heard 'a contrapuntal serpent hiss'.

Yeats paradoxically puts together both kinds of love – the love which enables him to explore his inner and his outer world, and which for that reason had to remain

> that monstrous thing
> Return'd but unrequited love

and the physical love from which primal energy derives. If his relations with the human being who had provided the first grew more and more remote, schematic and unreal, this can be paralleled in Dante and Petrarch, who continued to explore the relation of love after their ladies were dead. A fantasy relationship with a dead person is often of guiding importance for the inner life; and as was said at the beginning, Yeats's relations in his poetry and his relations in real life are extremely complex. For instance, his father, who obviously influenced him deeply, makes few direct appearances in the poems.

Hence those early poems, in which he wishes that his beloved were dead, are a truthful reflection of the need which drove him to the Mask and the Image, and kept him faithful to it, to the vision of art rather than the facts of life.

> A young man when the old men are done talking
> Will say to an old man, 'Tell me of that lady
> The poet stubborn with his passion sang us
> When age might well have chilled his blood.'
> ('Broken Dreams')

It was the poet rather than the lover whose stubbornness maintained the song.

Note

1 *In Elizabethan Poetry* (Stratford-upon-Avon Studies No. 2, ed. Arthur Brown and Bernard Harris, Edward Arnold, 1962).

XII.

Yeats and the Legend of Ireland

As the author of *The Wanderings of Oisin, The Land of Heart's Desire*, and *The Wind Among the Reeds*, Yeats by the opening of the twentieth century was established as poet of an Irish fairy-tale world. In 1900, he resigned also, after four years, from the Irish Revolutionary Brotherhood, having associated himself with the literary movement of the Irish National Theatre. In many countries other than Ireland, the poetic revival of a legendary past was seen as the surest way to recovering a national identity; it can be found from 1848 onwards in the ancient kingdoms swallowed by the Hapsburg Empire, in Poland and Bohemia; in Scandinavia, Ibsen began his career with such plays as *The Warrior's Barrow*, and *Lady Ingar of Østraat*; indeed, his contract at the Bergen National Theatre stipulated that this work must be sufficiently nationalist to counteract the Danish influences of the Norwegian capital, dominated from Copenhagen.

Max Beerbohm then might caricature Yeats presenting George Moore to the Queen of the Faeries[1] but he had edited Shelley, who had proclaimed poets as the trumpets that sing to battle, the unacknowledged legislators of the world; he had also edited Walter Scott, who, combining the Romantic and the anti-Romantic, had clearly recognised his own fantasies for what they were, whilst recreating, with their aid, a new Scottish nationalism: 'I can see as many castles in the clouds as any man. . . . My life has been spent in such day dreams' (*Journal*, 1 January 1827). Scott recognised, as Yeats was to do, the power of dreams to shape the world:

> What is this world? A dream within a dream – as we grow older each step is an awakening. The youth awakes as he thinks from Childhood – the full grown man despises the pursuits of youth as visionary – the old man looks

on manhood as a feverish dream. The Grave the sleep? – no, it is the last final awakening. (*Journal*, 13 May 1827)

Such beliefs were to take larger root in Yeats as he gradually developed a doctrine of reincarnation which linked the past to the present in new ways. Neither Scott nor Yeats used legends, except at the point of dynamic social involvement.

The constant Irish impulse of self-adulation had in Scott's time been found highly marketable by Tom Moore, author of the popular *Irish Melodies*; the prototype must be sought further back, in the Irish Sheridan's Lucius O'Trigger, the Sheamus and Teague of Restoration times. Against this coarse exploitation of the English market, which persisted down to the First World War in such popular war songs as 'Cassidy, Private Michael Cassidy', 'When Irish Eyes are Smiling' and 'Tipperary' (Kipling's Mulvaney had perhaps counted for something here), Yeats had set himself to create an heroic world from the medieval past, but to wed it to the present; to write for his own people, in the socially powerful form of drama – not a traditionally Irish form. *The Countess Cathleen* and *Cathleen ni Houlihan* were both written for Maud Gonne,[2] whom Yeats first met in 1891. As he continually revised *The Countess Cathleen*, the role of her poet-lover Aleel, who protests against her immolation for the cause of her people, gained power. As early as 1888, Yeats wrote to Kathleen Tynan: 'The early poems I know to be quite coherent, and at no time are there clouds in my details, for I hate the soft modern manner' (*Letters to Kathleen Tynan*, ed. R. McHugh (1953), p. 68). The original opening of *The Wanderings of Oisin* read:

> Oisin, tell me the famous story
> Why thou outlivest, blind and hoary,
> The bad old days

which becomes

> You who are bent, and bald and blind
> With a heavy heart and a wandering mind,
> Have known three centuries

where the 'famous story' has become more exact, crisp and bitter. Yeats, who lived out his dreams (which meant the past was continually being modified by the present), adopted the practical medievalism of William Morris far more than the personal explorers of legend – Tennyson with his idyllic purification of Victorian murk; Rossetti with his Blessed Damozel, deifying Lizzie Siddall.[3]

The most extraordinary rewriting, which amounted to a complete reversal of the original poem, was of a dedication written for a collection of stories from the Irish novelists. It first appeared in 1890 and was rewritten as late as 1924.

> There was a green branch hung with many a bell
> When her own people ruled in wave-worn Eri . . .
>
> Ah, exiles, wandering over many seas,
> Spinning at all times Eri's good tomorrow,
> Ah, world-wide Nation, always growing Sorrow,
> I also bear a bell branch full of ease.
>
> I tore it from green boughs wind-tossed and hurled,
> Green boughs of tossing always, weary, weary!
> I tore it from the green bough of old Eri,
> The willow of the many-sorrowed world.
>
> Ah, Exiles wandering over many lands!
> My bell branch murmurs: the gay bells bring laughter,
> Leaping to shake a cobweb from a rafter,
> The sad bells bow the forehead on the hands.
>
> A honied ringing under the new skies,
> They bring: u memories of old village faces,
> Cabins now gone, old well-sides, old dear places,
> And men who loved the cause that never dies.

The bell-branch remains, but little else:

> There was a green branch, hung with many a bell
> When her own people ruled this tragic Eire;

changes but one significant word; it is the present that has changed with the years:

> Ah, Exiles, wandering over lands and seas,
> And planning, plotting always that some morrow
> May set a stone upon ancestral Sorrow!
> I also bear a bell branch full of ease.
>
> I tore it from green boughs winds tore and tossed
> Until the sap of summer had grown weary!
> I tore it from the barren boughs of Eire,
> That country where a man can be so crossed;
>
> Can be so battered, badgered and destroyed,
> That he's a loveless man; gay bells bring laughter
> That shakes a mouldering cobweb from the rafter;
> And yet the saddest chimes are best enjoyed.

> Gay bells or sad, they bring you memories
> Of half-forgotten innocent old places;
> We and our bitterness have left no traces
> On Munster grass and Connemara skies.

One is a song of innocence from the young hopeful whose country was still a visionary place; the other a song of experience from Senator Yeats, who knew too well what government entails.

'By marriage with the Pollexfens, I have given a tongue to the sea cliffs.' Yeats's father in this praise of his son indicated in that indubitably Cornish name the only Celtic element in Yeats's inheritance, who otherwise came of Protestant Anglo-Irish stock; but Yeats's Ireland took what colouring events threw upon it, except that he usually preferred the unpopular cause. The development of his poetry traces a curve from early heroics, evincing the usual fantasy and wonder and worship, to critical and ironic response, tempered by a more rigid and more Byzantine form, reaching back, when his devotion to Maud Gonne remained unrewarded,[4] for its images to Helen of Troy, or an Elizabethan Phoenix. Fantasy and the medieval past of Ireland could reflect images that gave 'the detachment from the urgent present which ends by bringing the artist, if he is a great artist, into line with the spirits of the past and future.'[5]

Yeats's world was finally shaped by the rich compound of legend, poetry and experience; what he created and recreated was the mythical not the strictly historic Ireland.[6] He never let go of his dreams, but mastered and transformed them.

If, at first, he could indulge simple heroic poses at which Maud Gonne was so adept (these are revealed in her autobiography, *A Servant of the Queen*, (Gollancz, 1938), with the most naïve self-congratulation), the influence of Lady Gregory, at whose home he stayed every summer from 1897, and with whom he founded the Irish National Theatre, gave him new legendary material. She translated the legend of Cuchulain. Yeats saw himself as a descendant of the *fili*, the prophetic court bards, whom he depicted in Seanchan, the hero of *The King's Threshold* (1904), bringing the King to his knees; from 1904 he was production manager at the Abbey Theatre and then wrote the first of the Cuchulain plays, *On Baile's Strand*, nobly tragic, whilst two years later his *Deirdre*, the Gaelic Helen of Troy, was related both to heroic legend and to the pastoral lives of the country people in whose cause the whole enterprise was conceived. The Queen's ironic deception of her captor, after the death of Usnach's sons, begins:

> King Conchubar is right. My husband's dead,
> A single woman is of no account,

> Lacking array of servants, linen cupboards,
> The bacon hanging. . . .

But it was at that time that Yeats's ten years' adherence to the cause received a mortal blow, in the mob's angry reception of John Synge's *The Playboy of the Western World* (1907). Country people, so wedded to fantasy as to idolise a self-proclaimed 'slayer of his da' presented an unacceptable image to the self-righteous philistines of Dublin. And the phrase 'a drift of chosen females standing in their shifts' caused riots. Yeats stepped before the curtain to face the mob with the ringing words, 'The author of *Cathleen ni Houlihan* addresses you.' They produced no effect at all. Thirty years later, he was to recall among the 'beautiful lofty things' of the past his own much-loved father in a different stance:

> My father upon the Abbey stage; before him a raging crowd:
> 'This Land of Saints' and then, as the applause died out,
> 'Of plaster Saints', his beautiful mischievous head thrown back.
>
> ('Beautiful Lofty Things', *Last Poems* 1936–9)

In a savage epigram Yeats later compared the journalists, whom he considered to be responsible (they included Arthur Griffiths), to eunuchs; at the very end of his life he attacked in popular ballads, with equal force, those who supported the publication of the *Casement Diaries*. Yet he was also, in 'Remorse for Intemperate Speech' capable of denouncing his own practices. His irony against Ireland was always joined with irony against himself. Under stress he could strike a lofty pose; the poem 'Shepherd and Goatherd', a lament for Major Robert Gregory, his friend's son, is modelled on Virgil and Sidney, and designed to distance grief for her. Two bards, shepherd and goatherd, measure out tribute in a stilted ritualist pastoral which one critic stigmatised as 'the only thoroughly bad poem to be found in Yeats's post-1914 verse.'[7] What has been left out here – but comes so poignantly into the great verses 'In memory of Major Robert Gregory' – is the personal element. Twenty years later, in 'The Municipal Gallery Revisited', he succeeded in blending artifice and passion elegiacally.

By 1911 Yeats was appealing to Douglas Hyde to tell him the secret of popularity ('Dear Craoibhin Aoibhin, look into our case'), and by 1913 his hatred for the Irish philistines prompted the lament:

> Romantic Ireland's dead and gone,
> It's with O'Leary in the grave . . .
>
> ('September 1913', *Responsibilities*, 1914)

But 'In dreams begin responsibilities', and it was at this point that
Yeats began to make something different out of the legends he had
been weaving for a quarter of a century:

> I made my song a coat
> Covered with embroideries
> Out of old mythologies
> From heel to throat;
> But the fools caught it,
> Wore it in the world's eyes
> As though they'd wrought it.
> Song, let them take it,
> For there's more enterprise
> In walking naked.
> ('A Coat', in *Responsibilities*)

Far from walking naked, Yeats soon covered the face with a mask
and thickened the embroidery as the Easter Rising and the emergence
of an Ireland he had helped to create gave him a contemporary
mythology to blend with the old. Very rarely can great writing
come from immediate experience; his plays became now plays for
masked dancers and musicians: The ritual was stiff, alien. Later, he
wrote:

> The bravest from the gods but ask
> A house, a sword, a ship, a mask. . . .

That questioning of the heroic ideal which had begun with his
second Cuchulain play, *The Green Helmet* (1911), led on to the
third, and the first of the plays based on Japanese Noh drama, *The
Hawk's Well* (March 1916). It is located at a mountain well near
Sligo, his boyhood home, but written in free adaptation of a form he
learnt from his friend Ezra Pound, a student of Noh. The semi-
hypnotic action of drum and dancers was already his when the Easter
Rising occurred. His next play, *The Dreaming of the Bones*, includes
the figure of a fugitive from the fighting in Dublin, the ghosts of the
first betrayers of Ireland, Dermot and Devorgilla, a memory of
Dante's Paolo and Francesca, and the Japanese tradition of the holy,
haunted spot, with much power emanating from the locality itself,
the Burran in County Clare, where the play is set.

The violent events of Easter 1916 released Yeats from his dream of
love; after one last attempt to persuade Maud Gonne, he suddenly
married a young English woman who had never seen Ireland; in his
latest poems he recalled the progress of his poetry in a way that
almost identifies his younger self of *The Countess Cathleen* with the

pitying image of the young Keats, a boy with his nose pressed to sweet-shop windows:[8]

> It was the dream itself enchanted me.
> Character isolated by a deed
> To engross the present and dominate memory.
> ('The Circus Animals' Desertion', *Last Poems*)

The chosen hero Cuchulain, whose character had been isolated in *The Green Helmet* and *At the Hawk's Well* underwent many further transformations, including a humiliating death at the hands of a beggar, in the posthumous play, *The Death of Cuchulain*, which is introduced by an old man 'looking like something out of mythology', but speaking for the author. His own mask now presents his anti-self Cuchulain, the warrior, after whose death a goddess dances, only to fade before 'the music of some Irish Fair of our own day', and a modern ragged street singer who chants:

> The harlot sang to the beggar man
> I meet them, face to face,
> Conall, Cuchulain, Usna's boys,
> All that most ancient race;
> Maeve had three in an hour, they say.
>
> I adore those clever eyes,
> Those muscular bodies, but can get
> No grip upon their thighs.
> I meet those long pale faces
> Hear their great horses, then
> Recall what centuries have passed
> Since they were living men. . . .
>
> Are those things men adore and loathe
> Their sole reality?
> What stood in the Post Office
> With Pearse and Connolly . . .[9]
>
> Who thought Cuchulain till it seemed
> He stood where they stood?

In the fighting at the Dublin Post Office in 1916 'Pearse summoned Cuchulain to his side' and now, as the old man recalls,

> A statue's there to mark the spot,
> By Oliver Sheppard done. . . .

But the thought of his early poetry was no complacent memory for Yeats:

> All that I have said and done,
> Now that I am old and ill,
> Turns into a question till
> I lie awake night after night
> And never get the answers right.
> Did that play of mine send out
> Certain men the English shot?
> ('The Man and the Echo', *Last Poems*)

The play was *Cathleen ni Houlihan*.[10] His later allegiances also haunted him:

> Could my spoken words have checked
> That whereby a house lay wrecked?

The house was Coole Park. (Yeats did not live to know that the Irish government sold it and that it was pulled down, for the sake of £500 of lead in the roof. He might have stopped that.)

Thirty years earlier, in 1908 in the garden of Coole, he had already written lines to be quoted against him in the Irish Senate:

> All things can tempt me from this craft of verse;
> One time it was a woman's face, or worse –
> The seeming needs of my fool-driven land.
> ('All Things can Tempt Me', *The Green Helmet* (1910))

'The wild old wicked man' – who becomes one of Yeats's images from about 1921 – could still be tempted, when over sixty, by memories of a 'Ledaean body', but his rage was also roused by the modern images of Ireland. 'We are the people of Burke and Gratton', he declared in the Senate, defending private Divorce Bills against the Catholics, and speaking for the Protestant minority. In the *Last Poems*, 'journalist' became one of his strongest terms of denigration:

> Some have known a likely lad
> That had a sound fly-fisher's wrist
> Turn to a drunken journalist
> ('Why Should Not Old Men be Mad?')

and he retreated into a heavy armour-plating of his own old mythologies, a buried King Arthur, a Once and Future King:

> A statesman is an easy man
> And tells his lies by rote[11]
> A journalist makes up his lies
> And takes you by the throat,

So sit at home and drink your beer
And let the neighbours vote.
('Said the man in the golden breastplate
Under the old stone cross')

Impulse to exploit old poets' pathos is not absent from Irish journalism today. Maeve Binchy, in *The Guardian* (8 December 1975), opens her plaint 'I can remember the days when it used to be great to be Irish in Britain' (imagining that the English of London was a foreign language), going on to a self-dramatising conclusion:

> There used to be a happy role-playing thing about Irish songs, people who sang of Ireland's wrongs and woes and laid the blame on England for them all. . . . Songs stop being songs when you feel you have to explain them. . . . Life is too short for all this explanation. I'll just have to stop singing.

Though the final sob is hardly calculated to take anyone by the throat in a paper which also reported the Dutchman Dr Herrema's return to Limerick, the article skilfully plays on an image which since Yeats's death the English themselves have rather mercilessly exposed, in Yeats's own accents. Auden puts among sins to be atoned for

the impudent grin and Irish charm
That hide a cold will to do harm.[12]
('The Temptation of St. Joseph', *For the Time Being* (1945))

Yeats's own anger against his people taught younger poets outside Ireland. Not the least of Yeats's struggles in old age was with the image of himself that others, who also saw him as part of Irish history, had created. When he was proposed for the Senate and someone asked what a poet should do in the government of the Free State, St John Gogarty had magnificently replied, 'Without Yeats, there would be no Free State'; yet, like the hero of Pirandello's *Henry IV*, Yeats sometimes felt imprisoned by the role:

What matter if I live it all once more?
Endure that toil of growing up;
The ignominy of boyhood; the distress
Of boyhood changing into man;
The unfinished man and his pain
Brought face to face with his own clumsiness;
The finished man among his enemies? –
How in the name of Heaven can he escape
That defiling and disfigured shape
The mirror of malicious eyes

Casts upon his eyes until at length
He thinks that shape must be his shape?
('Dialogue of Self and Soul', *The Winding Stair* (1933))

Not that even this later phase kept Yeats totally immune from self-deception. He very much enlarged the role of his own ancestors, once he had begun to identify with the Anglo-Irish gentry instead of with the peasants:

> Old Dublin merchant 'free of ten and four'
> Or trading out of Galway into Spain;
> Old country scholar, Robert Emmet's friend,
> A hundred year old memory to the poor:
> Merchant and scholar who have left me blood
> That has not passed through any huckster's loin,
> Soldiers that gave, whatever die was cast;
> A Butler or an Armstrong that withstood
> Beside the brackish waters of the Boyne
> James and his Irish when the Dutchman crossed. . . .
> (Prefixed to *Responsibilities* (1914))

Yeats eventually confessed that 'free of ten and four' came from Villon, but he did not amend it, as he had amended the last lines which read at first:

> Pardon, and you that did not weigh the cost,
> Old Butlers when you took to horse and stood
> Beside the brackish waters of the Boyne,
> Till your bad master blenched and all was lost.

He found out and acknowledged that his ancestors had after all been Orangemen; but the careful distinction between wholesale and retail, merchants and 'hucksters', would have been unlikely to impress the world of Somerville and Ross[13] (his mother's family were flourmillers in Sligo). In another context, he would acknowledge among his forebears a smuggler ('Are you Content?', *Last Poems*), and after he had given six years to the drudgery of work in the Irish Senate, he turned away from politics, or broke into badly misconceived approval of violence.

> You that Mitchel's prayer have heard
> 'Send war in our time, O Lord!'

was written in September 1938 (the time of Munich), when there was some excuse for it, but the poet goes on to exhort the Irish poets to sing 'whatever is well-made', including the human products of the peasantry and 'hard-riding country gentlemen', monks and drunkards:

> Cast your mind on other days
> That we in coming days may be
> Still the indomitable Irishry.
> ('Under Ben Bulben', *Last Poems*)

That last flamboyant gesture is part of a testament, from an old man who ended by writing his own epitaph. He really wished to be and really is buried under Ben Bulben and 'under the old stone cross' by a road where the invisible riders of the Sidhe can be heard. He wrote his epitaph for the living travellers, though he unites them with the 'Pale invisible ones' of legend:

> Draw rein, draw breath;
> Cast a cold eye
> On life, on death.
> Horseman, pass by!

The old man who must remake himself as Timon and Lear (for Timon's tomb by the sea and his epitaph are recalled here) culminated in *Purgatory* with the blind beggar who, in the ruins of his ancestral home, kills his bastard son to quench the curse of his line when he 'sees' it re-enacted by his dead father and mother before his blind eyes. The figure harks back to the father who killed his son in the first of Yeats's plays on Cuchulain, *On Baile's Strand* – but that was a universal legend, best known in English in Matthew Arnold's tale of Sohrab and Rustum. In *Purgatory* (1938) this sacrifice is not a consciously chosen but futile one, since old tragic violence still reanimates the dead. Among Yeats's own visions, men-at-arms are still seen fighting medieval battles 'in the narrow pass' ('Crazy Jane on God'). The old crimes live a ghostly life; the final prayer

> Mankind can do no more. Appease
> The misery of the living and the remorse of the dead

could be Yeats's own prayer against 'the logic of fanaticism . . . drawn from a premise protected by ignorance and therefore irrefutable', so that he made his last songs too fantastic for any party (Commentary on *Three Songs*, *Variorum*, p. 835). As each event in Irish history assumes this loaded, legendary character, even the cooler mood of the statesman is imperilled, as Yeats was to confess:

I ranted to the knave and fool
But outgrew that school,
Would transform the part,
Fit audience found, but cannot rule
My fanatic heart.

I sought my betters; though in each
Fine manners, liberal speech,
Turn hatred into sport,
Nothing said or done can reach
My fanatic heart.

Out of Ireland have we come,
Great hatred, little room
Maimed us at the start.
I carry from my mother's womb
A fanatic heart.
('Remorse for Intemperate Speech',
The Winding Stair (28 August 1931)

Casement and Parnell were as alive to him as O'Duffy and his Blueshirts ('I am still their servant, though all are underground,' he sang in *The Curse of Cromwell*). Though in one sense, even for the politician there is living power in the image, this fatal confusion has always bedevilled Irish political debate. The Massacre of Drogheda and the Siege of Londonderry are still being enacted. This was not Yeats's attitude. He felt that a nation, in contemplating the drama of its own history, should each man be 'finding self and neighbour there, finding all the world there' (*Variorum*, p. 836).

Later, Yeats became even more passionate in the cause, and in 'Three Songs to the One Tune', cried, rather fanatically, 'Down the fanatic, down the clown!' Before the Second World War broke out he was dead. '"Time I was buried," said the old, old man.'[14]

Yeats, who had learnt to handle personal history and the history of his country in one, could now lament to see the Helen of his youth, dreaming of social welfare, 'climb on a waggonette to scream'.[15] In his later years he did not meet Maud Gonne, who continued to live in her early world of fantasy (as he depicted her in 'A Bronze Head'). By this time, all his friends and foes had become statues or pictures, they had passed 'into the artifice of eternity'. Dead or alive, he wrote of them all elegiacally. Yeats would not have been surprised to see in Winnipeg the Imperial lions confronted by the statue of Louis Riel.

He knew the dangers of fantasy as an instrument of nationalism; but for him his own images were sacred, being part of an ancient tradition.[16] The degradation of the modern 'image' in the hands of publicity agents has now reached depths that Yeats never dreamed of. According to Daniel Boorstin, it is 'synthetic, believable, passive, vivid, simplified and ambiguous'.[17] Yeats's images were syncretic, miraculous, active, multiform, complex and containing within themselves always their opposing image, being closely bound up with the metaphysical doctrines set out in *A Vision* (1925). He took Blake's view that 'contraries are positive. A negative is not a contrary.'

A certain modern poet, in 1968, declared at the beginning of the present Irish conflict, that Irish poets felt they had been given new songs. Maeve Binchy's journalism may at least serve to record that this is no longer the case; nor does the poetry of Yeats accord with the present state of Ireland.

Notes

1 Watercolour in the Municipal Gallery, Dublin, c. 1900.

2 The Irish Revolutionary, who eventually married John MacBride.

3 For William Morris see Yeats, *Memoirs*, ed. Denis Donoghue (1972), p. 20: 'Morris had not yet written the prose romances which were to delight me in later years. There were moments when I thought myself a Socialist and saw Morris more as a public man than a thinker. . . . I discovered in him something childlike and joyous that still leaves him my chief of men.' Yeats's sister was for a time May Morris's assistant at Kelmscott House.

4 However, 'The Folly of being Comforted', originally written in 1902, though still being amended twenty years later, was not changed in sentiment.

5 A. C. Benson to Yeats, quoted by Joseph Hone, *Life of Yeats* (1943), ch. 16. (A new *Life* has been prepared by the Provost of Trinity College Dublin, Prof. F. S. L. Lyons.)

6 See J. H. Plumb, *The Death of the Past* (Penguin, 1973).

7 Peter Ure, *Towards a Mythology* (Liverpool, 1946), p. 40. Major Gregory was killed in action with the Royal Flying Corps over Italy in January 1918. Cf. above p. 142.

8 The image comes in 'Ego Dominus tuus', written in 1915.

9 Compare 'The Statues' (*Last Poems*): 'When Pearse summoned Cuchulain to his side / What stalked through the Post Office? What intellect / What calculation, number, measurement replied?' This implies a Rosicrucian correspondence between the evocation and the result, the final statue.

10 See Stephen Gwynn, *Irish Literature and Drama*, p. 158; and *The Senate Speeches of W. B. Yeats*, ed. D. R. Pearce (Faber, 1961), p. 15, where one of the leaders of the IRB records that he was converted by this play.

11 Yeats had been a member of the Senate from 1922 to 1928; he voted

with the moderate Southern Unionist Party and joined the Kildare Street Club. He also replaced the image of the poet in the long black cloak by well-cut tweeds.

12 Even more savage treatment is meted out by Angus Wilson in two stories of his first volume *The Wrong Set* (1946): 'Saturnalia' and 'A Story of Historical Interest'.

13 E. O. Somerville's and Martin Ross's book *The Experiences of an Irish R.M.*, and its sequel is the best projection of the life of the Edwardian gentry in the west of Ireland.

14 Another of the 'Three Songs': he added a note in defence of ' "public order" and "the rule of educated and able men without which Ireland's noble history" would be "ignoble farce".'

15 'Why Should Not Old Men be Mad?', *Last Poems*. Cf. 'A Prayer for my Daughter', stanza 8.

16 See Ellic Howe, *The Magicians of the Golden Dawn* (Routledge, 1972).

17 Daniel Boorstin, *The Image: or. What happened to the American Dream?* (New York, 1962).

XIII.

Yeats and the Noh Drama of Japan*

When Yeats turned away from Irish National Theatre which had constituted his most considerable public achievement, he explained himself in a letter to Lady Gregory, entitled 'A people's theatre',[1]

> I want to create for myself an unpopular theatre and an audience like a secret society whose admission is by favour and never to many . . . an audience of fifty, a room worthy of it. . . . I desire a mysterious art, always reminding and half reminding those who understand it of dearly loved things, doing its work by suggestion, not by direct statement. (*Explorations*, 254–5)

Three years later, he was to find new dramatic talents in himself as an Irish Senator; his eloquence on the matter of divorce, as he spoke for non-Catholic minority groups, scandalised the Dáil. But he never returned to the popular stage, where he had so successfully worked to build national cohesion through cultural pride. As the author of *Cathleen ni Houlihan* he was to ask himself:

> Did that play of mine send out
> Certain men the English shot?

In 1925, on receiving the Nobel Prize, he rightly spoke of this as his chief claim to such an honour, wishing only that John Synge and Augusta Gregory could share the glory. But 'We make out of the quarrel with others, rhetoric; out of the quarrel with ourselves, poetry.'

---

* Lecture given at the Yeats Centenary Summer School, Sligo, 20 August 1965, revised. It was accompanied with a display of silks, fans, miniature Noh masks, dolls and illustrated works on Noh.

Cuchulain of Muirthemne had returned from the shades to succeed Parnell the lost King; he became Yeats's 'anti-self'. The severe blow which the popular fury at Synge's *Playboy of the Western World* dealt Yeats did not prevent his continuing to work for the Irish National Theatre, but his writing of *The Green Helmet* and *The Player Queen* took on a kind of stammer; he was constantly rewriting both. At the end of his life, in a preface to a projected edition of his plays, Yeats acknowledged

> two dominant desires; I wanted to get rid of irrelevant movement – the stage must become still that words might keep all their vividness – and I wanted vivid words. ('An Introduction for my Plays', *Essays and Introductions*, p. 257)

He asserted too that 'I have spent my life in clearing out of my poetry every phrase written for the eye and bringing all back to syntax that is for ear alone.' The prologue to the posthumous *Death of Cuchulain* reiterated the need for 'an audience of fifty or a hundred' – the Old Man, who appeals to 'Mr Yeats's plays' angrily insists:

> I wanted a dance because where there are no words there is less to spoil. Emer must dance, there must be severed heads – I am old, I belong to mythology. . . .

The contradiction between the stillness surrounding the 'vivid words' and the dance is resolved in that most fully integrated form of total theatre, the Japanese Noh. As Artaud was to turn to the Balinese theatre, and Brecht to the Chinese, Yeats, whose experiments in staging and décor had been as *avant garde* as his themes were traditional[2] discovered a form which he afterwards adapted and modified, but which led him to his later and more mature style.

Flash or contact came in the winter of 1913–14, when Yeats shared a small cottage in Ashdown Forest with Ezra Pound. They were close friends; Pound was to be groomsman at Yeats's wedding, their wives were step-sisters.[3] Pound, long a devotee of Eastern lyric, was asked by the widow of the great Oriental scholar, Ernest Fenellosa, who had died in 1908, to edit a group of Noh plays, the court drama of medieval Japan, created by Zeami, a contemporary of Chaucer, for the education of the young warriors, his Ashikaga patrons. Pound, evidently under the influence of Yeats, translated them into Kiltartanese; they abound in such un-Japanese idioms as

There never was anybody heard of Mount Shinobu but had a kindly feeling for it . . . so I may as well be walking along here. . . . I wonder now, would the sea be that way, or the little place Kefu that they say is stuck down against it.

. . . this silky wood with the charms painted it as fine as the web you'd get in the grass cloth of Shinobu, that they's still be selling you in this mountain.

These extracts are from the two opening speeches of *Nishikigi*, one of the plays that most deeply influenced Yeats. The Cuala Press published Pound's translation early in 1916, when the first of Yeats's four Plays for Dancers, *At the Hawk's Well*, was performed. Yeats's introduction of his new 'aristocratic form' was paradoxical: 'I love all arts that can still remind me of their origin among the common people.' In Noh, he was reminded of Irish legends, so that he concluded 'The men who created this convention were more like ourselves than were the Greeks and Romans, more like us than are even Shakespeare and Corneille.' Since by the fusion of poetry, song and dance this art penetrated with the intimacy of a small court group – or a small group round a country fire – it healed the breach between intellect, imagination and will: 'We only believe in those thoughts which have been conceived not in the brain, but the whole body.'

A filter that eliminated the trivial, purity that required a void, ritual devoid of belief, were found by Yeats through the Japanese dancer for whom he composed his first play. Without Ito achievement could not have been won:

> he was able . . . to recede from us into some more powerful life. Because that separation was achieved by human means alone, he receded but to inhabit as it were a deep of the mind. One realized anew at every strangeness that the measure of all arts' greatness can but be in their intimacy. All imaginative art remains at a distance, and this distance, once chosen, must be firmly held against a pushing world. ('Certain Noble Plays of Japan', *Essays and Introductions*, p. 224)

'A deep of the mind' in the Japanese Noh is reached by a discipline of which Ito could not partake; he was not a member of the five families who for 600 years had transmitted the Noh dances, in which the movement is very slow, far slower than the beat of the heart. A spectator at first finds it almost intolerable, but is gradually drawn into the rhythm – the only comparable rhythm known in the West being the muffled drums of some great funeral cortège.

Yeats never saw a Japanese Noh play; he absorbed intuitively those aspects that fed his own desires; and Ito, with aid of the artist Edmund Dulac, transformed Cuchulain to an image of heroic aspiration, staged in the drawing-rooms of Lady Cunard and Lady Islington.

The Noh play is very short, but they are matched together in a sequence. Its foundation is the meditative doctrines of Zen; the concept of Yugen which governs the Noh has been translated 'ideal beauty', or 'mysterious solitude'; it includes an element of the dark or the obscure, as it is found also in western neoplatonism with which Yeats was familiar. In each play two contrasted parts dissolve the pains of desire, of adherence to the world, which in Buddhism is symbolised by the Burning House. The six planes of existence depicted in Noh include that of the Azuras or angry ghosts, which for Yeats were the most significant figures.[4] If the spirit is imprisoned by some earthly attachment, it will return in ghost form to relive the moment of earth-bound desire, and finally may assume a demon form to symbolise its torment.

As in *Nishikigi*, translation to a higher state of being may be achieved through the prayers of another; in this play the prayers of a travelling priest release the ghost of a lover who had wooed un-availingly for a thousand nights by laying charm sticks outside the window where his lady sat weaving the narrow cloth Hoso-nuno, cloth too narrow to cover a woman's breast. Both ghosts appear to the priest first as two villagers, but as the story is told he realises their identity; they lead him to the cave where the lover lies buried and which is transformed into a bridal chamber full of light.

The sacred place, the travelling holy man, the redemption of past sorrow give the form of many Noh plays. The chief dancer or Shitē dominates the scene; the most powerful descriptive passages are sung by the chorus, drawn from master players – not a separate group like the musicians (three drums and a flute) or the clowns (*kyogen*). The action does not traverse an arc of experience in the Aristotelian manner of western drama; it brings together time and eternity, becoming and being, Earth and Heaven, of a drama of recognition and revelation, of epiphany. It is parallel in form to the Stuart court masque, or to the last plays of Shakespeare. A long past history is summarised in the supreme moment.

The Shitē is masked; the five families, who perform the Noh, treasure many beautiful ancient masks, as well as garments of court brocade, the gifts of former emperors, ancestral fans each designed for a particular part. The actors, who are all male, are trained from the age of four or five in one particular type of part only. The ascetic discipline of this life is maintained unchanged after 600 years; and the traditional form of the stage itself – which strangely resembles an

Elizabethan stage with its 'heavens' and its 'lord's room' – is unchanged likewise.

'Knowledge cannot be attained; it can only be embodied,' Yeats said later. The language of Noh is rhythmic and repetitive; many phrases are jewels lifted from other poets; but Noh performance does not neglect the effect of shock. The cedar-wood stage responds to a stamp, action in interspersed with sudden sharp cries, the musicians may release a sustained note with a drum tap and a sharp dropping sound that comes to the western ear like 'Yok!', whilst the slow entry down the 'flowery path' of the Shitē may be greeted by cries from the audience of 'Great hero!', or the like.

But the final effect is tranquillity. *Yoroboshi* is *kyoran-mono* – a 'madman's piece' (unknown to Yeats) where the Shitē plays a boy who, banished from home on the false accusation of his stepmother, has wept himself blind. His repentent father, seeking his son, is distributing alms in the temple grounds at Naniwa (the old name of Osaka) where the boy is begging, and sensitively responding to the plum blossom that drops on his outstretched sleeves. His father recognises him, but withholds reunion till nightfall. In the hour of sunset contemplation the stumbling boy reaches so clear a vision of the lovely scene that his sight seems restored; yet when he moves, he stumbles pitiably again. The Chorus chant the vision:

> In the sunset contemplation
> All, all stands bright and clear:
> Awaji, Ejima, Suma, Akashi,
> The sea of Kii drifts into view.
> All, all in vision comes,
> The beauty of the worldly scene
> Nothing of existence has
> Beyond the frontiers of the mind.
>
> *Shitē*: Everything I see,
> Everything so bright and clear.
> (*Japanese Noh Drama*, Nippon
> Gakujutsu Shinkokai (1960),
> vol. III, 110)

Finally, his father leads him away.

The transience of illumination is the theme of *At the Hawk's Well*, which is far closer to Noh than any of Yeats's later plays, and under the title *Taka no ido* adapted for the Japanese stage by Yokomichi to be performed in Tokyo in 1929.[5] In Yeats's play, all the main characters were masked, or made up to resemble masks; Dulac also invented a ceremony of unfolding and folding a piece of cloth to open and close the play, during which the musicians play and sing.

The Hawk's Well lies near Sligo, Yeats's boyhood home; its waters, though at the summit of a craggy rock, mysteriously rise and fall with the tides of Sligo Bay. To this 'aery spot' comes the young warrior, who has crossed the sea under 'a lucky sail' in search of the water of immortality. An Old Man, who has spent all his life waiting for the momentary plash of the magic water, is seated by a girl, the Well's guardian. Caught by the dance of the Hawk Goddess, who has entered the body of the girl, Cuchulain is cheated of his chance; the Old Man sleeps. The goddess has roused the 'wild women of the hills' against Cuchulain, but he, who has sought immortality through conquering her in love, shoulders his spear, and with the proud cry 'he comes! Cuchulain, son of Sualtim, comeś!' he goes to conquer Aoife the Queen-mother of his unborn son – whose death at his father's hand Yeats had shown in an early play, *On Baile's Strand*.

The epiphany of this play reveals the agony of frustrated desire, the pride of Lucifer in the hawk, and the naked clash of Life and Death – death remaining the price for immortality. There is no Buddhist doctrine here; rather Marlowe's line come to mind: 'That like I best that flies beyond my reach.'

The trance of the Guardian, of Cuchulain, and of the Old Man brings the moment of revelation, which is the dance. One of Yeats's best-known sayings from 'The Tragic Theatre' is 'Tragedy must always be a drowner of the dykes that separate man from man and . . . it is upon these dykes that comedy builds her house' (*Essays and Introductions*, p. 241).

Yeats was deeply experienced in trance. The 'secret society' that would furnish his ideal audience would replace for him the Order of the Golden Dawn, into which he had been inducted as early as 7 March 1890, and of which for some years he was Imperator.[6] The Order was in part Rosicrucian; but if he tested philosophy by poetry and not vice versa, Yeats required some basis, which he found in the ancient East, which would enable to 'keep that distance against a pushing world', and would give him a religion of ritual. The object of the Order was 'to obtain control of the nature and power of my own being'. His name within the Order was 'Demon est Deus Inversus' – truth and counter-truth must be held together. As the Order had survived till the First World War, Yeats lost this inner circle at the same time that he lost his total commitment to the Irish National Theatre; he wrote to Sturge Moore in 1929 that his work was not drama but the ritual of a lost faith.[7] Noh supplied this ritual; he treated it with the freedom that he had earlier applied to Indian thought.

The Tarot pack of cards supplied many symbols, and was used in the ritual of the Golden Dawn. The wandering Fool, the Tower and the Burning House belong to the Tarot. The hawk-headed goddess is Egyptian.

> The masks of tragedy contain neither character nor personal energy. They are allied to decoration and the abstract figures of Egyptian temples. Before the mind can look out of their eyes, the active will perishes.

Yeats told Sturge Moore the Hawk was one of his symbols; his adaptation of the Noh fused his secret knowledge with the still continuing struggle of his despairing love for Maud Gonne McBride, whose bronze-painted effigy years later took on for him the form of the Hawk:

> Here, at the right hand of the entrance, this bronze head
> Human, superhuman, a bird's round eye,
> Everything else withered and mummy-dead. . . .
>
> I thought her supernatural;
> As though a sterner eye looked through her eye
> On this foul world in its decline and fall . . .
> ('The Statues', Last Poems)

She had taken all his youth 'with scarce a pitying look' to serve her political ends. The harshness of this sacrifice is concentrated in the final ironies of the chorus for *At the Hawk's Well*:

> 'The man that I praise'
> Cries out the empty well
> 'Lives all his days
> Where a hand on the bell
> Can call the milch cows
> To the comfortable door of his house.
> Who but an idiot would praise
> An empty well?'
>
> 'The man that I praise'
> Cries out the leafless tree
> 'Has married and stays
> By an old hearth and he
> On naught has set store
> But children and dogs on the floor.
> Who but an idiot would praise
> A withered tree?'

The empty well, the withered tree, were to become the landscape of other plays – of Yeats and of Beckett; it was not neutral like the cedar-wood stage of the Noh with its single painted pine tree, its

Tsukurimono, or skeletal boat, coach, temple bell, house, well, rock, tomb. Yeats was writing of emptiness of spirit; as the good pagan he could neither give himself to Maud Gonne's cause nor escape from the world of the action. Tragedy showed 'character isolated by a deed'; it is 'character in action; a pause in the midst of action perhaps, but action always its end and theme.'

Drama remained for Yeats the contact between action and meditation; in drama, action encloses a space where finally words cease. Arthur Symons had seen the whole world as ballet; the core of drama, mime. For the Noh dancer too, the supreme moment comes in a pause, the foot sliding forward very slowly and lifting:

> Sometimes spectators of the Noh say that the moments of 'no-action' are the most enjoyable. This is one of the actor's secret arts. . . . When we are examined why such moments without action are enjoyable, we find it is due to the underlying spiritual strength of the actor which unremittingly holds the attention. He does not relax the tension . . . but maintains an unwavering inner strength. This feeling of inner strength will dimly reveal itself. . . . The actions before and after an interval of 'no-action' must be linked by entering the state of mindlessness in which the actor conceals even from himself his own intent . . . If it is seen, it is just as if a marionette's strings were visible. (Zeami (1363–1443), trans. Ryusaku Tsunoda and Donald Keene, *Anthology of Japanese Literature,* 1 (1956), 258–9)

The moment of silence for the poet is the equivalent of the moment of 'no-action' for the dancer, marking transformation from Becoming to Being, from the natural to the supernatural.

Less than a month after the first performance of *At the Hawk's Well,* the Easter Rising changed the course of Irish history, ennobled the common people with a new legend, widowed Maud Gonne McBride. It is the theme of Yeats's next play, *The Dreaming of the Bones,* a strange response to the violence. 'It is strong, too strong, politically,' he told Lady Gregory. The fighting in the Post Office is brought into touch with the love story of Dermot and Dervorgilla, whose guilty love first drew the Normans into Ireland.

A young fugitive from the Dublin fighting, seeking the Aran islands, appears in that most desolate landscape, the Burren in County Clare. An upland of basalt slabs, scarred and channelled, but almost as arid as the surface of the moon. In the dark, the young soldier meets a masked stranger and a young girl who guide him through the night to the ruined abbey of Corcomroe. They tell of the ghosts who haunt this place – among the accursed pair, who are kept apart by the curse even in death so that their lips may never meet. He passionately declares that Dermot and Dervorgilla shall never be forgiven; and as they dance, and fade in the dawn, realises who his guides have been.

The lovers are condemned; yet they recall both Dante's Paolo and Francesca, with the tale told by Lady Gregory of the ghosts of two peasant lovers who came to the priest to be married. They contrast most poignantly with *Takasago*, a play in which two old peasants who appear to a traveller are shown to be the spirits of two wedded pine trees; the old man has come to visit his wife and is later revealed as the Deity of the Sumiyoshi Shrine; for trees and plants, though not endowed with soul, in this auspicious reign

> Jewelled words, like glistening dew drops
> Light up our people's minds
> Awakening in all living beings
> The love of poetry . . .
> Herb or tree
> Earth or sand,
> Sough of wind and roar of waters,
> Each encloses in itself the universe:
> Spring forests stirring in the east wind,
> Autumn insects chirping in the dewy grass
> Are they not each a poem?
>   (*Japanese Noh Drama*, vol. I 11–12)

The desolate landscape of the Burren is shown in the opening chorus of *The Dreaming of the Bones*:

> Many a night it seems
> That all the valley fills,
> So passionate is a shade,
> Like wine that fills to the top
> A grey green cup of jade
> Or maybe an agate cup . . .

In the Order of the Golden Dawn every novice had to fashion a sword, which with the Cup, Wand and Pentacle, represent the four elements of air, water, fire and earth. Yeats who later received from a Japanese the gift of a ceremonial sword, used it for meditation. The jade or agate cup of the hills gave its title to the collection of essays where Yeats's study of the Noh appeared. *The Cutting of an Agate* represents the hardest of stones, and a few years later Yeats was to write of Dante:

> He set his chisel to the hardest stone.
> Being mocked by Guido for his lecherous life,

> Derided and deriding, driven out
> To climb that stair and eat that bitter bread,
> He found the unpersuadable justice, he found
> The most exalted lady loved by a man.
> ('Ego Dominus tuus', *The Wild Swans at Coole*)

Dante, 'the supreme imagination of Christendom', left a 'spectral image', and in this little play with its distanced echoes of the recent fighting, so strange in an Irishman – and so incompatible with the Noh, which throws all action into the heroic past – Yeats has also left the ghost of the love which had troubled him so long. His deeper self is with the guilty lovers. From the anguish of Diarmuid and Dervorgilla, a tragic joy still flashes, in the moment of recognition

> *Young girl:*   Seven hundred years our lips have never met.
> *Young man:*   Why do you look so strangely at one another,
> So strangely and so sweetly? all the ruin,
> All, all their handiwork is blown away
> As though the mountain air had blown it away,
> Because their eyes have met. They cannot hear,
> Being folded up and hidden in their dance.

The invasion of the present by the past became for Yeats the central transformation of his drama; it was the form in which the supernatural manifested itself. In this play the young man does not fear ghosts because they cannot stand him against the wall and shoot him; but for Yeats the presence of the ghosts was part of the conflict. The last song in his last play ends with questions:

> Are those things men adore and loathe
> Their sole reality?
> What stood in the Post Office
> With Pearse and Connolly? . . .
> Who thought Cuchulain till it seemed
> He stood where they had stood?
> (*The Death of Cuchulain*)

As Yeats evolved his own form, the later *Plays for Dancers* moved still farther from the Noh in form, but in two of his greatest, which are not written for dancers, the form of the Noh that unites the natural and supernatural worlds is more strongly presented in terms of the Irish mythology that Yeats evolved for himself, a highly eclectic one that included revolutionary figures, the heroes of the Protestant Ascendancy, especially the quartet of Swift, Burke, Berkeley and Goldsmith, and the friends of his youth – finally his own image – 'I am old, I belong to mythology' – as he looked on his lifework.

Two brief plays, one in prose, *The Words upon the Window Pane* (1930), and one in verse, *Purgatory* (1939), reanimate a tragic past in a squalid present that mirrors the bitterness of Yeats towards much in the new Ireland.

The demonic form of Jonathan Swift (demon est deus inversus) is at last seen by the ignorant Medium into whose seance his voice had burst with bitter refusal of Vanessa's love because 'I have something in my blood which no child must inherit', and as the sceptical young student eagerly suggests because Swift, 'the chief representative of the intellect of his epoch', foresaw its collapse. 'He foresaw Democracy, he must have dreaded the future.' As she is left alone, the Medium is invaded once more by the Old Man, with dirty clothes, and face covered with boils, the mad Swift of his last days.

> Where did I put that tea caddy? Ah! there it is. And there should be a cup and saucer. But where's the cup? (She moves aimlessly about the stage, and then, letting the saucer fall and break, speaks in Swift's voice) Perish the day on which I was born!

With this cry from Job, Swift (who, according to the most learned member of the seance, is in Purgatory) responds to the tender words of Stella's birthday poem, written upon the window-pane of the room.

The play named *Purgatory*, written in the last year of Yeats's life, is about the length of a Noh play. Its scene is 'A ruined house, and a bare tree in the background'. The ruined heir, now an old pedlar, waits with his bastard son under the tree once covered with 'green leaves, ripe leaves, thick as butter' for the apparition of his mother. Born of a noble house, she had married a handsome, drunken groom, who squandered the inheritance, as the Old Man tells his son:

> He killed the house: to kill a house
> Where great men grew up, married, died,
> I here declare a capital offence.

The Burning House, ancient symbol from the Tarot of immoderate desire, is also ancestral Ireland; and Castle Hackett, which though ruined might be 'suddenly lit up / From door to top' as Yeats had many times invoked it. Now, as the hoof-beats sound upon the avenue, the Old Man confesses that sixteen years after his mother had died in giving him birth, his father had burnt down the house in a drunken frenzy and within the burning house he had stabbed his father. But the crime now being enacted is the crime of his begetting, and his mother's remorse creates the dream. The old man turns upon his son and kills him to end the line, and end the curse. It is the decision of Swift in more savage form – 'my father and my son on the same jack-knife'. He sings the lullaby of that builder of a noble past, Scott:

> Hushaby, baby, thy father's a knight,
> Thy mother's a lady, lovely and bright.

As he does so, the house darkens, the tree stands illuminated; but then the hoof-beats sound once more, the woman's spirit remains earthbound; her son ends with a prayer

> O God. . . .
> Mankind can do no more. Appease
> The misery of the living and the remorse of the dead.

The three actors are in the classic Noh tradition; transmuted, it remains in this play of which Eliot was to say it solved the problem of poetic speech in drama. The words, as Yeats had wished, are for the ear alone; the rhythm of the rite is there, but the dancers have gone, and voices alone will suffice. *Purgatory* also gave a form to Samuel Beckett, as well as a landscape. The pride of Lucifer and the naked clash of Life and Death had been once more transposed.

Yeats's part in the Irish Literary Renaissance, according to Philip Edwards,[8] was 'to figure the deceptions we furnish ourselves with to avert knowledge of the nothingness underfoot' – nothing is concluded. The 'figuration' required an alien form, and something like the choristers' theatres of Elizabeth's time, where savage and disjunctive visions of a broken world were embodied in song and dance, by boy actors playing old men.

As Beckett was to turn to French rather than English, so Yeats had turned to a stage tradition ancient and inflexible, authoritarian and serene, unaltered in 600 years.[9] The distance of the Noh liberated the depth of his 'fanatic heart'; it was in the theatre that the greater tragic poet of his later days came into being.

Notes

1 This first appeared in *The Irish Statesman* in 1919, and was an answer to the earlier query 'What is popular theatre?'. It was published in *Explora-*

tions (1962). 'What is popular theatre?', the first essay in *Ideas of Good and Evil* (1896–1903), is reprinted in *Essays and Introductions* (1961).

2 See Karen Dorn, *Players and Painted Stage* (1983). Katherine Worth, *The Irish Drama of Europe from Yeats to Beckett* (1978) is more literary in approach.

3 Mrs Pound was the daughter and Mrs Yeats the step-daughter of Olivia Shakespear, the second of Yeats's loves.

4 The three volumes of translation by members of the Nippon Gakujutsu Shinkōkai (*The Japanese Society for the Promotion of Scientific Research*) Tokyo which gave the best introduction to Noh for the Westerner, are unfortunately almost unknown and unprocurable. Hiro Ishibashi, *Yeats and the Noh* (Dolmen Press, 1966) gives a brief survey with illustrations. Shotoro Oshima, of Wasada University, the chief Japanese authority on Yeats, wrote several books on him, including *W. B. Yeats and Japan*, (Tokyo, 1965); he also translated the poems of Yeats into Japanese.

5 The Old Man becomes a ghost, and the Shitē or chief role; the Hawk is part of his dream; Cuchulain wakens from his dream resigned, and his one line in Part II is 'the traveller is awakened from his dream'.

6 See Kathleen Raine, *Yeats, the Tarot and the Golden Dawn* (Dolmen Press, 1972, illustrated). Ellic Howe has also written on this subject, see p. 159 note 16.

7 See *W. B. Yeats and Sturge Moore, their Correspondence 1901–1937* (1953), 156. Sturge Moore made many designs for Yeats's later books.

8 See Philip Edwards, *Threshold of a Nation* (1979), p. 241.

9 Eliot likewise turned to late medieval drama for his first and most successful play, *Murder in the Cathedral*.

XIV.

Beckett, *En Attendant Godot*

'It invents a new form of dramatic expression,' observed Guichar-
naud of *En Attendant Godot*, first staged at the Théâtre de Babylone
in Paris on 5 January 1953; 'in fact, it seems like the end of a long
search.' At this distance of time, it is plain that here was a turning-
point in the theatre comparable with the first performance of *A
Doll's House* in 1879. The first French audience might stage a riot,
the English producer feel that he did not understand the script but
must start rehearsing. All were exhilarated, bewildered, captivated.
Younger playwrights learnt their trade from this one play, and in
its light the work of Beckett's contemporaries became more
intelligible.[1]

When Harold Hobson told Beckett that all London was debating
the meaning of his play, the author quickly replied 'I take no sides
about that.' In his early essay on Proust, the young Beckett repudi-
ated 'the grotesque fallacy of realistic art – 'that miserable statement
of line and surface' – and the penny-a-line vulgarity of a literature of
notations.[2]

An open myth, adaptable and flexible 'is not about something; *it is
that something itself.*'[3] It builds cohesion between man and that
'total object with missing parts' that may be termed his world.
Indefinite menace replaces the traditional conflicts of creeds, environment, events; Beckett makes a drama by leaving out conventional fillings ('there is no communication because there are no
vehicles of communication') yet response has preceded interpretation. To experience the play, to go through with it, exposes the
audience at the very least to an absence of the irrelevant.

It is not too difficult – though now becoming rather difficult – to
shock an audience. But to recharge the energies of separate individual minds in different ways is rare. Bewilderment and attraction

stirred up in the audience by *En Attendant Godot* show that this occurred.

A communal celebration of solitude, an intense inner activity based on the absence of external action might be either tragic or comic; the French version is nearer to tragedy, the Anglo-Irish to comedy. Actual presentation can vary, since statement is stripped down to its barest essentials. Yet shape, dialogue and sub-text are closely woven together. Images, which elsewhere in Beckett's work are fragmented, play on each other; an abundance of direct literary echoes witness to the magnetic power of the initiating forces within the poet's own psyche.

Act I.   Route à la campagne, avec arbre.
         Soir.
Act II. Lendemain. Même heure. Même endroit.

On a bare plateau, two companions, Vladimir and Estragon, wait for the mysterious Godot. We learn in the final sequence that Godot will punish them if they go. If he comes, they will be saved. The two companions, with nothing to do but wait, have nothing to amuse themselves with but their own wits, nothing to eat but a few roots, and the bones thrown from the supper of a rich passer-by, Pozzo, who enters with his slave Lucky, on the way to sell him at the fair of Saint-Sauveur.

In this barren scene Beckett embodies the existentialist anguish of life itself – the sin of having been born.[4] When Vladimir the thinker suggests they should repent, this is all that Estragon the poet can recall to be repented. Compared with the literature *engagée* of some of Beckett's French contemporaries, the play is uncommitted, but it shares with them the experience of *le néant*.

Aspects of Beckett's life would confirm this detachment. A Dubliner by birth, a student at Trinity College, Dublin, with A. A. Luce, the editor of *Berkeley* for tutor, he briefly taught languages there, but afterwards took to a literary life in London, Paris – where he met James Joyce and became his translator – and in Germany. With one exception (the radio play *All That Fall*) Beckett's later works, whether plays, novels, scripts for film or radio, grow increasingly withdrawn, set in that half-world which he defined in a poem written in the same year as *En Attendant Godot*.

> . . . what would I do without this silence where the murmurs die
> the pantings the frenzies towards succour towards love
> without this sky that soars
> above its ballast dust

what would I do what I did yesterday and the day before
peering out of my deadlight looking for another
wandering like me eddying far from all the living
in a convulsive space
among the voices voiceless
that throng my hiddenness.[5]

In avoiding reductive interpretations, it is not necessary to keep to such high generalities as Anouilh's observation that he had seen the *Pensées* of Pascal played by the Fratellini clowns (Beckett described himself as not gifted in philosophy). Any great play will be in one sense a history play, since the historic root constitutes a necessary part of any social art involving performance. Of course, any attempt to *explain* the work in terms of external events would destroy the elasticity of the open myth; but equally, the cohesive power of drama depends on some common assumptions, deriving ultimately from common experience.

By surviving, drama changes, outliving its origins and perhaps even the memory of those origins; nor does the artist himself directly recall its basis. Beckett has said, 'Voluntary memory is of no value as an instrument of evocation . . . We can remember only what has been registered by our extreme inattention and stored in that ultimate and inaccessible dungeon of our being to which Habit does not possess the key.'[6]

Certain facts are not in dispute. Between 1946 and 1950, in Beckett's great burst of creative activity, he took to composing in French, and besides *En Attendant Godot*, wrote poems, his trilogy of novels and other works that remain unpublished. *An Attendant Godot* erupted suddenly in the autumn of 1948, while he was engaged on the trilogy, demanding as it were to be set down. In 1956 he said that nothing written since 1950 seemed to him valid; since then his dwindling dramas and brief sketches (one play lasts about a minute and consists of a single cry twice repeated) are significant because they are by the author of *En Attendant Godot*. Beckett said of the painter Bram Van Valde, 'To be an artist is to fail, as no other dare fail, that failure is his world and the shrink from it desertion, art and craft, good housekeeping, living. No, No, permit me to expire.'[7]

Although he would keep an even more complete silence about those years, Beckett's identification with France in the 1940s made French his first language, the language of collective experience. He had been living in Paris since 1937, and returned there from Ireland on the outbreak of war. 'Je suis immédiatement retourné en France. Je préférais la France en guerre à l'Irlande en paix.'[8] Being Irish he was not politically implicated, but after the Occupation he joined the

Resistance, thereby becoming an exile at two removes, acting against
the official regime of his country of exile. During 1941 he served as
secretary and post office for a group of workers in Paris; in 1942,
escaping by moments from a visit of the Gestapo, he fled to unoccu-
pied France, where in the Vaucluse near Apt, at Roussillon, he
worked on the land. Subsequently he received the highest French
non-combatant award for his services.

In the play, one reference distinguishes the scene from Beckett's
refuge, but establishes a connection. Vladimir the thinker observes
that they are not in the Vaucluse, the mere reference to which cause
Estragon the poet to explode in protest. Who's speaking about it? he
asks. But you have been there, Vladimir reminds him.

> Estragon: Mais non, je n'ai jamais été dans le Vaucluse! J'ai coulé toute
>   ma chaude-pisse d'existence ici, je te dis! Ici! Dans le Merde-
>   cluse!
> Vladimir: Pourtant nous avons été ensemble dans le Vaudecluse, j'en
>   mettrais ma main au feu. Nous avons fait les vendanges, tiens,
>   chez un nommé Bonnelly, à Roussillon.
> Estragon: C'est possible. Je n'ai rien remarqué.[9]

The poet does not remember, but the thinker does. In the Anglo-Irish
version Vladimir too has forgotten the place-names.

Another thinker, Wittgenstein, ended his *Tractatus Logico-
Philosophicus*: 'Whereof one cannot speak, thereof one must be
silent.' Or as Beckett said elsewhere, quoting from Tommy Hand-
ley's wartime clown show, which he may have heard on the BBC, 'Do
not come down the ladder, I have just taken it away.'

By 1948, Beckett had experienced the period of deadness and
exhaustion that succeeded the war, the humiliations of peace so-
called, the exploitation of the past. Early in Act 2, Estragon has a
vision of being approached from all directions at once – Vladimir
thinks at first that Godot has come, secondly that they are being
rounded up ('Nous sommes cernés') but Estragon in great excitement
makes him take up a position of defence 'Dos à dos, comme au bon
vieux temps!'[10]

> The identification of immediate with past experience, the recurrence of
> past action or reaction in the present, amounts to a participation between
> the ideal and the real, imagination and direct apprehension ... such
> participation frees the essential reality that is denied to the contemplative
> as to the active life. What is common to present and past is at once
> imaginative and empirical, at once evocative and direct perception.[11]

It is less through matters of detail than through the general structure that Beckett evokes long periods of waiting at some imperfectly identified rendez-vous, where men dressed as tramps, each concealed under an alias, perhaps unknown even to each other, would come together. Constant deferments, obscure promises, ignorance of events occluded the men and women, youths and girls who passed on information they did not understand, carried out sybilline injunctions, and yet attempted in this featureless no-man's-land to remain human beings.

> Ce n'est pas tous les jours qu'on a besoin de nous. Non pas à vrai dire qu'on ait précisément besoin de nous. D'autres feraient aussi bien l'affaire, sinon mieux. L'appel que nous venons d'entendre, c'est plutôt à l'humanité tout entière qu'il s'adresse. Mais à cet endroit, en ce moment, l'humanité c'est nous, que ça nous plaise ou non.[12]

The absurd appeal for help to which this is a grandiloquent response, does not prevent Vladimir making his point – the free and gratuitous nature of his involvement

> Nous sommes au rendez-vous, un point c'est tout, Nous ne sommes pas des saints, mais nous sommes au rendez-vous. Combien de gens peuvent en dire autant?
>
> *Estragon:* Des masses.
> *Vladimir:* Tu crois?
> *Estragon:* Je ne sais pas.
> *Vladimir:* C'est possible.
> Pozzo: Au secours![13]

The instant deflation of any heroic gesture is really more like assurance than precaution. It is obligatory at any crisis. (King Lear's tragic statements are thrown into relief by the savage parody of his devoted Fool.)

Vladimir opens the second Act by singing a round about a dog that might well belong to a Fool – it occurs in other works by Beckett, including the novel *Watt*, which he wrote in the Vaucluse. Beaten to death for stealing a scrap of meat, the dog is buried by other dogs under a soldier's cross of wood.[14]

> Les autres chiens le voyant
> Vite vite l'ensevelirent
> Au pied d'une croix en bois blanc
> Où le passant pouvait lire
>
> Un chien vint dans l'office
> Et prit une andouillette
> Alors à coups de louche
> Le chef le mit en miettes.[15]

The sequence of dog-thief-crucifixion forms an image cluster, almost in the Shakespearean manner.[16] Since man lives at the animal level in this play, no brutes are introduced; it is man who freely sweats, urinates, belches, farts, sleeps, bleeds and suppurates. He gnaws bones, carrots and radishes. He sings, runs, dances and kicks. Smell, the most animal of the senses, is frequently invoked.

Humiliated, helpless – the Gestapo used to devise very simple humiliations like removing buttons, braces and dentures from their prisoners – the two clowns remain at their rendez-vous in a timeless void. It is in the second Act, when the pattern repeats itself with variations, that the reflection of history can be felt. Estragon soon joins Vladimir. As usual, he has been beaten up in the night by ten men, although he wasn't doing anything. In the French he repeats that they were ten. In the Anglo-Irish he repeats that he wasn't doing anything.

Between the first and second Acts the single tree, a willow that had shed its leaves, has put forth foliage (in the French version it is covered with leaves, in the Anglo-Irish version there are only a few). When Estragon had first seen its bare boughs his comment had been, 'Finis les pleurs!' Now the two companions move into the most powerfully orchestrated lyric sequence of the play, the threnody of the leaves, the lament for the dead. They talk in order to escape thinking, and in order to escape the voices of the dead, the 'voices voiceless'.

Vladimir:	Ça fait un bruit d'ailes.
Estragon:	De feuilles.
Vladimir:	De sable.
Estragon:	De feuilles. (*Silence*)
Vladimir:	Elles parlent toutes en même temps.
Estragon:	Chacune à part soi. (*Silence*)
Vladimir:	Plutôt elles chuchotent.
Estragon:	Elles murmurent.
Vladimir:	Elles bruissent.
Estragon:	Elles murmurent. (*Silence*)
Vladimir:	Que disent-elles?
Estragon:	Elles parlent de leur vie.
Vladimir:	Il ne leur suffit pas d'avoir vécu.
Estragon:	Il faut qu'elles en parlent.
Vladimir:	Il ne leur suffit pas d'être mortes.
Estragon:	Ce n'est pas assez. (*Silence*)
Vladimir:	Ça fait comme un bruit de plumes.
Estragon:	De feuilles.
Vladimir:	De cendres.
Estragon:	De feuilles. (*Long silence*)[17]

Vladimir senses the soul (*ailes: plumes*) and the body (*sable: cendres*) falling apart, Estragon feels only the continuity of the tree's life. At the end, they recognise that the voiceless voices alone can be said to live 'Seule, l'arbre vit.'[18] And so they prepare to hang themselves — another comedy turn of the old team, deflating the poetry. 'On se pendra demain. (*Un temps*). À moins que Godot ne vienne.'[19]

Direct recording of experience, when it is experience of extremity, of man at the edge of his being, is not possible. Sartre refused to release the play he wrote as a prisoner-of-war for his fellow-prisoners because it belonged only to that time and place — although later he wrote *Morts Sans Sépultures*. A direct conventional collection of tales, such as Elsa Troilet's *Le Premier Accroc Coûte Deux Cents Francs* may attempt to convey the hazards of rendez-vous, the bewilderment and sense of anti-climax when waiting gave way to action, the interminable waiting itself. But only by transmuting into an imaginative form what has been lived apart, only by uniting the living and the dead tree, can the poet communicate to those who have not shared his experience. Only so, can he recover it for himself, as an involuntary memory.

René Char, a leader of the Maquis in his native Provence, and a surréalist poet, kept a diary during 1943–4, which was published as *Feuilles d'Hypnos* (his name among the Maquis): Char said that he had only skimmed, not re-read it, for the notes belonged to no one — a signal fire of dry grass could have been their author.[20]

> If I survive, I know that I shall have to break with the aroma of these essential years, so concentrated; throw away — not repress — my treasure in deep silence, far from myself, take myself back to the beginning, bearing myself towards the world like a beggar, as in those times when I sought myself without ever attaining power, in naked want, barely glimpsed encounter, humble questing (No. 195).

A few of the *Feuilles d'Hypnos* (not those dealing with events of horror or heroism) may serve as footnotes to Act 2 of *En Attendant Godot.*

> Les enfants s'ennuient le dimanche. Passereau propose une semaine de vingt-quatre jours pour dépecer le dimanche. Soit une heure de dimanche s'ajoutant à chaque jour, de préférence l'heure des repas, puisqu'il n'y a plus de pain sec.
> Mais qu'on ne lui parle plus de dimanche. (No. 15)

> L'intelligence avec l'ange, notre primordial souci. (Ange, ce qui, à l'intérieur de l'homme, tient à l'écart du compromis religieux, la parole du plus haut silence, la signification qui ne s'évalue pas. . . .) (No. 16)

L'avion déboule. Les pilotes invisibles se délestent de leur jardin nocturne puis pressent un feu bref sous l'aisselle de l'appareil pour avertir que c'est fini. Il ne reste plus qu'à rassembler le trésor éparpillé. De même le poète. . . . (No. 97)

'Le voilà!' Il est deux heures du matin. L'avion a vu nos signaux et réduit son altitude. La brise ne gênera pas la descente en parachute du visiteur que nous attendons. La lune est d'étain vif et de sauge. 'L'école des poètes du tympan', chuchote Léon qui a toujours le mot de la situation. (No. 148)

Fidèles et démesurément vulnérables, nous opposons la conscience de l'événement au gratuit (encore un mot de déféqué). (No. 164)

Beckett has transmuted whatever of this kind formed the play, and he has united it with much from the conventional repertoire of stage clowns. If he left out a great deal of commonly expected filling material, the pace, rhythms, timing, jokes, all belong to the live theatre. Nothing may happen, but as an actor-critic observed, it happens very fast.

The clowns have aliases. Vladimir, a Slav name, and Estragon (he was originally given a Jewish name, Lévy) are not used at all: Didi and Gogo, the childish names they use, are said to be Chinese for Big Brother and Little Brother. The messenger addresses Vladimir as M. Albert; in one draft Estragon calls himself Macgregor, André; in the American text he is Adam; in the French and English, Catullus.

Pozzo is Italian for 'a well'; the Dantesque hint of an inferno is worth following. At first he is mistaken for Godot – which incenses him – but as Pozzo he could be god of the underworld – Pluto, god of riches, Dis, god of death. In the chthonic depth he finally discloses the identity of life and death: in the novel *The Unnameable*, the Voice asks 'Are there other pits, deeper down? to which one accedes by mine? Stupid obsession with depth.' However, on his second entry when he is blind and falls down, Pozzo is greeted as if he had fallen from the sky. 'Reinforcements!' cries Vladimir. 'Ça tombe à pic. Enfin du renfort!'[21] As he does not – after a certain amount of ill-treatment – reply to his name, Estragon addresses him as Abel. He replies with cries for help. Thinking therefore Lucky must be Cain, Estragon calls, but Pozzo replies again. Looking up to Heaven and seeing a small white cloud, Estragon concludes he is 'toute l'humanité'. When both join him on the ground they define themselves – 'Nous sommes des hommes'. But with some doubt, the second couple are described to the messenger as 'deux autres . . . hommes'.

Lucky is addressed always with animal epithets and encouraged with horse or dog language. In a grandiloquent moment Pozzo ironically terms him 'Atlas, fils de Jupiter'. The human race, especially himself, is of divine origin in Act 1; but then Act 1 is filled with lengthy discussions of God and Godot. In Act 2, Godot is referred to briefly, taken for granted. Godot's messengers – one tends sheep, the other goats – show some human timidity as distinct from panic; they are respectful but anxious to get away. The second messenger describes Godot with the traditional white beard which Lucky in his 'think' has ascribed to God the Father; Beckett, when asked 'Who or what is Godot?' replied 'If I knew, I would have said so in the play.'[22]

In the first production Pozzo wore a white beard, but this was not continued. The companions were dressed as clowns in France, as tramps – in the Chaplin style – in England. In the MS. Pozzo and Lucky are termed 'the very big one' and 'the little one'; in the first text they are 'les comiques staliniens'.

All four are old men although they act like babies and use baby-language at times. They are also learned – 'On n'est pas des cariatides,' exclaims the poet at one point, whereupon the thinker bursts into Latin.

Clowns always work in pairs, or the chief clown uses some kind of 'Double' to converse with.[23] They are intensely active without getting anywhere, or in doing the wrong things with pots of paint, or strings of balloons. The two companions use theatrical clowns' regular tricks, such as swapping hats, losing their trousers, arranging to hang themselves. They are allowed to recognise the audience and engage them in talk; they gaze into the auditorium with rapture ('Endroit délicieux! prospects riants!') or with horror. Vladimir, rushing off to relieve himself, is directed 'Au fond du couloir, en gauche' and replies 'Garde ma place!' The promise to be back again tomorrow can also mean 'The show will go on.'

Their dialogue is springy, gay, closely integrated; the brief speeches interlock, as if their minds overlapped. They are endlessly inventive ('nous sommes intarrissables'); their repetitions, rephrasings and inversions involve the spectator in a ballet of words, which replaces action. For example the first repetition is '*Vladimir:* Tu as mal?' To which, the indignant retort 'Mal! Il me demande si j'ai mal!' provokes Vladimir with equal indignation to recall his own past sufferings. Estragon responds '"Tu as eu mal?" *Vladimir:* Mal! Il me demande si j'ai eu mal!' Little brother's admonition, 'Ce n'est pas une raison pour ne pas te boutonner' calls up a dignified cliché – 'C'est vrai. Pas de laisser-aller dans les petites choses.'[24]

They are playing a game of words – when Estragon proves unresponsive to Vladimir's theological riddle, he cries impatiently 'Voyons, Gogo, il faut me renvoyer la balle de temps en temps.'[25]

They play at abusing each other (in the Anglo-Irish version, the final insult is Critic! in the French it is not specified but in one version it was Architect!), at being very polite to each other, at doing exercises, or being trees, at being Pozzo and Lucky.

Lucky's long 'think' is a word-game he plays with himself, a parody of a medieval theological disputation.[26] With its repeated 'mais n'anticipons' and 'je reprends', it appeals to the word-game as a most powerful defence against the decay of man — which happens 'malgré le tennis'. As Lucky's game gets faster and faster, 'malgré le tennis' bounces back again and again, and erupts among his final shouts before he is overpowered by the efforts of all the rest.[27]

In Beckett's translation the clowns talk in Irish idiom. (Ah, stop blathering and help me off with this bloody thing.) They have distinct characters, in spite of the formal pattern of their speech. Vladimir is protective, thoughtful, capable of remembering and generalising; Estragon is impulsive, vague, dependent. Vladimir is waiting for Godot, while Estragon is waiting for death. They are bound together as members of a family are bound, by habit grown into necessity; someone has spoken of their 'marital bickering'. The term 'pseudo-couple' which Beckett coined for the earlier pair Mercier and Camier, would not apply to these two; compared with the immobile Hamm, or the entombed characters of the later plays, they enjoy a full existence. Vladimir croons a lullaby to Estragon who can scream, punch and kick his enemies when they are down or ask Vladimir to smash Pozzo's jaw.

They can leap easily from theological heights to scatological depths, with the weightlessness of those inhabiting a vacuum. The opening lines sound heroic, but their immediate meaning is to record Vladimir's daily struggle with his bladder — 'et je reprenais le combat.' There is no need to exclude either the one meaning or the other. A quotation from *Proverbs* 'Hope deferred maketh the something sick, who said that?' replaces a French *bon mot* 'Le dernier moment . . . c'est long, mais ce sera bon', and again refers to Vladimir's difficulty with his bladder.[28]

Estragon can't remember if he has ever read the Bible — but at another point he compares himself with Jesus, and says he has done so all his life (and 'in Palestine they crucified quickly'). He cannot believe that Vladimir does not want to hear his dream or that he is satisfied with the daily world they see — 'Celui-ci te suffit?' he asks incredulously.

The climax of the play comes when Pozzo succeeds in communicating fully to Vladimir his blind man's vision of the pit of life and death, in another attempt to 'satisfy' the thinker.

Un jour nous sommes nés, un jour nous mourrons, le même jour, le même instant, ça ne vous suffit pas? Elles accouchent à cheval sur une tombe, le jour brille un instant, puis c'est la nuit à nouveau.[29]

Estragon tells him that what he has been thinking about Pozzo is only a dream.

> *Vladimir:*   Est-ce que j'ai dormi, pendant que les autres souffraient? . . .
> À cheval sur une tombe, et une naissance difficile. Du fond du trou, rêveusement, le fossoyeur applique ses fers . . . L'air est plein de nos cris. Mais l'habitude est une grande sourdine. Moi aussi, un autre me regarde, en se disant, Il dort, il ne sait pas, qu'il dorme. Je ne peux pas continuer. (*Un temps*). Qu'est-ce que j'ai dit?[30]

Vladimir's remorse – perhaps he has slept while others suffered – here echoes Lucky's 'think' about a God Who is above suffering yet will 'souffre à l'instar de la divine Miranda avec ceux qui sont on ne sait pourquoi mais on a le temps dans le tourment'.[31] The reference is to Miranda's opening words in *The Tempest*: 'Oh, I have suffered / With those that I saw suffer' (I ii, 5–6). God can see all suffering, but man may attain the greater compassion of suffering with those he does *not* see.[32]

Vladimir once more hears the cries of the dead upon the air. He keeps the hope that in turn there is someone who sees him, in the sleep of life.

This is the cue for the messenger, who this time appears to Vladimir alone, for Estragon is asleep, watched over by Vladimir. The different levels of being flow together; Vladimir no longer expects Godot, he asks only that the messenger shall say he was at the rendez-vous, that he has been seen. Here is a union of past and present, of the dead, the sleeper and the watcher. Vladimir's affirmation is of the barest and simplest; the act of receiving recognition provides in itself the catharsis.

There is a Chinese saying 'It is the way of heaven not to speak; yet it knows how to obtain an answer.' Estragon awakes to echo Vladimir's despair, 'Je ne peux pas continuer comme ça'; but both continue, none the less, as does the Unnameable, enclosed in his prison-jar, endlessly weeping, nothing but a head and a voice, 'Il faut continuer, je ne peux plus continuer, il faut continuer, je vais donc continuer.'

The game, too, continues, within its dereliction enclosing compassion. Beckett has said

> The only possible spiritual development whatever is in the sense of depth. The artistic tendency is not expansive but a contraction. And art is the apotheosis of solitude.[33]

En Attendant Godot, Beckett's first considerable work to be written in French, marked his transference to his adopted language at a deep level of feeling, some of the reasons for which have been suggested. *Watt*, the Anglo-Irish novel he wrote in the Vaucluse, is by contrast a dry and schematic work. The trilogy of novels has been considered his masterpiece; but in no other work but *En Attendant Godot* is there the same luminous ability to absorb other experience than that portrayed, the same power to invite participation at a variety of levels. With the trilogy he began the movement inward and downward, by which penetrating to a deep of the mind, he sealed himself off. The inner voice becomes more halting, under the burden of words. Krapp answers the Krapp of thirty years back, when he knew movement and love; the orders that Harry gives his body are like the orders Pozzo gives Lucky, 'On . . . stop . . . down'; Joe is imprisoned in his room listening to the voices inside his head — and what if God should speak? 'Wait till he starts talking to you . . . when you've done with yourself . . . all you dead dead.' The blind man, the child messenger, the death by drowning, the body in the jar may reappear, each time more flatly presented, more explicitly displayed. The grey world of Hamm, Krapp, Harry, Joe, M1 and W1 and W2 may faithfully embody the depths of the Self where in its solitude Beckett explores the silences beyond words. Only Winnie, the heroine of *Happy Days*, a play in which Beckett returned to English for his primary composition, shows the clowns' vivacity, their resources of poetry and song, where looking back to 'the old style' she creates a world out of a few scraps. Instead of the Tree of Life she enjoys the shelter of her tree-like expanding parasol (till it goes on fire in the true circus tradition). She flings it away with a gay 'Ah, earth, you old extinguisher!'

Winnie is a novelty in Beckett's *œuvre* by reason of her sex, although an earlier Winnie appeared in *More Pricks than Kicks*. Jean-Louis Barrault calls her 'gaie et reconnaissante'; others have found her trivial and the results disastrous.

Her speech is not Anglo-Irish but flat suburban, although she can quote Milton for her purpose. 'Hail, holy light' is her greeting at the opening of Act 2. 'Some one is looking at me still.' She can sing a waltz song ('the old style' — it is the *Merry Widow* Waltz) at the last moment, although she has given up saying her prayers, and forgotten most of her poetry. *Happy Days* (1961) is Beckett's last full-length play. It was translated by the author as *Oh les Beaux Jours*! Subsequent works became briefer, nearer to mime, more infrequent.

Beckett's power to speak through the gaps is counterbalanced by the careful craftsmanship with which he has presented his work since 1944 in both English and French. I have suggested that the social commitment of the author is implicit in the practice of his art. The choice of French for *En Attendant Godot* reveals something, I would think, of its origin in his life in France. The myth is based on memories that he could best communicate in French, and which have grown and changed since its first appearance. For like another of his plays, it is built on the tideline between the inner and the outer world – that tideline which he evoked in the second of his *Four Poems*.

> Je suis ce cours de sable qui glisse
> entre le galet et la dune
> la pluie d'été pleut sur ma vie
> sur moi ma vie qui me fuit me poursuit
> et finira le jour de son commencement[34]
>
> cher instant je te vois
> dans ce rideau de brume qui recule
> où je n'aurai plus à fouler ces longs seuils mouvants
> et vivrai le temps d'une porte
> qui s'ouvre et se referme.

Notes

1   The work of Pinter and Tom Stoppard shows particular indebtedness.
2   S. Beckett, *Proust* (Dolphin Books, Chatto & Windus, 1931), p. 57.
3   Beckett on Joyce: *Our Exagmination round his Factification for Incamination of Work in Progress,* (1929), p. 14.
4   Cf. Beckett, *Proust,* p. 49. 'The tragic figure represents the expiation of original sin . . . the sin of having been born.' In 'A Woman Young and Old', W. B. Yeats varied the phrase; 'the *crime* of being born Blackens all our lot.'
5   From *Four Poems* (written originally in French and translated by Beckett), *Poems in English* (1961), p. 51.
6   Beckett, *Proust,* pp. 4, 18.
7   *Three Dialogues with Georges Duthuit,* in *Transition* (1949), No. 5.
8   From L. Janvier, *Samuel Beckett par lui-même* (Editions du Seuil, Paris, 1969, no pagination; see Chronologie, 1939).
9   *En Attendant Godot,* ed. C. Duckworth (Harrap, 1966), p. 53.
10 Ibid., p. 66.
11 Beckett, *Proust,* p. 56.
12 *En Attendant Godot,* p. 71.
13 *En Attendant Godot,* pp. 71–2.
14 In the earlier work, *Mercier et Camier,* the rendez-vous is in the square St-Ruth, under a tree planted by a Marshal of France.
15 *En Attendant Godot,* p. 49.

16 The theological discussion of Christ and the two thieves opens Act I. In *Molloy*, a dog is killed and buried under a tree; the Rooneys mistake the smell of dead leaves in a ditch for a dead dog (*All that Fall*).

17 *En Attendant Godot*, pp. 54–5.

18 Yeats's play *Purgatory*, with its two tramps (father and son), its one bare tree that is finally lit up with a supernatural white light, as time passes over into eternity, provided an icon for this scene.

19 *En Attendant Godot*, p. 88.

20 The French text with translation is published as *Hypnos Waking*, ed. Jackson Matthews (Random House, 1966). The following translation is my own. Char dedicated his journal to Camus – whose *Mythe de Sisyphus* reflects also the pangs of waiting.

21 *En Attendant Godot*, p. 69.

22 Beckett has dissociated himself from any religious sentiments (*Janvier*: 'Je n'ai aucun sentiment religieux'). His family was Protestant; his mother, the most pious member, belonged to the Society of Friends, whose worship is silent.

23 See William Willeford, *The Fool and his Sceptre* (1969), pp. 34–47, for examples of the pseudo-couples – the fool and his bauble, his coxcomb, his doll, or his 'second banana'.

24 *En Attendant Godot*, p. 4.

25 Ibid., p. 7. Compare *Endgame*, which is a game of solitaire; Hamm's opening is 'A moi . . . de jouer.' Love is found only in the dustbins, between Nagg and Nell.

26 Beckett used such forms in his early novels; and Joyce made frequent use of them also. Lucky cites all sorts of bogus authorities for the existence of God and the decay of the world.

27 Beckett in his youth was excellent at games and played cricket for Trinity College, Dublin in international matches.

28 'Hope deferred maketh the heart sick, but when desire cometh, it is a tree of life' (Proverbs, 13, xii). This incomplete verse may be compared with the reference to 'the divine Miranda' below; neither could be meant to convey the full message to the audience.

29 *En Attendant Godot*, p. 83.

30 Ibid., pp. 84–5.

31 Ibid., p. 37.

32 Beckett had made the point much earlier in *Proust*, p. 30. 'Unlike Miranda he suffers with those he has not seen suffer.'

33 *Proust*, p. 47.

34 Cf. Pozzo and Vladimir above, pp. 182–3.

Acknowledgements

Many of the articles have been published elsewhere. I am grateful for permission to include them here, and would like to express thanks to all concerned: 'Peele's *Old Wives' Tale*; a play of enchantment', *English Studies* (Amsterdam) 1962, XLIII, 323–30, published by Swets and Zeitlinger; 'Hero and Leander', *Scrutiny*, 1933, II, 59–64; 'Shakespeare's Debt to Marlowe', *Shakespeare's Styles*, ed. P. Edwards, I-S. Ewbank and G. K. Hunter, 1980 (Cambridge University Press); 'Shakespeare and the Use of Disguise in Elizabethan Drama', *Essays in Criticism*, 1952, XI, 159–68; 'Virtue is the true Nobility: a study of the structure of *All's Well that Ends Well*', *Review of English Studies* n.s. 1950, I, 289–301 (Oxford University Press); 'The Origins of *Macbeth*', *Shakespeare Survey*, 1951, 4, 35–48 (Cambridge University Press); 'Time, Fate and Chance in *The Duchess of Malfi*', *Modern Language Review*, 1947, XLIII, 281–94 (permission of the Editors and the Modern Humanities Research Association): 'Beaumont, Fletcher and the Baroque', preface to the Everyman (1962), *Selected Plays* (Messrs J. M. Dent and Sons Ltd); 'Thomas Heywood, Shakespeare's Shadow' appeared in a shortened form in *Essays in Theatre*, 1982, I, 2–13, Department of Drama, University of Guelph, Ontario, but in this form was given to the Société Shakespeare Française at the Sorbonne in November 1982; 'Yeats and the Elizabethans', *The Dublin Magazine*, Summer 1965, 40–55; 'Yeats and the Legend of Ireland', *Mosaic*, a journal for the comparative study of literature and ideas, 1977, X.2, 85–96, the University of Manitoba, Winnipeg; '*En Attendant Godot*' from my book, *Literature in Action, Studies in continental and Commonwealth Society*, 1972, 13–33 (Messrs Chatto & Windus Ltd).

I should like to express my gratitude once again to the staff of the Harvester Press and especially to Sue Roe for her editorial help.